THE 24-HOUR SOUP KITCHEN

"Like most of us, Stephen Henderson felt guilty about eating well in a hungry world. Unlike most of us, he did something about it. This fascinating tale is incredibly inspiring. Wondering what you can do? Reading this book would be a good place to start."

—Ruth Reichl, Chef, Food Writer,
and host of PBS's "Gourmet's Adventures with Ruth"

"A captivating and original book. This quest to learn more about gastrophilanthropy is at once a vibrant travelogue and deeply moving search for self. I devoured it and still wanted more!"

—Cynthia Nixon, Actress and Activist

"Giving food to the hungry is a sacred responsibility and joy. This beautifully written series of autobiographical vignettes relates how a minister's child turned world-traveled writer discovered the various ways needy people are fed around the globe. Honest, colorful, and at times even humorous, I highly recommend it."

—Gregory E. Sterling, Dean of Yale Divinity School

"When figuring out how to help the needy, our choices are actually quite simple: clothe the naked, give shelter to the homeless, and feed the hungry. We all know this but too often we're not sure where to begin. Stephen Henderson decided to start small by baking up a few batches of cookies. From there, his culinary volunteerism grew and took him to soup kitchens around the world. His unusual and poignant book may inspire you to light a fire—under a charitable fry pan, and under yourself!"

—Charles King, CEO, Housing Works

"An inspiring philanthropic account that deftly displays the author's affability, knowledge, and passion. . . . Henderson's writing bubbles with enthusiasm. . . . A graceful, well-balanced, and enlightening work."

—Kirkus Reviews

Alexis Soyer, 1810 – 1858

THE 24-HOUR SOUP KITCHEN

SOUL-STIRRING LESSONS IN
Gastrophilanthropy

Revised Edition

S T E P H E N   H E N D E R S O N

Radius Book Group
New York

Distributed by Radius Book Group
A division of Diversion Publishing Corp.
www.RadiusBookGroup.com

www.the24-hoursoupkitchen.com / www.stephenhenderson.com

For more information, email info@radiusbookgroup.com.

The 24-Hour Soup Kitchen is a work of nonfiction.
Some names and identifying details have been changed.

100% of the author's net proceeds will be donated to
Food Bank of New York City, a hunger-relief organization
working to end hunger throughout the city's five boroughs for over 35 years.

First edition: April 2020
First paperback edition: October 2021
Paperback ISBN: 978-1-63576-746-9
eBook ISBN: 978-1-63576-690-5

Library of Congress Control Number: 2019913589

Manufactured in the United States of America

10 9 8 7 6 5 4 3 2 1

Cover design by Erin Kirk New
Interior design by Neuwirth & Associates
Drawing of Alexis Soyer by Guno Park

Radius Book Group and the Radius Book Group colophon are registered trademarks of Radius Book Group, a division of Diversion Publishing Corp.

*There are people in the world
who are so hungry,
God cannot appear to them
except in the form of bread.*

—Mahatma Gandhi

CONTENTS

AUTHOR'S NOTE

Julia Child famously once said that chefs should never admit fault or try to explain what went wrong with something they've cooked. Her theory was that most diners would not sense anything amiss, or even if they did, an apology wouldn't make dinner taste any better.

While I always attempt to follow Child's advice in the kitchen, before I serve you this book I can't resist a few words of context.

The experiences described in the chapters ahead took place over the last ten years in many different countries and often necessitated the help of native speakers as my translators. Some of the interviews I conducted were recorded and transcribed; on other occasions I took notes, but there were also times when I had to reconstruct conversations from memory.

Although I've worked hard to fact-check things and tried my best to accurately record places, names, events, and quotations, if there are any errors, omissions, or things misconstrued in the following pages, please forgive me.

I'm trying out a new recipe here. I hope you like it.

MISE EN PLACE

I AM A BOY, STANDING IN A CHURCH BASEMENT AND STARING up at a long line of serving tables. Arranged on top of these tables are more groceries than I've ever seen in one place other than a supermarket. Rising in stacks that nearly touch the room's ceiling are countless boxes of rice and pasta, glass jars of spaghetti sauce, plastic tubs of margarine and peanut butter, and teetering towers of tuna fish cans. Interspersed among these loose items are bulging brown paper bags stamped with the bright logos of Waldbaum's, A&P, and Pathmark, as well as white Styrofoam coolers filled with frozen items—bricks of hamburger, cartons of fish sticks, and stubby tubes of orange juice concentrate.

"Really? You mean, it's all . . . *ours?*" I ask my mother.

She smiled down at me, nodding her head, though her brow was creased with confusion. Mom didn't know what to make of this cornucopia either. We'd recently come to a new city, and people we didn't yet know had assembled this perplexing quantity of food to make us feel welcome.

My father, William Douglas Henderson, was a Baptist preacher. When I was five years old, Dad believed God gave him a clear command: he was to accept a new job (and step into a new pulpit) in Levittown, a hamlet in Long Island's Nassau County about thirty-five miles from New York City.

We arrived here from Connecticut slightly more than a decade after the builder, Abraham Levitt, broke ground in 1947 on his eponymously named community. Designed for returning veterans of World War II,

Levittown is now considered the first mass-produced suburb in America. Using precut lumber and assembly-line techniques, Levitt's construction crews managed to build neat rows of identical houses, which sprouted up at an astonishing rate of thirty a day in what were formerly onion and potato fields. My parents, three sisters, brother, and I squeezed into one of these small houses, which was the parsonage for Levittown Baptist Church.

Situated just off Hempstead Turnpike, a busy east–west state highway, Levittown Baptist in the early 1960s was still a work in progress, with a dark and gloomy unfinished basement that parishioners optimistically referred to as the "Fellowship Hall." In years to come this space would be spruced up with paint, vinyl flooring, and a dropped ceiling of acoustic tile, but on this Sunday after Dad preached his first sermon in the sanctuary upstairs, the Fellowship Hall was made less drab by crepe paper streamers, balloons, and those tables piled high with groceries. At the center of this dazzling display was a poster board with a funny caricature drawing of my father. Depicted with a large wooden mallet dropping onto his head, Dad's eyes were x-ed out in the cartoonist's symbol for unconsciousness. The good folks at Levittown Baptist were "pounding the preacher."

This long-standing culinary tradition in several American religious denominations, especially beloved by Baptists even to this day, is actually constitutional in origin. "Congress shall make no law respecting an establishment of religion," the U.S. Constitution's First Amendment begins, thereby outlawing those churches that were publicly funded before the American Revolution whose preachers (primarily Anglican and Congregational) were paid as if they were government employees. Subsequently, all churches would be supported only by their members, who were now required to pay their leaders' salaries and ensure their comfort in other ways too, such as providing a parsonage, along with the occasional "pounding." The name probably derives from staple items that were sold by the pound such as sugar, cornmeal, and coffee.

On that Sunday morning in 1963, however, my family was nearly knocked senseless by a Warholian quantity of Campbell's soup, boxes of

Rice-A-Roni, instant mashed potato flakes, Kellogg's Froot Loops cereal, Cheez Whiz, and Heinz Tomato Ketchup. While the church's members chuckled affectionately at our consternation, the Henderson family was encouraged to admire these nonperishable goods and take them home with us.

Back then, I was really, really, *really* excited by this largesse. More than half a century later, however, and older now than my parents were then, I can only imagine what they must have felt.

Dad had food issues long before the phrase became popular. A natural athlete, he thought any excessive body weight was a sign of laziness, if not moral depravity. My father also had a horror of any foodstuff that was too brightly colored. When he was a boy, or so the story went in our family's folklore, Dad was seduced by the siren call of a bakery cake—one of those gaudy numbers with piped icing and flower petals made from sugar. He greedily devoured piece after piece until he ended up with such a terrific stomachache, he'd later claim it lasted for several days. As a result, my father swore off anything "candy-colored," and his prohibition become our family's too. Jell-O, soda pop, Halloween treats, and ice cream in any flavor but vanilla were frowned upon in the Henderson household.

Dad expressed his chief eccentricity about food, though, when he evoked the threat of starvation. Having served in World War II, where he saw great poverty in Italy as well as North Africa, he developed what was almost an obsession about never letting anything edible go to waste. (I think of him whenever I shear mold off a neglected chunk of cheddar rather than throwing the cheese away.) If any of his children began to whine about, say, the living room being too cold, the difficulty of a homework assignment in math, or the injustice of only having permission to watch a half hour of television on school nights, Dad would level his gaze at us and say, "I hope you never know hunger."

What he meant was "if you think this is bad [a 52-degree indoor temperature, the challenge of algebra, or an incomplete viewing of *The Carol Burnett Show*], just imagine if your insides groaned from lack of food." The unspoken implication, of course, was that we were weak and coddled and wouldn't be able to tough out any real deprivation.

My mother's experience of eating was also fraught with distress. A deeply religious woman, Mom lived a circumspect life, carefully cordoned off from what she habitually referred to as "the world." She had no interest in movies, the latest novel, or fashion magazines. Her rigorous self-restraint even extended into the kitchen. Mom wasn't a bad cook; rather, there was something nearly ascetic about her complete disregard for new flavors or recipes. It was as if she believed blandness was next to godliness. By far the most exotic spice I knew her to deploy was paprika—and this sparingly. For her, food was something of a necessary evil; it had to be prepared but preferably with a minimum of effort. Any undue fuss over dining was suspicious to Mom if not downright sinful. She wanted her food served plain, save for a pious pinch of salt and pepper.

In fairness, even if my mother had wanted to be a more adventurous chef, she didn't have oodles of free time to devote to culinary experiments. As with most Baptist preachers' wives of this era, Mom was my father's unpaid assistant. Whenever there was a meeting at the church—morning and evening services on Sunday, Wednesday evening prayer meetings, the Women's Missionary Fellowship on Thursday—she was required to be there. Mom had other pressing obligations too: counseling a distraught wife who'd just found out her husband was having an affair, typing a mimeograph for the church bulletin, and leading a weekly gathering of young women called the Pioneer Girls. She also took it upon herself to read early drafts of my father's sermons to edit out his more recondite verbal tics, including his fondness for words such as "recondite."

Almost every night, seven days a week, the seven of us—Mom, Dad, Deborah, Martha, Douglas, Ann, and I—would gather for a family dinner. We were too poor to eat at restaurants or order takeout, and the recently invented Amana microwave oven had yet to become a standard kitchen appliance. With all my mother had on her plate, what ended up on ours each evening was mostly a last-minute scramble.

That's where I came in.

For reasons only she understood, over time my mother excused my older siblings from kitchen duty. Instead, she conscripted me as her sous-chef and dishwasher, then gradually expanded my responsibilities to include menu planner, grocery shopper, and eventually chef de cuisine. I didn't mind. On the contrary, these chores in the kitchen delighted me. I loved reading recipes and making a list of ingredients. Some of my earliest, happiest memories are of accompanying Mom to the supermarket. Once our order was rung up, it thrilled me to watch the cash register spool out a long receipt, like it was a gift ribbon. Unpacking all those bags from A&P at home and organizing various items into our cupboard, refrigerator, and freezer was like pounding the preacher all over again.

I probably knew how to cook meatballs before I could spell "meatballs." By doubling and tripling recipes, I learned how to multiply. Eventually, I grew comfortable with preparing large quantities of food. To be sure, the mainstays on our family's menu were quite ordinary: pot roast, fried chicken, or baked ham. Nonetheless, their preparation required mastery of basic skills such as peeling, dicing, measuring, sautéing, timing, and tasting. I took each step very seriously; making the family supper made me feel useful and like I'd found my place.

As I grew older, I became more daring. I'd rush home from school to learn new techniques from public television's broadcast of *The Galloping Gourmet*, starring a Scottish chef named Graham Kerr. Looking back on it now, I realize he was probably one of my first crushes. I'd marvel at the magnificence of Kerr's lantern jaw and puzzle over what I considered his bizarre insistence on using only clarified butter—whatever that was. Eventually, I began to mimic his boozy, louche sense of humor.

Mom and the rest of my family seemed amused more than anything as I concocted new recipes, or at least new to the Henderson household. One weekend morning, though, when I'd gotten up early to experiment with my version of *les oeufs à la méditerranéenne*, a fairly complicated recipe for which I needed to mince garlic, dice tomatoes, pit black olives, and make a chiffonade of basil leaves, Mom was not pleased. "Can't we just have eggs?" she complained.

Such outbursts were rare. Really, the main discouragement I experienced was mechanical, thanks to our HotPoint electric range, a standard feature in all Levittown homes. Like a slowly deflating balloon, the Hot-Point's oven would lose its oomph during any prolonged period of baking. Because I was as yet unaware of the simplest of kitchen tools—an oven thermometer—I would constantly jiggle the temperature dial upward, guessing how this might affect the interior. This dubious calculus often resulted in a turkey bloody at the bone or lasagna blackened about its edges. Teaching myself through trial and error, mostly the latter, I thought this was how all stoves worked: they were fickle and had minds of their own.

FAST-FORWARD A FEW decades.

At the age of fifty, a time when many men indulge in embarrassing acquisitions designed to make themselves feel younger—a Porsche Spyder sports car or a billboard-size television for their man cave—I found myself flying to France, about to buy an absurdly expensive oven. This was one of those it-made-sense-at-the-time decisions that can only be understood within the context of a fiscal madness known as "household improvement."

In early 2008, my husband, James, and I bought a prewar co-op apartment in New York City that needed a lot of work. A key part of the gut renovation, which I oversaw, was our wish to create a kitchen that wouldn't really look like a kitchen. This required finding an oven that didn't really look like an oven. Eventually my research led me to Lacanche, a classic French range made in Burgundy, near Dijon. The stream-lined design of these powerful cooking machines hasn't changed much since the 1920s, the same era when our apartment building in Manhattan was built. Lacanche ovens aren't kept in stock. Rather, each is made to order, with only a few thousand produced every year. Lacanche has passionate devotees; you might even call them cult members. There are newsletters, online fan clubs, and Tumblr, Instagram, and Pinterest pages filled with reports from home chefs telling of their latest culinary triumphs cooked with a Lacanche range.

Perhaps due to my religious upbringing, I'm usually skeptical that any material object will provide long-lasting satisfaction. As I learned more about Lacanche ranges, however, the possibility of owning one began to take hold of my imagination. I fell in love—madly, blindly, and imprudently. Soon enough, when I should have been working on other projects, I'd find myself sneaking away to the Lacanche website to gaze yet again at various ways a range could be tailored to my precise wishes.

Did I want two gas ovens, two electric, or maybe one of each? A cooktop with five gas burners, six, or—*gasp!*—eight? One morning, I imagined my range in a sexy black color; the following afternoon, it was a ripe persimmon. After much dithering and internal debate, I made the leap and placed an order for a Cluny model. I also wangled a journalistic assignment from *Gourmet* magazine to make a pilgrimage to the Lacanche factory to see where my oven would be born.

After a few days in Paris I traveled on to Lacanche, a cozy village in a region that is traditionally associated with France's steel industry, as iron ore was discovered nearby in the seventeenth century. A gentleman named Jacques-Étienne Caumartin selected Lacanche in 1797 as the spot where he planned to produce kitchen cookers and radiators. Today, of the seven hundred people who live there, nearly two hundred work at the oven factory.

I had an appointment to meet with Jean-Jacques Augagneur, the director of Lacanche, who proved to be something of a philosopher and historian as well as a businessman. In his office, as we flipped through old sales catalogs, Augagneur told me Lacanche reached its peak of glory as the Industrial Revolution trickled down to domestic products.

"Manufacturers thought it important for household items to not only be functional but beautiful," he said. "Browse a spare parts brochure from those days, and it's like looking at an art book."

Augagneur smiled. "Do you want to see your Lacanche?"

"*Absolument!*" I replied.

We entered the factory, where all workers wore a uniform of gray cargo pants and a navy blue T-shirt with the logo "SIL"—for Societe Industrielle de Lacanche—stitched over the left breast. It's a secret club, and I was being tapped to join!

Placed on a wooden pallet, about to be crated, was my range. The hardware, as I requested, was polished nickel. Despite the factory ceiling's dim lighting, I could see the oven's color—a pale gray-brown called "frangipani"—was luscious. I crouched, bringing my face close to admire the glossy enamel finish.

"Do you hear a heartbeat?" Augagneur joked.

Earlier I had mentioned feeling like I was about to meet my baby for the first time. Now I laughed, first with a gush of pride, then a spasm of fear. Did I really deserve such a splendid thing?

THAT EVENING, AUGAGNEUR asked me to dine with him at Hotel de la Côte-d'Or, in the nearby town of Seaulieu. This famed spot was created by Bernard Loiseau, who in the 1990s was France's most celebrated chef. He leveraged himself into debt while building this restaurant, but finally attained a three-star rating for Côte-d'Or in the all-powerful *Michelin Guide*. Some of these facts I was familiar with, as I had read *The Perfectionist: Life and Death in Haute Cuisine*, a biography of Loiseau.

Augagneur, who knew Loiseau personally, told me more. Surviving, much less flourishing, is difficult in the competitive realm of fine dining. Loiseau began to see himself as surrounded by enemies, all wanting him to fail. In February 2003, worried he was about to lose a Michelin star— which, he feared, would cause his business to collapse—Loiseau committed suicide with a shotgun he'd received as a gift from his wife.

Augagneur and I were seated in a garden behind the restaurant. It was a mid-autumn afternoon. The air was warm, and butterflies flitted among the day lilies as we sipped a cocktail of prune juice mixed with Cremant, the sparkling wine of Burgundy. Every few minutes, an attendant would arrive with another delectable nibble—eel mousse with leek gelatin, or snails en croute. This was all marvelous, aside from a nagging thought that the man who'd overseen the laying of every brick and the planting of each flower bulb had blown his own head off when the job was done.

As if he'd been reading my mind, Augagneur broke the silence. "Bernard had a physical presence that lit up a room. Full of energy, he was a visionary who was excited for the future."

"Then why did he kill himself?" There could be no answer to this question, but I blurted it out anyway.

"Bernard truly was a perfectionist, which never makes life easy," Augagneur replied with a shrug. "There should be a sign along the highway as you drive into Seaulieu. It would read: 'Warning, Your Passions May Kill You.'"

After sunset, we moved into Côte-d'Or's octagonal dining room. Our meal began with radish soup garnished with a foam made from the vegetable's leaves. Then came a *spécialité du maison*, frogs' legs laid out as spokes around two concentric rings, one of parsley jus and, at the center, a perfect circle of garlic puree. This appetizer brought Loiseau international acclaim, its secret being that the garlic is slowly braised, with the water changed several times to mellow its flavor. For my entrée, I selected pigeon served in a red wine reduction. I savored each bite, including a final crusty and crunchy bit that, Augagneur informed me, was the bird's claw. Taking a sip of wine, I smiled at how far I had come from battling with a HotPoint electric range in the parsonage at Levittown.

Our leisurely meal wended its way to dessert: peach sorbet with tarragon along with strawberries covered with a cloud of fennel-flavored spun sugar. Still unnerved by the ghost of Bernard Loiseau, I began to have buyer's remorse about my Lacanche. Could I cancel my order? I would pay some sort of penalty, but then I could donate whatever I was refunded to charity, right? When I mentioned this half-baked idea to Augagneur, he smiled.

"You Americans! You love this sort of either/or drama. You are either a saint or a sinner. A wise man or a fool. Why can't you be both?"

I had no reply to this.

"Listen, my friend," Augagneur continued. "You seem to know a little something about food and French culinary history. You've heard of Carême, Escoffier, and Bocuse, yes? But, have you ever come across a chef named Alexis Soyer?"

"No."

"Well, you should," he said, with a sly chuckle. "Learning about his life might help you. He was equally content to cook for the richest, and poorest, of men. If he could, Soyer would tell you to enjoy your new oven, especially since he's the one who practically invented it."

ONCE BACK IN New York, I followed Augagneur's advice and started to look into Alexis Soyer's story. What I found wasn't an either/or, but rather an "everything plus . . ." scenario. His life was a jumble of high and low, grotesque and grand. Soyer tried to do too many things at once and sometimes promised more than he could deliver. Yet, he also accomplished acts of tremendous generosity.

In the mid-nineteenth century, Alexis Soyer was the world's best-known chef. He became a culinary celebrity while working as the chef de cuisine at the Reform Club on London's Pall Mall, where he fed some of Britain's greatest men. While at the Reform, he designed and built a commercial kitchen of such technological virtuosity—Soyer pioneered cooking with gas—it astonished Victorian England and attracted visitors from across the globe. His best-selling cookbooks essentially created this genre of literature, and his brazen acts of self-promotion set the template for our own pantheon of cooking luminaries such as Martha Stewart, Rachael Ray, and Emeril Lagasse. Nearly everything they've done, Alexis Soyer did first—and did better.

What's more, Soyer is credited with inventing the concept of soup kitchens. He first experimented with this idea while volunteering to feed London's neediest inhabitants in 1845 and 1846. Then, when the great potato blight of 1847 struck Ireland, he set off for Dublin, where he devised a recipe for "famine soup" and served it to many thousands of starving peasants. Poor people had been fed before, certainly, but Soyer turned charitable cookery into an organized system—a feeding machine.

Once introduced to this fascinating man, I needed to know more. There are several biographies to which I am indebted, especially Ruth Cowen's *Relish: The Extraordinary Life of Alexis Soyer, Victorian Celebrity Chef.* At the British Museum Library in London, there's a complete set of Soyer's books, and I read most of these too.

Alexis Soyer was an operator, always angling for a better deal and a get-rich-quick scheme. Something of a lush, he frittered away vast sums of money on creating his distinctive wardrobe as well as on champagne. He understood the vulgar mechanics behind maintaining his place in the public eye and was willing to be the butt of jokes in newspaper cartoons and caricatures—as long as they spelled his name correctly in the caption. A dear friend of his, Lady Stratford, once wrote to Queen Victoria and expressed what was a general opinion of Soyer among London's upper crust: "He is a most ridiculous man, but quite perfect in his own way."

How can someone be both ridiculous and perfect? Doesn't one cancel out the other? With Alexis Soyer, no. It was the cataclysmic contrasts in his life that made him so remarkable—and aspirational. Soyer, for me, seemed an all-too-human hero. I didn't have to worship him, revere him, or even look up to him. I could regard him honestly—man to man, eye to eye.

Alexis Soyer died in 1858, exactly a century before I was born. He was at the pinnacle of success, making a fantastic wage cooking delicacies for the most powerful people in the world, when he first became aware of those living in the squalor of London's Spitalfields neighborhood. Did he feel it necessary to give up his fat salary or stop wearing his gold-threaded waistcoat before he could make soup for the hungry? He did not. Instead, Soyer chose to live in a style he called *à la zoug-zoug*, his preferred way of zigzagging between conflicting realities.

Jean-Jacques Augagneur was right. Learning about Soyer helped me. I began to consider the possibility that by following his example, I might begin to reconcile the twists and turns of my life. Even so, I found myself haunted by Bernard Loiseau. At this highest level of refinement to which Loiseau ascended, it's slightly sickening how wasteful it is to produce something like garlic puree or fennel-flavored spun sugar. If junk food causes heartburn, haute cuisine can sometimes singe your soul.

These thoughts continued to bother me after the Lacanche range arrived from France and was installed in my apartment's kitchen. Just looking at it, I began to experience something like dread. There it sat, a thing of exquisite engineering and style with two ovens and six gas burners. I felt nervous and embarrassed about what now seemed an inexcusable indulgence.

My love affair with Lacanche blossomed during the heady days of early 2008, when I felt financially flush and bullish about the future. By the time the range was delivered to New York only a few months later, America had plummeted into an economic crisis nearly as severe as the Great Depression. The United States was burning while I fiddled with how to sauté fiddlehead ferns.

Besides, who was I kidding? I didn't cook enough to deserve such a professional-quality oven. "I'm ready to feed multitudes," my Lacanche announced in a voice steely and reproachful, "and all you've got is plans for steamed broccoli and roasted salmon for two?"

Whether or not I needed to be forgiven for my "sin" of buying it, I started to think that I'd never feel comfortable with my Lacanche unless I could figure out ways to use this range more generously. But how? Starving people weren't showing up at my door, nor would it make much sense to wander the streets of New York with Tupperware containers full of home cookin', hoping to find takers.

While continuing to brood over this, however, I was reminded of how wonderfully useful I once felt when helping my harried mother get supper on the table. I thought again of the people at Levittown Baptist Church who wanted to show their love by making sure our family's pantry was well stocked. I also recalled how, years later at another church where my father had lately begun to preach, a shy young man named Gary Hewitt showed up at the parsonage's front door with a large grocery sack filled with maybe thirty pounds of ground beef and sirloin steaks. The plastic wrap around this meat had leaked, and the brown paper bag was moist with blood and about to burst at its bottom. Yet, Gary presented the bag to Mom with great solemnity because, he explained, "God laid it on my heart you might need this."

Okay, that last scene is slightly creepy, I'll admit. But food is love, and this was an act of what I began to think of as "gastrophilanthropy." What was God laying on *my* heart that I was suddenly remembering these long-forgotten events?

"I HOPE YOU never know hunger," my father used to say.

Well, funnily enough, his threat came true. That's what this book is about—it recounts my experiences of getting to know people who are hungry as well as the people who feed them. I'm not an authority on global poverty, famine relief, or the economic, political, and social problems that plague the world's food supply. Ill-equipped to tackle such macroquestions, I've deliberately chosen a smaller, much more personal approach by seeking out opportunities to cook alongside gastrophilanthropists in India, Iran, Israel, Mexico, Japan, Peru, South Korea, and in soup kitchens all across America.

When in doubt, I frequently asked myself, "WWAD?" What would Alexis do?

I hope the soul-stirring stories in *The 24-Hour Soup Kitchen* will help you get to know hunger too. You may discover that no sooner do you begin to stir the pot than you'll find a way to feed someone—maybe even a person you don't know but whose stomach needs to know you.

Case in point: I'd barely begun to consider the idea of gastrophilanthropy when I heard from an old friend of mine, Alan Burks, former president of the Haggar Pants Company. Alan's oldest son, Peter, decided to enlist in the U.S. Army after the September 11, 2001, terrorist attacks in the United States. Tragically, Second Lieutenant Peter Burks was killed in November 2007 when a bomb planted just outside the Green Zone in Baghdad blew up his Stryker armored vehicle. He was twenty-four years old.

As a way of managing his anger and grief after his son's death, Alan became a tireless champion of U.S. soldiers in Iraq as well as other Gold Star families (relatives of those killed in combat). When Alan arranged with American Airlines to fill a cargo jet with supplies for soldiers still fighting in Iraq, he sent out an email soliciting donations. Scanning his list of suggested items—pencils, soccer balls, athletic socks—I had a sweeter thought. Couldn't I bake cookies? Alan thought this was an excellent idea.

List in hand, off I trotted to the grocery store, and soon enough my cart was full of everything I needed to make oatmeal-raisin, chocolate chip, and gingersnap cookies. In an excess of exuberance, I planned to make six hundred, or a dozen cookies for each state in America. I was grinning as the cash register unspooled a long ribbon of a receipt. Back in my kitchen, however, when I considered for whom I was about to start baking, I was overcome with a terrific sense of imbalance. Men and women in the military are daily risking their lives, and I show my appreciation with gingersnaps?

Then again, wouldn't it be worse to do nothing? Yes, I decided, it would. Food is love. So, I set my Lacanche oven to 375 degrees, and it stayed at that temperature—steadily, I might add—for the better part of two days while I turned out batch after batch of cookies.

Did these cookies end the war? Sadly, no. But baking them was a baby step, one slightly *à la zoug-zoug*, that gave me the courage to begin volunteering my culinary skills at other times and in other places.

2

SIKH, AND YE SHALL FIND

M Y NEXT BIG LESSON IN GASTROPHILANTHROPY CAME about by accident when I was invited to write a story about India's Fashion Week. I'd long wished to travel in the subcontinent, so I jumped at this chance when a friend of mine named Harmeet Bajaj asked if I'd be willing to spend a few days watching shows and then give her my impressions about Delhi's growing sophistication as an apparel center. I told Harmeet I wasn't a fashion expert, but I'd be pleased to go. The Indian press might want to chat with me, she added. Would this be a problem?

"If someone asks what you think, just say everything is *amazing*," my husband, James, told me. "When people are interviewed during Fashion Week in New York, that's all they ever say. Calvin's amazing. Michael's amazing. Ralph's amazing. Everyone's amazingly amazing!"

Enlightened by this sage advice, I took off for Delhi.

Textiles are one of India's biggest industries, and the country is a major producer of cotton, silk, and jute. With a population of one billion people, Harmeet explained, "Even if everyone in India buys only two new items of clothing a year, and each garment on average takes two meters—though a woman's sari takes five—that's four billion meters of fabric that must be made." What she neglected to mention is that much of this fabric, especially the dazzlingly fine materials that are strutted on the "ramps"—what modeling runways are called in Delhi—is often made by children in what amounts to slave labor.

The Grand New Delhi, the hotel where I lived for a week, loomed in solitary glory above a dust pit a few minutes' drive from Indira

Gandhi International Airport and directly across from the construction site of what promised to be an enormous shopping mall. As my driver turned off a superhighway that sped by the hotel, I noticed what appeared to be a whole family at work paving the road—by hand, that is. Apparently, a new surface of asphalt was about to be poured on top of the old one, and the previous layer needed to be perforated in order to make it more adhesive. The mom had a basket of small rocks, and her young children were placing the stones neatly in a grid. Dad then beat them down into the old asphalt with a sledgehammer, while a grandmother and grandfather pried them free and tossed the rocks back into the mother's basket so this whole process could start over again. It was after midnight and terribly warm outside, but these people were slogging away by the firelight of several blazing torches while cars and eighteen-wheel trucks whizzed by them so closely, the women's saris were constantly frothed up around their heads.

I was being driven in a Range Rover so robustly air-conditioned that my teeth were chattering. Yes, I keenly felt the dissonance here, but this grim roadside scene was erased from my consciousness with shameful speed as bellhops fell upon me, practically carrying me into a brilliant bubble of opulence. As I stepped into the Grand New Delhi's lobby, two women brushed past me, and I overheard one say, "I am here buying clothes for the royal princesses of Saudi Arabia. They are invited to an important wedding in Mumbai."

Much of Indian fashion, I soon learned, is driven by the nation's customary style of wedding ceremonies. These can last up to a week and include a marathon of parties spread across each day, at which no self-respecting woman would be caught dead wearing the same garment twice. Just as these nuptials tend to take on a larger-than-life aspect, so do Delhi's fashion shows, which feature probably twice as many looks as a designer would dare display in New York, London, or Paris.

Each show was a spectacle, hypnotically scored with Hindi house music played at spine-shaking volume, with tabla drums banging and jangling. The models wore so much sparkle they seemed like avatars: half human, half divine. Golden bracelets connected the women's wrists to belly button piercing, ear lobes were lashed to nostrils, and jewels dangled at the center of their foreheads like a third eye. There was a lot of bare skin on display as well. Women would writhe down the ramp, naked save for pasties in the form of lotus blossoms. And the men! They were absolute gods, clad in backless loincloths, with their perfect bodies glistening with saffron-tinted oil. Fire-breathers belched out tongues of flame, and acrobats suddenly fell from the ceiling on hidden wires or rose from trap doors in clouds of smoke. It was exhausting, like taking a tab of ecstasy over and over and over again.

Too much of a good thing, India Fashion Week might have proved oppressive had I not been assigned a design student, who acted all week as my personal assistant. His name was Meet Mohan Singh, and he would proceed in front of me, forcefully pushing people aside if necessary, so I could pass by undeterred. Meet always had bottles of chilled water in his purse in case I felt parched. If a shimmer of perspiration appeared on my upper lip, he daubed it. When I asked him to do something, instead of replying "yes," he would always say "100 percent!" Though I implored him to call me by my first name, he stubbornly insisted on calling me "Mr. Henderson." Meet was twenty-one and an adorably dizzy young man. When he saw what he called a "super-duper model" swish past, he'd start to hyperventilate. "Oh. My. God! There is Sheetal Mallar!" he'd whisper, naming a dazzling brunette who, he assured me, was soon to leave the ramps behind and become a super-duper star in Bollywood.

From Meet, I actually learned a great deal about American pop culture. Obsessed with Jay-Z, Will Smith, and above all Sarah Jessica Parker, Meet bragged that he'd seen every episode of *Sex in the City* at least twice. My admission that I'd never watched the show led to such a convulsive meltdown in Meet's mood that I was forced to revive him by describing a time I'd interviewed Parker backstage at a Broadway theater and how she'd chatted away charmingly, clad only in her bra and panties. Hearing this, Meet's hands fluttered about like they were ablaze. "Oh. My. God!" he shrieked. "Ohmigodohmigodohmigod!" Meet flew off to find his friends, with whom he shared this fabulous news.

Because he was a Sikh, Meet had never cut his hair and always wore a bulbous turban that resembled a black water balloon swelling from his scalp. Toward the end of Fashion Week, Meet asked if I would like to come to a Sikh temple with him. I readily accepted his invitation, and off we went to Gurdwara Bangla Sahib in central Delhi, which was once a maharaja's palace. This impressive building has gold domes and is surrounded by what seems to be several acres of marble plazas as well as a vast pool of water, a plunge into which is thought by Sikhs to cure all ailments.

As Meet showed me about this extraordinary place, I was intrigued to learn that all Sikh temples (which are called gurdwaras) operate 24-hour soup kitchens. They serve nutritious vegetarian fare called *parshad* to anyone who arrives, be they rich or poor, Sikh, Muslim, Hindu, Christian, or Jew. They also make no distinction between castes, so Brahmans sit with Dalits, or "untouchables." Subsequent to the much-ballyhooed arrival of the Beatles in 1968 at Rishikesh, India, where they studied Transcendental Meditation with Maharishi Mahesh Yogi, hordes of penniless hippies who followed in their wake often ate their meals at gurdwaras.

Ideas for future stories are like eggs lying in the nest of a journalist's mind. Some hatch, others don't. Perhaps someday, I thought, I would get to write something about these soup kitchens.

A FEW YEARS later, I was asked to return to India—this time to report on the Leela Palaces, a chain of luxury hotels undergoing a rapid expansion. I wasn't thrilled by the prospect of a week spent in earnest discussion of thread counts, in-room amenities, and spa treatments. However, I accepted this magazine assignment after I realized I could stay on in India for another week and learn more about Delhi's soup kitchens.

I emailed my young friend Meet, and he put me in touch with his father, Bunty, who is a fabric exporter in Delhi and a well-respected member of the city's Sikh community. Bunty said he'd be happy to pull some strings and arrange for me to stay at a small guesthouse on the property of Gurdwara Bangla Sahib, the very spot I'd visited with his son. (This was an unusual honor, as Bangla Sahib is a pilgrimage spot for all Sikhs and the biggest gurdwara in Delhi; normally only monks, priests, and other visiting dignitaries are allowed to stay at the guesthouse.) Bunty would also secure permission for me to cook in the temple's soup kitchen day or night, working as much or as little as I liked.

First, though, Meet suggested that I should spend a night at his parents' house to get situated. Bunty was waiting outside when I arrived, and I liked him at once. He was a tall man with a bushy black beard. He wore his long, never-cut hair under a black turban that swooped around his head. He had magnificent eyebrows and dark, piercing eyes. At age sixty, he looked forty and attributed his youthfulness to eating raw garlic in the morning and washing his skin with yogurt instead of soap. Bunty insisted on paying the taxi driver and grew agitated when I made a polite feint to grab for my wallet.

Bunty's house, of which he was proud, was large, three stories tall, and made of marble. For all its exterior luster, the house wasn't very comfortable inside. Its rooms were numerous, but each was smaller than the last and stuffed with oversized furniture upholstered in bright red fabric and draped with nylon antimacassars. Lit with a great quantity of florescent bulbs, my skin appeared a sea foam green. Bunty liked to watch television at fantastic volume, and the dull gray stone everywhere served to amplify the TV's blare.

Keeping things in order was a whippet-thin servant, a boy named Santoosh who appeared to be twelve but, I later learned, was twenty-two with a wife and two sons back in his home state of Gujarat. Santoosh was so skinny that the too-large belt he wore had its end wrapped all the way around one hip to the middle of his back. He looked perfectly terrified, as you would be if you had to jump every time your master called. The first few times I heard Bunty shout the kid's name— *SAN-TOOOOOSH!*—I thought my heart would burst.

Many minutes into our house tour we came across Bunty's wife, Bier, who emerged from nowhere like a vapor. Frail, quiet, and pale, she was like an Indian version of Mrs. Rochester from *Jane Eyre*.

When I tried to express my gratitude to Bier, Bunty answered for her. "It is the LEEEEEEEEEAST we can do," he said, drawing out the word to comical length. He then took my hand and stroked it. "If someone visits you, it is because he loves you, he thinks about you. Your visit blesses our house!"

Up to this moment I'd not understood the expression "killing with kindness," but Bunty's style of hospitality did seem to verge on homicidal. I couldn't make a move without him offering to do something for me. For example, he showed me to my bedroom and pointed out the adjoining bath. Less than three minutes later, I was taking a shower when Bunty yanked back one end of the curtain and popped his turbaned head into the steam for a few quick solicitations. Was the water hot enough? Did I need more towels? Would I like some yogurt?

"No, thank you, Bunty," I sputtered.

Cleansed and dressed, I went downstairs. Entering the living room, I saw Bunty had changed into a new costume and was resplendent in snow white linen pajamas. He'd sprawled on a sofa, feet up on the coffee table, while Santoosh was down on his knees giving Bunty a vigorous foot massage. The peculiar combination of intimacy and servility in this scene slapped me across the face, and I tried to back out of the room before I was spotted. Bunty was not embarrassed in the least and invited me to sit with him.

Bunty asked many questions about my travels, New York, and American politics. Talking to him was like body-surfing. I got tossed about, rolled over, yet it was stimulating and fun. I quickly discerned that he was a sensitive and spiritual man. Our conversation went beyond the mere exchange of pleasantries to a more tender place, as each of us struggled to speak of things such as love, ambition, and mortality. Twice he said a Hindi phrase and thumped his chest with an extended finger as he translated: "To conquer your heart is more difficult than to rule the world."

Indeed.

Meanwhile, Bier hid in the kitchen hovering over another servant, a girl named Matuli, as she prepared something like a small crepe sandwich, filled with finely shredded ginger and scallion, then fried. I ate about twenty of them, and this was just a snack.

At some point, we two men, alone, went into the dining room, where a wall at one end of the room was dedicated as a shrine to Meet's artwork. Pride of place in this assemblage was given to a surprisingly well-rendered painting of the fashion model Naomi Campbell. The primary palette for this canvas was bright yellow, with Campbell's visage— all dagger-sharp cheekbones and pillow lips—rendered in bold strokes of chocolate brown. It was as lovingly idealized an image as those I'd seen elsewhere in India of goddesses in the Hindu pantheon such as Parvati, Radha, and Lakshmi. Naomi Campbell! I couldn't stop looking at Meet's depiction of her. It reminded me, painfully, of a similarly star-struck painting I made as a teenager of the actress Karen Black when she was in the 1975 movie *The Day of the Locust*. My "Karen" did not hang in the dining room of my parents' house. I didn't even show it to Mom and Dad; I knew they wouldn't be pleased.

The servant girl, Matuli, brought in dish after dish of vegetarian food: lentil dal, curried cauliflower, potato, the yogurt sauce called raita, and a crispy flat bread known as chapati. I made something of a blunder when I reached for a platter of food. Bunty gently took the spoon from my hand and made it clear he would serve me. Occasionally Santoosh arrived with more bread, fresh from the oven. Indian respect is shown to guests by always presenting them with the hottest slice. Each time Santoosh appeared, pieces of flatbread were shuffled around between plates, with Bunty always getting the chilly chapati.

While we ate (and ate!), Bunty bragged about his children. Santander, his twenty-five-year-old son, managed a Circuit City store in Alexandria, Virginia, outside Washington, D.C., and had asked his parents to start looking for a suitable spouse. Bunty believed arranged marriages—as his was to Bier—are preferable to love marriages.

"Look at it this way," he said. "In a love marriage, it comes about between two people who think they know one another completely. Then, they get married, and the wife discovers the husband is a slob, or the husband learns his wife takes a very long time to get dressed in the morning. Suddenly, you find these foibles to be hugely upsetting, because you feel deceived, as if the loved one has been hiding this fact from you, and you become angry and intolerant. In an arranged marriage, practically nothing is known, everything is a surprise, so you fully expect things will, at first, be awkward and difficult. Minor problems don't get blown out of proportion. How can you argue about any one thing, when there is everything to argue about?"

I heard Bier fretfully pacing in the hall outside the dining room while Bunty offered up this paean to marital bliss.

A third son, Arjun, lived with Santander and hoped to become a model. I'd already heard much about Arjun from Meet. He'd told me that Arjun spends all his time at the gym, or in front of the mirror, and I didn't even want to guess how much money Bunty had spent for photo shoots, personal shoppers, diction lessons, and eyebrow threading.

"Let me show you Arjun's portfolio," Bunty said. "*SAN-TOOOOOSH!*"

The servant came running with a large leather-bound book full of excruciatingly odd photographs in which Arjun strained mightily to look like a hot stud. Here he was emerging from a pool, astride a motorcycle, or wearing only a scant loincloth made of gauze.

Santoosh was on the floor again, massaging his master's feet, as Bunty laid his hand on my thigh and asked me why I did not have a wife. I was not an unattractive man, he told me. Why could I not find a woman? Was I too choosy?

"It is not good for you to be alone, Stephen. Especially as you get older. You will want companionship."

This was beyond awkward. In most circumstances, I would not have hesitated to say that I am gay, James is my partner of many years, and we have a wonderful life together. However, homosexuality is a famously taboo topic in India. Not to mention that with one of his sons being a fashion designer who paints portraits of Naomi Campbell in his spare time, and another a would-be model with a fondness for see-through miniskirts, it seemed like I might upset the apple cart if I now announced I'm queer.

"Won't you promise me you will try to find a wife?" Bunty urged. "Won't you try harder?"

He was speaking to me sincerely, like a concerned father. He was dear, generous, and kind. Yet, his hand was heavy, warm, and had come to rest practically on top of my crotch.

"Yes, Bunty," I promised. "I will try."

"Excellent!" he replied. "Let us have some more chapati, shall we?" With this, Bunty gave Santoosh a kick, and he scurried out from under the dining table and raced off to the kitchen.

THE NEXT MORNING, Bunty arranged for me to meet with his lawyer, Parvinder Singh, another Sikh, who was willing to explain more about his religion and help me understand what I would experience later that day when I arrived at Gurdwara Bangla Sahib.

Bunty's driver took us over to Parvinder's house, where we found the lawyer in his study, contemplating a glass vitrine in which there was a scale model replica of the Golden Temple in Amritsar—sometimes called "the Vatican of Sikhism." Parvinder had a gray beard flattened by a thick mesh chin strap that held his turban snug to his head. Unlike Bunty's basic black, Parvinder's turban was a two-color affair of maroon and bright orange. Parvinder's wife (whom I later learned was a pediatric surgeon) seemed genuinely insulted and affected a convincing sulk when I wouldn't let her serve me a second breakfast. I sat on a sofa and leaned back against throw pillows so hard they must have been filled with sand. A servant brought tall glasses of orange soda and a plate with sugary balls of coconut fudge.

Parvinder talked, and I listened, unable to get a word in edgewise, for the next hour. I had arrived, he told me, at a time of tremendous excitement in the Sikh community: it was the three hundredth anniversary of the Guru Granth Sahib, which is the holy scripture for Sikhs. Two hundred years prior to this, Sikhism began in the fifteenth century as a pushback against Muslims, who were forcibly trying to convert Hindus to Islam. Ten historical gurus are revered, and the first was Guru Nanak. Once I recognized him, I began to see Guru Nanak's picture all over Delhi. To my eyes he looked like Santa Claus, only he was wearing a mustard-yellow turban.

Guru Nanak's birthplace was in Punjab, once part of India but since the partition now in Pakistan. Born in 1469, Guru Nanak grew up to become a missionary, spreading his message of tolerance and love while walking the entire length and breadth of India, from Tibet to Sri Lanka, Burma to Iraq. A much-told story has it that one day Nanak's father, a rich businessman, gave his son twenty rupees, or gold coins—then quite a sizable sum—and told him to turn a profit with it. Nanak felt called into the world for a different purpose than his father's. So, when Nanak met a group of sadhus (holy men) who hadn't eaten in some time, he spent his money to buy them food and satisfy their hunger.

"The twenty coins have multiplied," Parvinder concluded. "It is out of the grace of this experience that today's practice of langar, or feeding the hungry, has grown."

"The central tenet of Sikhism is to protect the weak," Bunty agreed, as he tossed into his mouth what I counted as his fifth ball of coconut fudge.

Langar is performed not just at Gurdwara Bangla Sahib in Delhi but at all Sikh temples—including those in the United States. (Parvinder suggested I must visit a gurdwara in Richmond Hill, Queens, for instance.) At Amritsar, there is a machine that can make up to ten thousand chapatis an hour, but they don't use it too often, as there are so many people eager to do volunteer work at the golden temple that the bread is all rolled out by hand.

"Really?" I found this a little hard to believe.

"Oh, yes. Prayer alone will not bring me to God. Knowledge alone does nothing. It is the practice of what we learn that's important," Parvinder replied. "When people cook this food, what's called the parshad, they say prayers—they put God's blessing into the meal. When we eat parshad, this is why it tastes different and is so satisfying to us."

I was still mulling this over as Bunty and I left Parvinder's house and immediately found ourselves stuck in a three hundredth anniversary parade that had brought traffic to a standstill in this part of Delhi. We were going nowhere, so Bunty and I quit his car and begin to walk. Free food was being served everywhere alongside the parade route, and Sikh women were stern in their demands for me to sample their food. It was considered a grave insult to refuse, Bunty assured me. In short order, then, I ate deep-fried samosas, a plate of lentils and rice, almond paste, ice cream, biscuits, spicy popcorn, cotton candy, and three mangoes. One woman, dressed in a psychedelic sari emblazoned with swirling paisleys, was particularly vehement, insisting I try some of her lamb kebabs.

When I laughingly explained that I didn't want to get fat, she said, "No matter how much you eat of parshad, you will never gain weight. Even a diabetic person can eat unlimited quantities of sweets; if they are parshad, it will not affect them."

Finally, we arrived at the gurdwara, and Bunty escorted me to a guesthouse where I would stay. I was introduced to Mr. Gulshan Singh, Mr. Gaaet Singh, Mr. Tony Singh, and Mr. Satnam Singh—none of them related to each other. They were dressed identically in the official regalia of Sikh temple guards, long purple tunics over tight white pants. They wore orange turbans, and each had a sword at his side, the scabbard dangling from a leather belt strapped across the chest and falling to the hip at a sharp angle. These guys were fearsome; I guessed they hadn't smiled more than a couple of times in the past six months.

Although Bunty held a letter of welcome he'd arranged to have written for me by the head priest at the gurdwara, there was much discussion in Punjabi over who I was, what I was doing here, and if I should be allowed to touch the parshad. These were my guesses, at least. Frankly, I didn't know what they were talking about, but it went on for a long time with much dramatic gesturing, fists brandished, turbans touched, and foreheads bowed. I sat, smiling and trying my damnedest to look passionately engaged in these incomprehensible proceedings, as an attendant entered, carrying a tray. He poured out glasses of water, which were handed all around. I thought of Parvinder's earlier lecture—all water at the temple is holy, he said, and will cure any sickness I may have. Yet, since arriving in India ten days ago, I'd not had a sip of anything but filtered or bottled water. I was about to spend a week alone, surrounded by total strangers. Did I really want to get "Delhi belly" now?

Everyone else had already gulped their water in one slosh. I looked at the temple guards' swords and realized not drinking this water would probably be more injurious to my immediate future. Bunty's words from the night before rang in my ear: "To conquer your heart is more difficult than to rule the world." I bowed to the men and dumped the water down my throat.

When Bunty eventually saw my berth at the guesthouse, he erupted in a fit of rage. In truth, the room was pretty shabby and about the size of a hall closet at a Leela Palace Hotel. The bed was unmade, with sheets that appeared well used. Thankfully, the room had its own bathroom, but there was no hot water, towels, or soap, and a few unusual-looking bugs. Only with the greatest of effort was I able to convince Bunty that I could survive in these less-than-luxurious accommodations. I pleaded with him not to complain to any of the four Mr. Singhs downstairs. Couldn't he understand this would set the tone for my time here and I'd be branded as the spoiled and bratty American? Eventually Bunty relented, but I could see that doing so gave him nearly physical pain.

Before he left, Bunty made sure I was given a tour of the temple complex by Sukwinder Kaur, a soft-spoken young woman who was dressed in a sherbet pink sari. Breakfast, lunch, and dinner were all served, she said, though officially the kitchen never closed, so someone who was hungry could get a meal any time, round-the-clock. They feed upwards of twenty thousand people a day, Sukwinder noted in passing.

"Excuse me," I interrupted, thinking either I'd misheard or Sukwinder had misspoken. "Don't you mean two thousand?"

"No. Twenty thousand. Sometimes more."

This outrageously large number put me into a temporary state of shock, which was perhaps why I made my next—altogether clueless—request. "Is there some sort of booklet, or an instructional video, to show me how I should go about working here?"

Sukwinder was flummoxed by my question, as if I'd asked if there was an instructional video to teach me how to breathe. "Anyone can cook, if they're willing to try," she said. "The only thing required is that you must go barefoot."

Following her directions, I removed my shoes, and we walked together over a dirt, rock, and rubble-strewn courtyard, through a crowded parking area, and to an enormous tin-roofed langar, where dozens of people were preparing that day's lunch. Sukwinder introduced me to her cousin, Biswajit Singh, a twenty-nine-year-old man with whom I would spend many hours in the days ahead. His dark beard dangled down to where his navel must be. Biswajit was the boss and the only paid employee in this entire kitchen. When we met, he grinned brightly as if he didn't have a care in the world. Biswajit spoke Punjabi and Hindi but no English. Sukwinder translated, and as I heard what her cousin said, I was incredulous at the calm bliss of his demeanor.

Thousands upon thousands of hungry men, women, and children appear at the gurdwara. They line up for hours, waiting in the hot sun, and eventually are herded into a queue that corrals them into groups of six hundred at a time. When a signal is given, they rush forward into an open-air dining area and seat themselves on the concrete floor in three parallel lines. Food on a tin plate that's put on the floor before each guest is probably the only sustenance they will eat all day.

As if this isn't enough pressure, Biswajit doesn't know from one moment to the next what supplies will be on hand for him to cook. His kitchen, like most in India, does not have any refrigerator. Instead, vegetables, grains, and beans (all meals served at the gurdwara are vegetarian) are primarily donations that arrive on an indeterminate timetable. For instance, while Sukwinder, Biswajit, and I were talking, a flatbed truck loaded with a small mountain of cauliflower pulled up—a gift from some anonymous Sikh who apparently thought this morning "Maybe I'll send a little something over to the temple."

"You didn't know this was coming?" I asked Biswajit.

"No, it is a surprise. A good surprise!" At the end of this comment, he said something that sounded like "Sat Sri Akal."

When I asked Sukwinder what this meant, she translated. "God is truth."

Not only did food appear spontaneously, but everyone who would now unload the truck of cauliflower, cut it up, cook, serve, and wash the plates it was put on were volunteers who arrived on their own capricious schedule. There was no "org" chart, no directory of staff. Every person—now including me—who was working in this kitchen just decided today "I guess it is time to spend an hour or two over at the langar." Think of trying to feed your family this way, and then imagine you're having twenty thousand surprise guests.

Sukwinder asked me if I was ready to start.

"Yes," I said. "What would you like me to do?"

"Oh, just jump in wherever you like," she replied.

With this being the big anniversary of the Guru Granth Sahib, Sikh pilgrims were arriving from all over the world, and Sukwinder was busy with many other people's needs. She'd been gracious to give me these few minutes, but I could tell she was anxious to move on. Bunty was gone; I was on my own. For a moment, I experienced a panicky realization that I was the only white face in this vast kitchen; no one around me spoke any English.

What was I doing here?

Lentils were simmering in copper cauldrons the size of Jacuzzi bathtubs and set above open flames stoked by firewood. This looked exciting, and eventually I'd put in several sizzling hours working over these fires. In my apprenticeship afternoon, though, I opted for something less challenging when I saw two slate troughs built low to the ground, each as big as a children's swimming pool in a public park. A pair of women were stationed at either end of each trough, where they sat behind tall mounds of chapati flatbread dough. Working quickly, they pried off a hunk of this dough, separated it into smaller pieces, rolled these into balls, and tossed them out, in turn, to dozens of other people who were positioned at low benches along the troughs' long sides. After catching the balls, these men and women rolled the dough out into flat disks that they stacked up like pancakes.

This is what Parvinder Singh had told me about—it's because of volunteers such as these people that the chapati-making machine goes unused at the Golden Temple in Amritsar.

There were many small rolling pins lying about. I'd made a pie crust or two in my time. I could do this, couldn't I? Nonetheless, after sitting down, it felt at first that everyone else knew what they were doing and my efforts were a hindrance. I saw Indian women take a dough ball and, with a couple of deft motions, flatten it out into a perfect patty. I wasn't nearly this agile, but I put my head down and tried to silence the doubt and self-reproach in my mind.

THIS KITCHEN AT Gurdwara Bangla Sahib was my world for the next five days. Every morning, I'd wake up early and head over to the langar barefoot, the soles of my feet blackened before I arrived at the cooking shed. There, I'd chug a few cups of very hot, very sweet chai tea. For the next fourteen hours, from 8:00 a.m. to 10:00 p.m., I worked harder physically than just about any other time in my life.

I rolled out many hundreds of chapatis, and I learned how to cook them over a wood-fired griddle. While stirring those copper "jacuzzis" full of beans, I also tended the embers smoldering beneath them. Under a rippling tarpaulin, I sat outdoors surrounded by tall piles of potatoes, tomatoes, zucchini, or ginger root. It was up to me to pick over, clean, and chop every last piece of produce I could see. There was no one to help me; all other volunteers were busy doing something else. How was this possible? What if I hadn't come to Delhi? Who'd chop the vegetables then, huh? But I had, and here I was, up to my shoulders in eggplant.

I was starting to know hunger. I thought of my father often in these long days in Delhi. What would Dad have to say about an ever-rotating cadre of sadhus who wandered through the kitchen at all times of day and night? Usually they had their heads bowed, praying silently to themselves. However, at some inner prompting of their own, they sometimes felt the need to shout at the top of their lungs. Were these the prayers that were supposed to make the food taste so good and be calorie-free?

Hours would pass—and once an entire day—when I didn't hear a single word of my native tongue; every interchange I had was done strictly through pantomime. There was one notable exception, though, and remembering it still makes me blush with shame.

It was lunchtime, and yet another group of six hundred had just rushed in to take their places on the concrete floor. I was carrying a heavy pot of lentil stew, working my way down a line of hungry people, plopping a spoonful onto each outstretched tin plate. As I moved quickly, most of the diners became a blur. Sometimes, though, I looked up and saw a face smiling at me, and felt a flood of happiness at what I was doing. Gradually, I began to allow myself the occasional human touch. I would squeeze an old woman's shoulder encouragingly or tickle a child's ear. I hoped this made the whole interchange a little more compassionate.

I'd been doing this for a few hours one afternoon when another volunteer, a guy with a brilliantly turquoise turban, suddenly jerked on my elbow and pulled me aside. Speaking in plummy tones, his accent sounding like he'd just stepped off a wide green lawn at Oxford or Cambridge, he said to me, "My friend, it's all very dear these caresses I see you are giving, but any physical contact here is quite forbidden. Many of these people have cholera, leprosy, tuberculosis, or something far worse. And, have you even considered that you, too, might have germs of your own you could pass on to them? Now, go wash your hands, and then get back to work!"

The man pushed me toward a door in the kitchen, where there was a bathroom I didn't know existed until this moment. Inside, I spotted the first and only piece of soap I saw in my entire time at the Sikh temple in Delhi. As I scrubbed my hands, I felt a choke of anger rising in my throat—not for the guy who'd scolded me, but for myself. I'd been indulging in Mother Teresa fantasies and gotten busted for it.

My hands clean, I went back to serving lentils. I didn't touch the guests anymore. And, after I'd worried over it for a while, I eventually became glad that this man pulled me aside with his reprimand. Squeezing someone's shoulder is easy. What's much harder, I decided, was to focus my energy into the food and infuse this humblest of meals with love.

"Prayer alone will not bring me to God," Parvinder Singh had said. "Knowledge alone does nothing. It is the practice of what we learn that is important."

The rest of my week went by quickly. When it was time to go, I was sorry to leave the Gurdwara Bangla Sahib and India.

Sat Sri Akal. God is truth.

3

ALL ABOUT ALLAH

L EARN A NEW WORD, AND OFTEN A STRANGE THING HAP-
pens. Though blind to it your entire life, this freshly acquired vo-
cabulary suddenly jumps before you in the most unexpected ways.
Similarly, when I returned from India and told friends about my experiences of cooking at the gurdwara, people who'd never expressed any
knowledge of how the poor were fed began to suggest other instances of
charitable cooking. They ranged from awesome to gruesome.

Had I ever heard of Daniel Rakowitz, a drug dealer in New York's
East Village who in the summer of 1989 killed his girlfriend, dismem-
bered her body, and cooked the remains up into a stew that he fed to
homeless people living in Tompkins Square Park?

I had not.

Did I know of the Restaurants de Coeur in France? They were
started by Coluche (Michel Gérard Joseph Colucci), a comedian whose
coarse humor and profanity-laced routines earned him a title of "the
French Lenny Bruce." When Coluche found out in the mid-1980s that
the French government spent more money to store surplus food products than it would cost to distribute them free to the poor, he was
spurred into action. Today, the Restaurants de Coeur feed over 600,000
people a day in France.

Was I aware that Mort Zuckerman, the real estate tycoon and
owner/publisher of the *New York Daily News* and *U.S. News and World
Report*, gave many millions each year to fund Meir Panim, a chain of
soup kitchens across the state of Israel?

Or, had I heard about a method of gastrophilanthropy called *nazr*, which occurs in Iran? An Arabic word that means "to make a spiritual vow," *nazr* is a supplication to Allah. Charity is a key pillar of Islam, and the Qur'an is filled with stories of people assisting the needy. One of the most popular forms of nazr involves voluntarily cooking for others and is mostly practiced by women. In hopes of making her heart's desire come true—perhaps it's for her daughter to give birth to a healthy baby, or for a son to find a suitable wife—an Iranian woman brokers a deal with Allah. She promises to prepare a particular dish, then distribute it to a specified number of people. Typically, she'll observe the date her prayer request was answered by cooking on this anniversary for the next five years, ten years, or even longer.

Curious to see how such arrangements played out in Iran, I made plans to visit this country, once known as Persia. Before leaving, I sought advice from Najmieh Batmanglij, reaching her on the telephone at her home in Washington, D.C. Batmanglij has made it her life's work to adapt Persian recipes to Western tastes and is the author of many books, including *New Foods of Life: Ancient Persian and Iranian Cooking and Ceremonies*, which the *Los Angeles Times* called "the definitive book of Persian cooking."

Arranging nazr is common among rich and poor Iranian women alike, Batmanglij told me. Those who are better off will usually prepare dishes such as biryani, which is lamb meat cooked with rice, raisins, and almonds, or fesenjan, made with walnuts, pomegranates, and chicken. A nazr can also be something simpler: dates or apricots that are picked green and eaten with salt.

"During times of crisis and misfortune, Persian women believe that making charitable food will ward off danger and evil spirits," Batmanglij said. "Everyone has private wishes. A nazr feeds those hopes; at the same time, it nourishes the hungry."

YAZD IS A desert city in central Iran famed for its silk-weaving industry. It also boasts a distinctive style of Persian architecture designed to mitigate the punishing summer heat (100-degree days and higher are not uncommon) and make the most of this region's scant breezes and rainfall.

In Yazd, I dined one afternoon with a woman named Maryam. When I stopped by her house, Maryam, who is a conservative Muslim, was dressed in a chador, despite the triple-digit temperature. This is the body-concealing black robe that women are required to wear in Iran since the Islamic Revolution in 1979, when Ayatollah Khomeini overthrew Shah Reza Pahlavi. With one hand Maryam gripped this robe tight about her chin, forcing her to do all cooking with one free hand. If I had not been present, she would not have done this, as Muslim women usually shed their chadors in the privacy of their own homes. Watching Maryam work at a gas cooktop, its flame turned quite high, I felt responsible for this extreme modesty and worried that her garment would catch fire. Such kitchen mishaps are distressingly common in Iran.

Maryam's *batterie de cuisine* was a small number of pots and pans, each with a bottom dented from much hard use. She used no measuring cups or spoons; every ingredient was added with a practiced dispatch. One of her secrets, she shyly divulged, was a homemade tomato paste. She would cut up tomatoes, leave them outdoors to dry for a day or two in Yazd's brutally strong sunshine, and then puree them with olive oil. We chatted about a few more cooking tips until I worked up my nerve to ask Maryam if she had ever entered into a nazr.

"Yes. My husband had a very bad disease when we were engaged to be married seventeen years ago," she replied. "I did my first nazr during Muharram [an auspicious month on the Shiite Muslim calendar], and my husband, Amir, was soon well again." Every year since, on the anniversary of Amir's return to health, Maryam has cooked enough to feed approximately 150 poor people.

She had done this for seventeen years? I was dumbfounded by this fact, but Maryam did not find it noteworthy. "Some people do it every week, or every month—it happens frequently in this neighborhood," she said.

Acts of nazr bind the local community, Maryam believes, by letting people know if a nearby family has either a sorrow or an event to rejoice over. "When someone else's food arrives at your house, it reminds you of them, and you may think to pray and seek Allah's help on their behalf."

Just at this moment, a young girl showed up at Maryam's door bringing a small dish of halvah—a confection Iranians call a "sweetie" made from sugar, lard, nutmeg, and cinnamon. "Someone in that house had a bad car accident," Maryam explained in hushed tones after the girl left. "They are praying for this person to recover quickly and completely. This is their nazr."

Everything in her house was spotless, though Maryam, Amir, and their two small daughters lived, ate, and slept together in one room. A few well-worn carpets were on the floor; throw pillows leaned up against the walls. It was here, after I watched her prepare our lunch, that we sat down together to feast on lamb cooked with yellow split peas and an eggplant stew called bademjan. I could almost taste the sun's rays in the tomato paste she'd stirred into the eggplant. Without much arm-twisting from Maryam, I ate seconds and then a third helping—as did Amir. After he put his empty plate aside, he laid back on the floor and folded his hands on top of his waist. Within seconds, Amir was asleep.

Theirs was an arranged marriage, Maryam told me, her voice a whisper. They didn't know each other when they were introduced but liked each other at once. Amir has worked in the same textile factory since he was fifteen years old, but after thirty years of seven-days-a-week labor, he's recently been able to retire.

Maryam had been wonderfully kind. Welcoming me, a total stranger, into her home, allowing me to stand beside her while I watched and took notes as she cooked, and then serving me this fragrant food. It might have been polite to show gratitude by ending my incessant inquiries about the meaning of every single movement she had made. I was still bothered by something, though, and couldn't resist one more question. Speaking softly not to disturb Amir, I asked Maryam if she was truly convinced that her promise of cooking food for the poor had caused Allah to heal her husband.

"Can a nazr really be that powerful?" I asked.

Maryam turned a fond gaze toward Amir, who was snoring softly. This sound, the proof that he was alive, provided her only answer.

As I learned more about Iran, it began to make sense why this devotional practice is so beloved by Persian women. After all, they face constant reminders that they're considered second-class citizens, and they endure blatant prejudice. Cooking a nazr can make a woman feel that she has at least some agency as well as a chance to influence her own destiny.

Consider these facts. When I visited, women still were made to ride at the back of the bus. A woman's opinion was worth half of a man's in a court of law. Women could have no contact with men to whom they were not related—even a handshake—without the presence of a male relative. They weren't to be seen on the street unless accompanied by a man. Given these daily deprivations, it is no wonder many Iranian women like to believe that whipping up a charitable batch of biryani might help things to go their way. You've heard the old cliché "the way to a man's heart is through his stomach." With a nazr, it's Allah's stomach that's being enticed.

The nazr custom also flourishes because Iran's is a home-based culture. "We are the reverse of café society," Morteza Barharloo, an Iranian poet and novelist, told me one evening when he had me over to his apartment for a cup of tea. "You can't really get anything good to eat at restaurants; all the best cooking in Iran happens at home," he said. "And Iranians are obsessed with hospitality, especially with giving a warm welcome to strangers."

This absolutely was my experience, as I was repeatedly charmed by the friendliness of Iranians. Few foreign tourists visit, especially from the United States, a country with which Iran has no diplomatic relations. As I made my way about cities and villages, people I encountered on the street smiled, waved hello, and sometimes rushed up to me. When they learned where I lived, their grins would widen. "Obama!" they might say. Or, "America. Good country!" From those who spoke more English, I got the sense that they were embarrassed by their then president, Mahmoud Ahmadinejad.

To really feel the love, you need to be invited into an Iranian family's house for a meal, which is not hard to do. In slightly less than two weeks of traveling, I was offered a home-cooked meal three separate times, twice by people I had just met.

At one of these occasions my hostess asked, "Would you like to eat as an American does, in a chair? Or, like an Iranian—on the floor?"

"Like an Iranian," I immediately replied.

With a big smile, she spread out a plastic sheet in the center of her living room and placed a fine cloth over it. She then served her family and me a plate of rice topped with stuffed peppers in pomegranate sauce. As I learned at Maryam's house in Yazd, the wonderful thing about dining this way is that when you overeat—as you'll be encouraged to do—you can simply stretch out at meal's end.

Cooking a nazr is not only a spiritual practice, my hostess explained, but also makes psychological sense. "When you feel out of control because a bad thing has happened, you desperately wish there was something you could do," she said. "Praying and worrying are two favorite pastimes for women, but they don't truly distract you, do they? Cooking for a big crowd takes your mind off your worries completely. It is busywork, but the result helps others and helps you."

How well I understood this! During those years when I was growing up in Levittown, with those countless hours spent fretting over confusing things I was learning about in school—the Scopes Monkey Trial, for instance, or nocturnal emissions, or did I truly believe what I heard Dad preaching each Sunday morning—how comforting it was to push those anxieties aside, at least for a while, by the labor of making dinner for my family.

BASED ON THE abundant hospitality I experienced, it seemed Iranian women like to cook for a crowd, even when a small number of guests are expected. One night, in the enchanting city of Shiraz, I was invited to a dinner party for eight people, but there was enough food on the table to easily satisfy three times as many. Before dinner, we sipped hot tea and nibbled sohan, a crunchy, sweet Iranian confection that's something like a praline. I asked a few of the other guests what sorts of food they'd make for a nazr. These were cultured and prosperous women. I sensed that for them this custom was a benign superstition, like saying "bless you" after someone sneezes.

"Charity foods are usually high in calories," one lady suggested. "So something like saffron brownies."

"Rice pudding with butter and saffron."

"Or, noodle soup, with meatballs, and a broth made from lamb bones boiled with saffron."

"It really doesn't matter," another woman concluded. She then cited a famous Persian poet. "'The best recipe is always hunger,' Rumi said. When someone is hungry, they will eat any food you give them."

Why, I wondered aloud, was saffron included in every dish they'd mentioned, sweet or savory? Oh yes, the ladies agreed, saffron is not only good-tasting but also good for you.

"It steadies your nerves," one woman claimed.

Another lady mentioned Persepolis, a ceremonial capital from the sixth century BCE, ruins of which were only a few dozen miles from where we were sitting. In my visit to this UNESCO World Heritage Site earlier that day, I heard how Darius the Great as well as his son Xerxes would come to Persepolis each spring to receive tributes from all the lands and peoples under their rule.

"Give tributes to the king, because you want something from the king," the lady explained. "Nazr is only a supernatural version of this idea. If you please Allah by feeding the poor, Allah may give you what you want."

After dinner, Kvos drove me back to my hotel. He was a handsome and dapper man whom I guessed to be in his mid-seventies. I asked Kvos if it was typical in Iran to serve sweets before a meal as an appetizer, as his sister had done that evening. No, he replied. This was only the case on special occasions, such as a wedding or some other festive meal. His sister was spoiling me, in other words.

"We do things differently at festive meals in the United States," I explained. "We offer our guests salty snacks as hors d'oeuvres, which causes them to become thirsty. They drink liquor, get into a relaxed mood, and the party becomes livelier."

Kvos smiled ruefully and assured me that he was perfectly aware of how a cocktail hour functions. Things worked the same way in Iran until the Islamic Revolution banned all consumption of alcohol.

The Park Hotel where I was staying, he said, was once the pride of Shiraz. Today it is a hard-worn spot, grimy and tattered, but Kvos recalled that when the Park was first built, in the late 1960s, he'd spent many pleasant afternoons there sitting by a pool in the courtyard, sipping whiskey, and admiring young women in their bikinis. He found it incredible, and I agreed, that in his lifetime the clock had been turned backwards in Iran. The courtyard pool is long gone, and it's now a serious crime to get a little tipsy while ogling pretty girls on a lazy summer day.

FOR MANY WEEKS, I thought of all the amazing things I saw in Iran. I wrote a couple of design stories about the handicrafts such as blue and white painted pottery, or zellige, an intricate form of mosaic tile work found in many mosques in Iran. To anyone who would listen, I insisted that Esfahan, the third-largest city in Iran, which was built four centuries ago but still has its old town mostly intact, must be one of the most beautiful man-made spots on Earth.

Mostly, however, I kept thinking of how Iranian women volunteer to make food for others. My thoughts would return to Maryam and her pledge to Allah to feed 150 people. She was planning to keep this yearly charitable effort going for the rest of her life—all prepared in the cramped kitchen of her small cottage.

Could I cook this way, for needy people, from my house?

Inspired, I started showing up one morning a week at a soup kitchen on Ninth Avenue hoping that after the management there got to know me, I could suggest bringing over a dish now and then. A kale salad? A huge platter of spicy meatballs? Regrettably, I was informed that New York City's many laws and regulations about food service prevented nonprofessionals from bringing their cooking into the kitchen. I had to content myself with standing in the serving line passing out apples or pieces of bread, which I did, but it seemed like a neutered form of nazr.

I suppose it was unrealistic for me to expect anything different. Yazd and Shiraz have a totally different culture than New York City's. In the Big Apple, we don't rely on, or even particularly trust, the kindness of strangers. We pride ourselves on not knowing our neighbors, even when we share a wall with them. So, I couldn't just show up at the apartment building next door with a box of saffron brownies or eggplant cooked with my sunbaked tomato puree. People might think my nazr was trying to poison them or, worse, that I'd cooked up my lover like the druggie Daniel Rakowitz.

I was still traveling for journalistic assignments, though. So, whenever I possibly could, I decided to add a few days to future trips and continue to learn more about gastrophilanthropy. This was a goal I thought the Persian chef Najmieh Batmanglij would support.

"Cooking isn't just a duty," Batmanglij had told me. "When you prepare a meal, whether it's a nazr or just dinner for your family, you must try to pass on something positive through the food. Something is missing in the world when we don't do this."

4

YES, WE (SOUP) CAN

WHEN THE GREAT RECESSION OF 2008 BEGAN, ELKHART, Indiana, was suddenly in the national news. President Barack Obama visited four different times as he tried to push through his economic stimulus package. While it once boasted some of the lowest unemployment numbers in the United States, Elkhart now had the highest. This sudden shift, which occurred within a thirteen-month period, was caused by a one-two punch of high fuel prices and shrinking consumer confidence. Almost overnight, the city's main industry—the manufacturing of recreational vehicles, what critics call "whales on wheels"—was rendered obsolete. With gasoline at $4 a gallon, Elkhart couldn't give away these fuel-guzzling RVs.

Reading about this, I realized more than three decades had passed since I lived in Elkhart. How had the years and a soured economy changed this place I briefly called home? I also wondered if I could meet a gastrophilanthropist to show me how charitable cookery was done in Indiana. A couple of computer clicks, a phone call or two, and this last question was answered, as I'd arranged to cook for a few days in the kitchen at Faith Mission of Elkhart.

SITUATED ON A pretty hill about three blocks from Elkhart's Main Street, Faith Mission of Elkhart is a Modernist steel structure with dramatic planes of sheet glass. This imposing building was formerly the Recreational Vehicle Hall of Fame Museum, where visitors paid to see exhibits detailing America's love affair with RVs. Today, this facility is a harbor for the homeless, many of whom became destitute when they were laid off from their jobs at Elkhart's RV factories.

The residents of Faith Mission, which has accommodations for 135 people, are either addled by drugs and drink, mentally impaired, recently released from prison, or some combination of these issues. They sleep in bunk beds, packed tightly together, in three small dormitory rooms. Breakfast, lunch, and dinner are served to them—as well as to an equal number of walk-in guests—every day. The mission is adjacent to Washington Gardens, a federally subsidized housing project, and another complex for low-income senior citizens. People living in these places usually receive food stamps, social security, or disability checks, but these funds tend to run low by month's end. This is when meal attendance peaks at Faith Mission.

Mike Perez, a development director, escorted me around on the morning I arrived. The atmosphere is tightly regulated, with many rules for residents to follow. Wake-up is at 6:00 a.m., lights out at 10:00 p.m. There is zero tolerance for anyone found with an intoxicating substance while on the premises. This is a *working* mission, Perez told me more than once. No one gets a free ride. Some earn their keep by doing grounds maintenance and custodial work; others help by cooking meals. A worship service occurs every evening at 7:00 p.m. and features the singing of gospel songs, Bible readings, a sermon, and prayer. Attendance is mandatory for residents at Faith Mission, the majority of whom are men.

"Men are more stubborn in their sense of pride," Perez explained. "Women? They will ask for help. They'll go back to their families and somehow make it work. But men get drunk, get angry, and burn bridges. Men would prefer to live under a highway overpass, out in the cold, rather than admit they need assistance. When all else fails, though, they end up here."

Our tour ended in the kitchen, where Perez introduced me to Kerry Czoch and Ann Conner. These two women had worked together for many years and enjoyed the affectionate banter of an old married couple. They called each other "dear" and "sweetie pie"; they said they're best friends.

"Best friend besides God, that is," Czoch added, and Conner nodded in agreement.

Czoch had a husband and grown children, but she dressed like a teenager. When we first met, she was wearing a long-sleeve blouse completely covered with Valentine's hearts. Over this she had a red short-sleeve T-shirt on which were printed the words "One World, One Love!" What appeared to be the fragment of a red feather boa was looped around her hair and yanked up into a ponytail that dangled, somewhat lopsidedly, from the crown of her head. Czoch had a frenetic, ready-for-drama personality and a piercingly loud voice.

A widow since her husband died nine years earlier, Conner had two adult sons who no longer resided in Elkhart. Soft-spoken and very thin, she wore a shaggy wig anchored to her head with a baseball cap. A veteran of nearly thirty years of working in nursing homes before she came to Faith Mission, Conner had the tranquil mien of a person who is seldom angered.

"This is a Christian place, but we don't push it down people's throats," Czoch said. "We don't stand up on tables and yell about Jesus, but the message still gets served."

"Food is very powerful," agreed Conner. "If you do not eat, your body begins to break down, and you become a weak, negative person. It's the one thing everyone in this world has in common!"

Mike Perez called them "Soup Can Kerry" and "Can Opener Ann," a not-so-gentle jibe at how often they served food that was simply dumped from a metal cylinder into a heating tray. I saw Perez's point when I heard the menu for lunch: roast pork, canned boiled potatoes, canned peas and mushrooms, canned fruit cocktail, and chopped iceberg lettuce mixed with canned green olives and covered with a blizzard of packaged grated cheese. For dessert, there was an enormous bowl of M&M's in a speckled shade of salmon unlike anything I'd encountered before.

It turned out these M&M's were factory rejects and a tax-deductible donation for their manufacturer. Such botches—candy with the wrong mix of food coloring, mutant donuts with the hole closed up—arrive regularly, as do oddments from fast-food chains such as Olive Garden, Little Caesar's, and Pizza Hut that are past a company's accepted expiration date but are still edible and, more important, still a write-off for the corporations. Can Opener Ann and Soup Can Kerry must be creative in devising new ways to make such gifts palatable. When all else fails, they sometimes arrange a buffet that they wishfully call the Taco Bar.

Czoch and Conner gave me a fast tutorial, but barely five minutes had passed before Czoch asked, "Ya ready to boogie?"

"Put me to work," I replied.

Conner pointed to three stainless steel vats full of pork ribs and tenderloins she'd roasted the afternoon before and set in a refrigerator overnight. I was to cut this meat into individual portions. There was a several-inch-thick sludge of congealed fat on top of each pan. Conner instructed me to scoop around with my fingers, discarding most of this, but leaving some "for flavor."

My eyebrows must have raised, as she quickly added, "We also have tuna salad, if people don't eat pork for religious reasons or because they have hypertension."

That's not what worried me. I was thinking about the vegetarian recipes I helped cook at the langar and how much more healthy, wholesome, and economical the food was in India than here in Indiana. Ribs, I later learned, are a rare treat on Faith Mission's menu; usually the protein is either chicken or beef. There was somehow a glut of pork at the Indiana Food Bank, and Czoch bought it at pennies a pound. This explanation only confounded the issue. How could pork be plentiful enough in America that nearly two hundred pounds could be bought for $30?

Once I chopped up the meat, I began my attack on countless cans. The opener was a medieval-looking contraption that plunged a dagger into the lid; then, a large manually operated crank rotated the cylinder around this sunken blade. When one of Faith Mission's residents showed me how to work this device, he overdid it, crushing a five-gallon can with such force that it exploded, shooting up a mushroom cloud of, well, mushrooms.

"It's not a test of strength," Conner murmured gently, as she helped wipe up the mess. "There's some skill involved."

WHILE WE LABORED together over the next few days, I became friendly with several of my coworkers at Faith Mission of Elkhart. I talked with Phil, a carpenter who lost his job at Four Seasons Housing, a modular home builder in nearby Middlebury, Indiana, and was subsequently evicted from his home. David was a nurse laid off from a managed-care facility in South Bend and had lost everything but his cell phone. And John, a PhD, was at one time a professor of biochemistry at Southern Illinois University. Some of the incidents these men described had a certain logic to them; many didn't. What sort of details had they failed to mention? When you tumble down a rabbit hole, I guessed, it is tough to remember your precise rate of fall.

Mark Caldwell was a powerfully built man suffering from an infection he called "pink eye." Flat broke, he needed help in paying for his medicine. This would only cost $6, so I offered to fund his purchase and tagged along as Caldwell headed off to a pharmacy. Without much prompting, he spilled out his story.

When he was still a carpenter at several different factories where recreational vehicles were manufactured, Caldwell supported a girlfriend and two ex-wives with whom he'd fathered a total of four children. A resident at Faith Mission for one month, he'd arrived here straight from prison, where he had been serving time for a drunk driving charge.

Caldwell readily admitted that he was no angel. A convicted felon, he'd previously been in prison for an assault and battery charge. Still, at the time of this latest scrape with the law, he insisted, he was not drunk. In a breathalyzer test, he claimed, the amount of alcohol in your system is less important than how recently you swallowed it. You are much more likely to "blow numbers" if you've just had a drink, as was the case with Caldwell. As he told it, for the crime of drinking two Budweisers, he was locked up for twenty-six months. Meanwhile, he lost his job, one of his ex-wives got killed, and his girlfriend became a prostitute.

Then there was Lonnie Spearman, a young man from Erie, Pennsylvania. Spearman's troubles began when he had a fight with his father. On the day after their argument, Spearman decided to run away from home. With money he had saved, he bought a one-way Amtrak ticket to Chicago because he longed to see the Sears Tower, which he was shocked to learn was now called the Willis Tower. En route to the Windy City, Spearman impulsively decided that he also wanted a look around the football stadium at Notre Dame University and got off the train in South Bend. A weekend spent at a $40-a-night hotel and what he vaguely described as a couple of "bad situations" depleted the rest of his fortune. Penniless, he was left with no alternative but to travel by foot back home to Pennsylvania. Spearman got as far as Elkhart, where he was arrested by county police, who informed him that walking on railroad tracks was a misdemeanor. The cops brought him to Faith Mission, and here he was, opening cans of fruit cocktail.

Feed the hungry and help those in trouble.
Then your light will shine out of the darkness,
And the darkness around you will be as bright as day.
—Isaiah 58:10

This Bible verse was painted in large letters on a cinderblock wall outside Faith Mission's kitchen. A lunchtime crowd—mostly black men, a few Latinos, a couple of white guys, and a handful of women and children—had gathered. Several dining tables were equipped with wooden high chairs for the youngest of visitors.

"We are a family-friendly environment," Conner said. Most of the children who come to lunch, often lugging along an infant brother or sister, don't know where their parents go during the day, she told me, and are left alone to fend for themselves. The gurgle and laughter of these youngsters was sometimes the only noise I heard in the dining hall. Adults ate in silence.

Czoch prayed out loud at each meal and demanded the men remove their hats before she would begin. This often took a while, with much singling out of laggards—"Hey, bozo! Yeah, you in the knitted red cap! Get it off your friggin' head!"—before she was satisfied that everyone was ready to offer their bareheaded thanks to God.

"We are grateful you've given us all another day in which we can try to get it right," Czoch usually said at her prayer's conclusion. "Bless this food to our bodies, oh God! May we learn to love and take care of each other, and will you continue to shake the ground beneath our feet."

I squirmed at this last request. Things seemed shaky enough for most guests here, if the experiences of Lonnie Spearman, Mark Caldwell, and Tonnes Lovelady-Malone were typical.

She was the mission's emergency care director and the first person most people who showed up here got to see. I sat with Lovelady-Malone one afternoon, and she explained that she interviewed five or six new people a day. Lately, she'd noticed an uptick in the number of teenagers who showed up, alone and scared.

"There is crisis and chaos in the world today, and our young people are just falling through the cracks," she said.

Lovelady-Malone was all too familiar with crisis and chaos, I learned. She had a trim figure, with her hair in thin, neat braids, and she dressed like a schoolteacher in prim gray slacks with a white blouse. So, I was shocked when she divulged that for twenty-seven years of her life, she was a crack addict and sex worker.

"I was really hard-core," she said. "Once, I went eleven days without sleep, high the whole time."

Her father was a Baptist preacher, and her upbringing was middle class. "But, I didn't understand my mother. I was not getting any attention from her. I discovered that if you have money, and if you have drugs, you can make friends easily, and people want to be around you. This was a big discovery for me at the time. But when the money ran out, I had to start turning tricks to get more. Even when I was on the streets, I still had my faith in God. It may sound funny to say this, but I would pray before I got into every man's car, asking God to please help me get out of there alive."

Lovelady-Malone had two children but realized she couldn't take care of them, as drugs became more important to her than parenthood.

She dropped them off one day with her mother, disappeared, and did not return for twenty years. Her parents put out a search warrant with the Indiana police, but she was never found, even though in all that time she had barely left Elkhart, only going out at night. Her weight dropped to under seventy pounds. "I didn't ever see the light of day and didn't want to, either."

When she finished talking, I was about to commiserate and say that I was also a preacher's kid and I understood how difficult it was to grow up under the gaze of so many churchgoers. However, to make this analogy between her experience and mine seemed too much of a stretch— even something of an insult. I kept silent.

On my last morning at Faith Mission I arrived in the kitchen, where I found Czoch munching away on what she admitted was her third Krispy Kreme donut. "These are really bad for you, aren't they?" she asked.

"Yes, they are," I agreed.

"Why do they taste so yummy then?"

"It's cruel, isn't it?"

Czoch's husband was the publisher of a group of trade magazines that serviced the RV industry, with titles such as *Truck Industry* and *Pavement*. She had worked with him as an advertising sales representative. Good at her job, Czoch liked the hurly-burly of meeting new clients and wining and dining them. At just the right time, pre-recession, they decided to sell the business. They bought a fixer-upper and took two years to make it the dream house they wanted. Age fifty and retired, Czoch was soon bored.

"I'd been lucky. I felt like I needed to give something back. So, one day, I am on my way to the supermarket, and I say to God, 'Listen! I'll tell you what. My life is in your hands. Do with me what you want.' Well, be careful what you pray for!"

As she told it, Czoch soon saw a copy of the *Elkhart Truth*, and in the newspaper's classified section she spotted an advertisement announcing that Faith Mission needed a chef. She knew she enjoyed being in the kitchen but had no professional experience cooking for crowds. None-theless, she decided to stop by where the mission was before it moved to its newer, nicer location.

"So, duh! I got the job," she said. "Ann was already there, and good work was going on, but oh my! It was pretty dismal down there, and grim. There was a pest problem, the rooms were not well lit, there wasn't enough equipment, and no air-conditioning. I swear, it got up to about 125 degrees in the summertime, back in the kitchen!"

"Still, right away, I liked it," Czoch continued. "I liked seeing people grow and rise up. They graduate from here, go on with their lives, and get back their jobs and their houses."

"Does that really happen?" I asked.

"Sure, it happens. It happens a lot!"

I hadn't seen too many "most likely to succeed" stories in my talks with the residents, I told Czoch. Listening to them, I admitted, was difficult. I became increasingly self-conscious, feeling guilty about how fortunate I have been in comparison to what life had given others. "Sometimes I feel like I am rubber-necking at a car accident, and I'm staring at things it's not polite to look at," I said.

"Yeah, it's hard. Working in a place like this really changes the way you think," she agreed. "Everyone has a story. There are a million of them! Some are hilarious, others are horrific and will just break your heart. But you can't let it!" Czoch was nearly screaming now. "What good will it do for you to get depressed? It's not your fault! Besides, these guys are lonely and used to being ignored. I'll bet they're flattered you are listening to what they have to say."

I told Czoch how impressed I was that Conner and she had created an atmosphere in their kitchen where these guys straight out of prison would help them get meals ready. "It's really something of a miracle," I said.

"Well, I tell you one thing. You can't beat people over the head with the Bible! We try to just be a light. And, you have to have lots of patience. Some people don't have linear thinking when it comes to performing tasks. I always thought this was innate, but I've come to see that this is a learned way of thinking. I'll say to one of these guys, 'do this, this, then this and this,' and the poor thing will be halfway through step one, and he's already lost. He's not being lazy. He has a mental problem!"

Czoch sighed and reached for another donut. "I guess it's a maternal thing. It's an environment we nurture, and somehow it softens these guys up. It makes them feel important and included. Ann and I are everybody's mom."

Our conversation concluded, Czoch asked me to supervise a guy named David Loken. He told me right away that he was a Mormon, and my failure to react to this abrupt admission seemed to disappoint him. Balding, chubby, and good-natured, Loken told me he was "forty-seven and a half." He asked permission to pretend that he was my younger brother.

Was he mentally challenged, or had he just spent too much time by himself? Mike Perez told me the single biggest problem most homeless people face is not hunger or cold. Instead, it's loneliness. Maybe Loken had gone for many years without having any close friends.

He followed my directions with unnerving exactitude. Czoch hoisted two cardboard crates of green peppers onto a stainless steel table and asked him and me to wash, core, and remove their seeds. She didn't offer any further specifics on how she wanted the peppers cut, an omission that made Loken visibly upset. To placate him, I suggested a quarter-inch dice. Loken shook his head in vigorous agreement and set to work, methodically producing tall piles of green peppers cut to precisely this shape.

Lunch that day was the Taco Bar. Conner told me to scoop several large containers of sour cream into an ugly gray plastic tub that would be placed on the buffet. To amuse my little brother, I decided to use some of Loken's oh-so-carefully chopped peppers to spell out the word "Hola!" on top of this white lake of dairy product.

When I reminded him of the word's meaning in Spanish, Loken chuckled and snorted like this was the funniest thing he'd ever seen.

When it was time for lunch, Czoch got the men to take their hats off before she prayed and again asked God to shake the ground beneath our feet. Loken and I assumed our positions. I spooned up ground beef; Loken served the sour cream and was extra vigilant in not disturbing the peppery lettering.

As each and every person came through the serving line, Loken pointed and said, "See? It says 'Hola!' That's Spanish for 'hello.'"

5

YOUR QUESTION IS MUKI!

WHAT DOES IT SUGGEST ABOUT THE UNITED STATES THAT when hungry people come to one of our nation's soup kitchens, they might be served discolored candy, or pizza that is several days old? If you are what you eat, aren't we telling the poor they are garbage when we feed them things deemed unacceptable by the rest of us?

On the contrary, wouldn't it be wonderful if all soup kitchens were places of healing where the hungry could rely on finding truly life-enhancing food? Almost like remedial training centers, people could learn to eat differently and eat better than they had before. While this may sound like a utopian fantasy, it's one shared by *shojin ryori*, a form of gastrophilanthropy that once flourished throughout Japan and still is practiced today in the country's many Buddhist monasteries, especially those in Kyoto. For centuries, shojin ryori has been guided by rules of healthy dining—eat seasonal, eat local, eat little or no meat—we in the West have discovered only recently.

Because Buddha lived as a mendicant, many believe an experience of poverty is necessary in order to understand Buddhist principles of nonattachment. In a practice known as takuhatsu, young men training to become Buddhist monks are given a begging bowl and required to go forth every morning to seek donations of food.

Both parties understand themselves to be engaged in a spiritual exercise: novitiates obtain sustenance for their religious study, while benefactors expect to be blessed for their generosity. Monks are taught to accept without complaint what is given to them, even if it's not necessarily what they might want to eat.

When they return from their daily rounds of begging, monks bring this bounty to a tenzo (head chef in a Buddhist monastery), who acts as a combination of psychoanalyst and dietician. Not only does he advise the Buddhist priests and those in training, but people from the community will also talk to the tenzo about their complaints—emotional, physical, and spiritual—and he'll prescribe what he believes to be the most effective dietary cure.

AFTER LEARNING ABOUT shojin ryori, I was anxious to visit Japan. I had the opportunity to do so when I successfully pitched a magazine story on rice growing and the rising popularity of microbrews of premium sake in Niigata Prefecture, four hours north of Tokyo.

Locating a temple that would allow me to cook in its kitchen, however, proved much more difficult. While there were once thousands of young men studying the tenets of Buddhism in Kyoto, as so beautifully described in *The Temple of the Golden Pavilion* by Yukio Mishima, current enrollment of novitiates is down. Centuries-old monasteries are being turned into boutique hotels, and shojin ryori is fast being made obsolete by ramen noodles eaten from microwavable cups.

After many dead ends and leads that didn't pan out, I suddenly started getting emails from a priest named Giko. He typed out short, declarative sentences that sounded like a drill sergeant's orders.

"Okay. You come my temple!"

"You stay four days. Okay. Then, you must leave!"

"You cook. You learn from my wife!"

His wife? Weren't Buddhist monks supposed to be celibate?

I allowed these questions to go unanswered. From years of working as a journalist, I have learned to be improvisational. Gaining access to any foreign place is a step into the dark. Pressing too hard for everything to be spelled out in advance can scare people away. Doors suddenly close, and appointments for interviews get canceled.

Instead, I tried to read between the lines of Giko's cryptic notes: "Okay. We are poor! You know we are very poor, okay?" In no time, I had dreamed up a fully formed scenario, a Japan-tasia, with me learning culinary cures for acne, heartburn, and other stress-related health disorders while I cooked alongside Giko's wife, whom I imagined as a geisha version of Adele Davis. The student monks, their heads shaved, wearing maroon robes, would be neatly lined up to have their rice bowls filled by Mrs. Giko and me before they went back to practicing calligraphy or puzzling over the sutras.

"Itashimashite!" I practiced saying. This is Japanese for "you're welcome."

A BLUR OF such preconceptions was whirling around in my mind as a Kyoto taxi driver dropped me off before an intricately carved wooden gate, plunked down in the middle of a suburban neighborhood of contemporary houses. Impressive as this ancient arch appeared, standing several stories high, its entryway was small in height. Doubling over at the waist while passing through, I dragged my suitcase up a winding stone path and past a statue of the seated Buddha. In case someone was watching me from inside, I made a respectful bow.

Mrs. Giko answered the door. Her first name was Hiromi. She was an attractive woman, with thick black hair pulled back into a loose French twist, and smooth, faultless skin. Her voice was high and delicate, almost as if she were singing a lullaby when she talked. I instantly had a crush on Hiromi. I couldn't decide if I wanted to protect her, hug her, or be her.

At her elbow stood a girlfriend of hers, Takago, who would be Hiromi's translator and our constant companion. Takago had a saucy, sarcastic manner; she was primed to make a joke about everything and punctuated many of her sentences with a wink.

Before I entered the house, Takago demanded I remove my footwear. Already familiar with this Japanese custom and impatient to comply, I kicked off my boots too quickly. They fell with a thud to the floor. Hiromi whispered something to Takago, who informed me that there was no excuse for such careless noise making. I must make every effort

to slip my shoes off silently—especially when Giko-san was around—
and line them up neatly next to the front door.

Trying to make up for this clumsy entrance, I made yet another faux
pas when I brought forth my hostess gifts: a bottle of organic sake and
a box of macrobiotic candies made from green tea. They'd been appall-
ingly expensive, and I hoped Hiromi would be impressed.

Takago grabbed my arm and pulled me after Hiromi as we scuttled
down a shadowy passageway. We entered the main meditation hall, or
zendo, a large room where the floor was covered in tatami mats and the
back wall was made of sliding shoji screen doors overlooking a garden.
Hiromi arranged my presents on an altar in front of a gilded statue of
Buddha. She lit an incense stick and then several candles. Takago, she,
and I got down on the floor and prostrated ourselves here for many
minutes. The sake and candies remained on the altar all week, un-
touched. Every morning when Giko and I went there to meditate at
4:00 a.m., they were the first and last things I saw. I grew weary of
looking at them and increasingly sorry I had purchased them in the first
place. If this was a lesson in nonattachment, it was an effective one.

Where were the young monks, those eager novitiates whom Hiromi
and I would be cooking for after they brought us their begging bowls
full of fruits and vegetables?

There were none.

It turned out this temple was a subsidiary of Ryoanji, which is a few
blocks away and world famous for its rock and sand garden. Centuries
earlier, rich patrons wanted to live near the main temple and its tenzo,
so a constellation of twenty-two subtemples encircled Ryoanji, each
with its own priests and monks in training. Over time, most of these
structures have been desacralized or burned down. (Fire is a constant
worry in Kyoto, as almost all temples are built solely of wood.) Now,
Ryoanji has only two subtemples. Giko and Hiromi are the caretakers
whose selfless devotion is keeping this one, a treasure of fifteenth-century
architecture, from being turned into a sushi restaurant or Pilates studio.

Theirs is a life of much prayer and sacrifice and not a whole lot of
perks other than the shojin ryori cuisine Hiromi cooks for them. I

couldn't be sure they even collected a salary for their custodial labors, as Giko teaches sociology at the University of Osaka. He was celibate until age fifty, when he met and fell in love with Hiromi. She'd never married either and was forty-five when they wed.

Hiromi explained all this to me as we drank tea together on that first afternoon. Takago would translate her friend's words, sometimes adding her own caustic commentary through a side-of-mouth whisper. I got the impression she was a little afraid of Giko-san, and I began to be wary of his imminent arrival. Takago also confessed that she didn't know the first thing about cooking and was unfamiliar with the names of most vegetables, even in Japanese. With the help of a Japanese-English dictionary, I would look up words and point them out to Takago, who'd speak to Hiromi. It sounds cumbersome, yet somehow the awkwardness of communication was humorous and ice-breaking. The three of us were soon merrily peeling taro root, frying tofu, and shredding daikon radish.

"In winter, the body gets cold," Hiromi said. "To warm up, it is good to eat warm foods like root vegetables—potatoes, carrots, and turnips. In the summertime, it reverses. Cucumber and tomatoes make the body cold."

Shojin ryori's plain though not exactly bland flavors are designed to not unduly stimulate the digestive system. During prolonged periods of meditation, Hiromi explained, it's inconvenient for a monk suddenly to be burping from onions, garlic, or spicy red peppers served at lunch. Her father is a rice farmer in Japan's Shimane Prefecture, so she knew a lot about rice. Hiromi instructed me to wash it several times before cooking or the rice grains would stick together. I learned how to make a simple soup stock by boiling dried seaweed and dehydrated fish.

I grew up in a house where we were made to "clean our plates"—eat everything we were served—at each meal. Under Hiromi's tutelage, this phrase took on a still more sanitary meaning. She demonstrated how I was to wash my own dishes, at the table, by swirling green tea around in my bowl to dislodge those two or three uneaten grains of rice, then pour the fluid into my dish of radish, lifting up fragments here too, bowl to bowl, until I had a swill in which all leftover bits floated. This, I was to quaff as an after-dinner drink.

"Nothing go to waste," Hiromi concluded.

She, Takago, and I were cooking and gabbing away, finally having hit our multilingual stride, when suddenly Hiromi froze, her entire body paralyzed.

Takago gasped, "Giko-san is home!"

Substitute "Godzilla" in that last sentence, and you have a better sense of the frightful expressions both Takago and Hiromi had on their faces. I couldn't hear a sound. How did they know he was here? The tension built. I decided it was best for me to stop breathing.

As he walked into the kitchen, Giko led with a scowl. He turned with a sour glance to his wife, then Takago, and lastly, to me. He didn't appear pleased to see any of us. He was short, with a blocky physique like that of a sumo wrestler. Giko had a shaved head and fleshy, protuberant ears. His nose was shaped like an isosceles triangle, small at the bridge but swelling forth into a thick base with two nearly fuming nostrils. His vigorous exhalations ruffled the hairs of his wispy black mustache.

Takago had prepared me for this tense moment by providing a little script to say in Japanese, which I had carefully written out in capital letters. I did my best to set this phrase to memory, but upon Giko's arrival I became rattled, and it was lost inside my head. I rifled through my notebook until I found the words, which I read aloud slowly but forcefully.

"KONBONWA! HAJIMEMASHITE STEPHEN DES. OSE-WANI NARIMASU!"

Takago told me this meant something like "Good evening, master. I am your humble guest, Stephen. Please take care of me." It was, or so I inferred, a Buddhist way of saying "I'm an intruder. You could kill me right now, but wouldn't it be fun if you didn't?"

When I finished, Giko responded with the barest flicker of a smile. Then, he went off to meditate.

Hiromi said, "He's really a kitten."

After translating this, Takago winked at me and whispered, "He's really an asshole!"

This was going to be an interesting few days.

AT DINNER THAT evening, Giko was still grumpy and didn't hesitate to correct my smallest of errors. Shojin ryori required an even more intricate dining etiquette than Hiromi had let on. While eating, I had to sit with my knees together and calves folded back under me so that I was perched on my feet, back rigidly erect. There was much adjustment until I managed to hold my chopsticks to Giko's satisfaction. My rice dish must always be placed to the left of the miso soup, and if I rested my elbows on the table, all hell broke loose!

My father presided over family meals with a strict set of rules. When I was about ten, he once reached across the table and gave my thumb a whack with his knife because he was disgusted by my childish habit of manually shoving food onto a fork. But Dad was a marshmallow in comparison to Giko. It was as if all the priestly lessons Giko had stored up to teach his nonexistent novitiates must now be drummed into me.

Gradually, his mood began to improve. This could be explained by the knee-touching intimacy of eating at a squat piece of furniture called a kotasu, which is something like a hybrid of a coffee table and a tea cozy. Hiromi set out the food—"Our poor supper," Giko apologized. "We are very poor, okay?"—on top of the kotasu, and then we all hurriedly jostled to sit on the floor, get our knees and thighs in underneath it, and cover them with heated blankets that draped from the table's four sides. Most Japanese houses do not have a furnace and make do with a few strategically placed electric heaters, along with the kotasu. Here we huddled while Giko held forth on various topics. He spoke almost perfect English, only rarely mangling a word or two. Giko's sense of humor was so dry I could never tell if he was trying to be funny. Still, I ended up laughing a lot at what he was saying, and he took no offense.

Giko was the second son of a Buddhist priest in Kyoto. His brother is also a priest and oversees a temple that is bigger and better funded than Giko's, he wanted me to know. Giko did a stint at the Yokoji Zen Mountain Center in Southern California, and he liked to complain about American egotism. "People in your country suffer from a nearly incurable me-ism," he said. "I am the best! I am smart! I am pretty! Me, me, ME! I found it extremely embarrassing."

Tibetan Buddhism is popular in the United States, he believed, partially because of the Dalai Lama's charisma but mostly, he said, "due to that American actor."

He fiddled with his mustache as he tried to remember the performer's name. I really didn't want to be the one who had to say it, but I suspected that Giko would not stop pulling on his nose hairs until the dreaded syllables were spoken.

"Richard Gere," I said, in a voice so soft I could barely hear myself.

"That's right!" Giko shouted. "RICHARD GERE!" He then frowned at me, another dumb American who only knew about Buddhism because it had a celebrity spokesperson.

AFTER THIS BUMPY beginning, we settled into a satisfactory, if spartan, routine. Up at 4:00 a.m., Giko would pound on a giant and fantastically resonant brass gong. I was expected to rise immediately and join him for morning meditation. Buddhists speak of the "monkey mind" as a way of describing how difficult it is to relax our consciousness. The secret of meditating? Don't try too hard, Giko advised. Lightly close the eyes, gaze upon the back of your forehead, and let your mind drift. When distracting thoughts arise, watch them but don't stare, he said. They are twigs on a stream. They'll pass. He suggested a good mantra to repeat is "Let it go."

During our breakfasts together, tucked under the kotasu, I would interrogate Giko with questions about Buddhism before he got on his train to Osaka. Did he really believe a carrot dropped into a begging bowl would taste any different or have more health benefits than carrots purchased in a market? It's my preferred way of conversing: I ask clever questions; the other person supplies memorably wise answers. Giko quickly figured out my game. Then, he refused to play.

There are no rules in Buddhism, Giko said, and no definitive answers. This makes it especially difficult for Christians to understand, because the Judeo-Christian ethos is based on tradition, on received wisdom, and honors a blind faith unaffected by anything observed on a daily basis. Buddhism, in every possible way, is the opposite. Buddhism rejects all dogma and insists that the only way to enlightenment is through experience.

"Don't believe anything that anyone tells you, including me," Giko said one morning. "No one is holier than you are." He mentioned a Zen master, Lin-Chi, who went so far as to proclaim "if you meet the Buddha, kill the Buddha!" In other words, don't unquestioningly do what anyone tells you to do, no matter how enlightened they may seem—even the Buddha.

Let's see. Giko was counseling me not to follow anyone else's advice. But wasn't that a piece of advice? This perfectly circular conundrum is the sort of head-scratcher Buddhists call a koan.

Far more confusing for me, though, was Hiromi. At first she'd appeared excessively meek, but I soon understood her to be a woman of strong will. Hiromi had her own belief system with very definitive answers—not about Buddhism but concerning food and design. Hiromi wanted to teach her lessons just as badly as Giko wanted me to "unlearn" his.

Hiromi, Takago, and I spent hours each morning in Nishiki Market, Kyoto's open-air food street. It's only six blocks long but crammed with hundreds of shops, some scarcely more than a few feet wide, that sell everything from eggplants smaller than my pinkie finger to cabbage heads larger than a beach ball. We sampled dozens of varieties of tofu and countless types of apples. One day, we searched to find the perfect sesame seed roaster—a delicate mesh contraption you can whisk through flames to gently brown the tiny seeds. To my mind, it's a tool of somewhat limited use, but Hiromi was adamant I needed one.

We would carry food home and spend the afternoon cooking it while Hiromi explained the various health benefits of each vegetable. As a result of this diet, I was sleeping better and feeling remarkably energized during the day.

Bong! Bong!! *BONG!!!*

When Giko rang for me to join him in meditation, I woke, chilled to my innermost core, as I had been sleeping, or attempting to, on a tatami mat in an unheated room. This morning, as an extra "bonus," he decreed that we would do two sessions, back to back, of forty-five minutes each. When this finally ended and the sun was just beginning to rise, Giko went to stand by the sliding doors overlooking a small garden behind the temple.

"Now we do some genital cleaning," he said.

I knew it! I just knew this visit was going to end badly, but I didn't think it would be quite this terrible. I have read a lot about Buddhism over the years, been to a zendo or two, and once spent an entire weekend on a "silent" retreat at a Buddhist monastery in the Catskills. I was aware peculiar things occur—such as the monk whose job it is to give you a whack with a wooden paddle if you're not sitting up straight during meditation. There are complicated customs about the washing of one's hands and mouth before entering a temple. However, I wasn't yet familiar with any rituals involving the gonads. With a feeling of revulsion— and, I will admit, some morbid curiosity—I slipped on a pair of wooden sandals and clop-clip-clopped behind Giko along a stone path until we arrived at what looked like an outhouse.

"We are very poor," he said, pointing to this rickety structure.

The door was off its hinges and simply leaned into place. I could stick my hand in between most of the vertical wood slats that comprised its walls. Were we going into this dark shed to, um, clean ourselves? I glanced up and back at the temple. There was Hiromi, standing at one of the windows, and our eyes met for just a moment before she darted away from view with a stricken look.

Giko removed the outhouse's door, set it to one side, and stepped inside. With great solemnity, he handed out a set of personal grooming tools: a wooden comb, a bamboo-handled brush, and what looked like an ancient set of iron tweezers. Good God! Does he think I have lice down there? I shifted back and forth on my sandals—clip, clop—unsure what to do. Giko reached up to the waist sash of his kimono. I dropped my eyes, fearful of what would happen next but thinking I might have to take some sort of peek. Was it something I did to myself, or was it a two-man job?

After giving his sash a tightening tug, Giko grabbed his own set of tools and turned around. "Don't just stand there," he said, giving me a shove. "Go! Okay? The lawn! Rake! Okay? Give it genital cleaning."

Giko's back garden was planted with dwarf bamboo at the edge and miniature ficus, maple, and cedar trees I could have cupped in one hand. So Lilliputian was the scale of the landscaping, it looked like a child's toy railroad set. The ground cover was a fuzzy emerald moss onto which, overnight, a sprinkling of tiny leaves had fallen, each the size of a dime. So that's what the tweezers were for! It was hard work, but I felt lighthearted as I swept and cleaned, all the while snickering quietly at Giko's garbled pronunciation, or my mishearing, of "general." A flood of puns poured through my monkey mind. The price for a movie? Genital admission. What's required before a group decision is made? Genital agreement.

As I learned later from Takago, when Hiromi saw me in the back window, the reason she'd ducked away in such fear was that I was the only man, other than Giko-san, who had ever seen her without makeup. This unprecedented degree of personal exposure terrified her. I didn't feel able to reciprocate by explaining what I thought was going to happen back at the garden shed.

Some things truly are lost in translation.

GIKO ANNOUNCED AT breakfast that Osaka University was on holiday. His schedule was free, so we could spend the day on a tour of other Buddhist temples and Shinto shrines in Kyoto, an itinerary that would conclude with a tea ceremony. I was pleased by this unexpected development, mostly because I had the distinct sense that Giko didn't like me very much. This kind offer seemed to suggest otherwise.

Off we went on what turned out to be a crash course in Japanese history—or at least Giko's interpretation of his country's past, particularly its religious heritage. Over our few dinners together, I'd learned Giko liked the sound of his voice and preferred to lecture, uninterrupted, for long periods of time. Only reluctantly did he allow questions to redirect his stream of thought. Fine. I was ready to listen and learn. Our sightseeing expedition would be my version of takuhatsu, and my notebook a begging bowl, ready to receive whatever words of wisdom Giko cared to drop into it. We had a lot of ground to cover, as there are an estimated 1,600 Buddhist temples in Kyoto.

Of these, we could only see a handful, such as Daitoku-ji, Myoshin-ji, Tenry-ji, and Tofuku-ji (*ji* is Japanese for "temple"). This last, Tofuku-ji, is one of the five most-visited Zen temples in Kyoto. Built in the middle of the thirteenth century, it has the biggest and oldest main gate of any Buddhist temple in Japan. There was no blueprint for this building; carpenters simply had to envision the whole structure.

Fascinating as all this information was, Giko cautioned me not to focus on architecture: *we* are the temple; finding what's truest, holiest, and best within ourselves is the goal of Zen Buddhism. By now he was speaking rapidly, his mind at full gallop. Enlightenment does not come all at once like a Christian "born again" experience. It is a gradual process, slippery and slick, like trying to use chopsticks to pick up a hardboiled egg. True liberation of the mind is being able to simultaneously think conflicting ideas.

I scrawled many more sentences such as this into my notebook.

As we were leaving Tofuku-ji, I asked Giko how long ago this place became a museum.

"It is not a museum!" he answered, his voice shaking with a barely suppressed fury. "All temples in Japan are still working temples. Monks are still in residence, but they keep themselves hidden away during hours when tourists like you are swarming around."

We ended our round of visits at Daitojo-ji (founded in 1326), which is where Giko trained as a novitiate. Since the sixteenth century, this temple has cultivated monks who are experts in the matcha tea ceremony, one of which Giko had arranged for us to attend together.

Before we entered an exquisite pagoda where this tea ritual would take place, Giko pointed to a stone-rimmed basin of water with a ladle where Buddhist monks cleanse themselves before prayers. There were four Japanese characters carved here in a circle, and they signified the words "I," "Only," "Understand," and "Sufficient." Though placed at the noon, three, six, and nine o'clock positions on this basin's perimeter, these words could be randomly shuffled, he noted, with no loss of meaning. "Only I understand sufficient." "Understand, only I sufficient." "Sufficient, I only understand." No matter how you arranged the characters, they signified everything and signified nothing.

"But what does it mean?" I asked while gazing down at the basin.

"It *means*," Giko said, mimicking my urgent tone, "each of us is alone. We can only attempt to understand ourselves. And that is enough. Don't be eager for more."

We went into the tea ceremony. This was no simple affair of plopping a bag into hot water. Instead, I witnessed a ritual that's been practiced with great care for hundreds of years. In this slow-moving spectacle, lacquered bowls were placed carefully on a tabletop, jade-green powder was spooned into them, steaming water poured with great care, and the mixture whipped into a bubbly fizz, something like a tea frappe. Called *gyokuro*, or "jewel dew," it was the harvest of bushes that are covered for several weeks before being picked. Lack of direct sunlight is believed to make tea leaves sweeter tasting.

We were sitting—Giko, a priest friend of his, and I—on a wooden floor beside a window. This overlooked a manicured garden with bonsai trees and plazas of carefully raked gravel. I was in a swoon over how beautiful everything was and wished I could understand how Giko's philosophy might be merged with Hiromi's. In a Buddhist understanding of aesthetics, was beauty considered a pathway to the divine? And could eating the perfect diet really bring one closer to being enlightened?

Instead of either of these questions, I asked, "Giko-san, do you believe there is life after death?"

"I have no idea," Giko immediately replied. "Who knows? No one knows! Okay? It is a stupid question, really. In Japanese, there is a word, 'muki.' It means something that is unimportant, something not worth thinking about. Your question is muki!" He then laughed, waving his hand in front of his nose as if I had farted and he was trying to dispel the odor.

"How do you live, at this moment?" he continued. "That is the only important thing! Eating, praying, meditating, shitting, fucking—they are the same! All are holy. All should be taken seriously, okay? It's not good or bad, sacred or secular, Heaven or Hell. Okay? It all just is!"

Giko was shouting, and I imagined the delicate rice paper walls of the pagoda might be quivering. My heart was beating wildly. Giko, I realized, was out of patience with me and sick to death of my questions. But isn't this what students do—try to learn from their teachers?

Lightly closing my eyes, I gazed upon the back of my forehead and let my mind drift. When distracting thoughts arose, I watched them but didn't stare. They were twigs on a stream. They would pass. Silently I began to repeat my mantra: "Let it go."

6

ATILLA THE NUN

"**B**EGGING CHANGED MY LIFE," SISTER LIGUORI ROSSNER, a Catholic nun, told me. "Notice I didn't say 'fundraising.' No, I said begging."

It was early summer. Sister Liguori and I sat together in her second-floor office overlooking the dining hall of Jubilee Soup Kitchen in downtown Pittsburgh. She was explaining how she'd struggled to create this haven for her city's hungry and homeless.

Now in her late sixties, Liguori suffered from rheumatoid arthritis and had difficulty getting upstairs each day. Once settled at her desk, she deployed a low-tech but highly effective public address system. If she wanted something or someone, she started yelling.

"Stephen! Get in here!"

After I was summoned into her presence, I spotted a Xerox page framed on her office wall. This colorful photoshopped image revealed the startling possibility that Sister Liguori was the "love child" of Leona Helmsley, the Manhattan hotelier famous for her imperious demeanor, and Mother Teresa, defender of the downtrodden.

"I would go into an office building, ride the elevator up to the top floor, and work my way down," she continued, allowing herself a smile at this youthful bravado. "In each lobby, I would introduce myself to the receptionist and ask if I could speak to the company's president. This was the 1970s; I was still wearing a habit. Pittsburgh is a Catholic town and was even more so then. No one could say 'no' to me. I would simply tell the man—and at this time, all chief executives were men—I wanted him to write me a check so I could build a soup kitchen in Pittsburgh's Hill District. I found I was good at this. It got to the point that I could beg anything off anyone."

Jubilee Soup Kitchen opened in November of 1979. There were fifteen people at the first lunch. Today, an average lunchtime crowd is 150, and Jubilee has a child day care center, a job placement office, primary health care services, and a prison ministry.

After she told me the bare bones of her life story, Liguori demanded, "Tell me what you're doing here."

I had driven from New York City to see my niece, Amy, who had just completed the first year of her doctoral program at Duquesne University. When traveling in Iran not too long ago, I told Liguori, I learned about a culinary custom called nazr whereby people promise God they'll cook food for the poor and hungry if their prayer request came true. Inspired by this tradition, I decided to create a nazr for my niece. To celebrate each year Amy completed of her PhD program, I would come to Pittsburgh and cook a meal for the needy.

This far into my tale I paused, not sure how much more to share with this busy woman. Did she need to know about "pounding the preacher," my career in public relations and journalism, or how my guilty purchase of a Lacanche oven led me to explore charitable cookery? Should I tell her about Alexis Soyer and how I was making a conscious attempt to live as boldly as he did and welcome the zigzags of life?

Probably not.

So, I simply informed Sister Liguori that I planned to cook my first large-scale charitable meal right here at Jubilee Soup Kitchen. I assured her I was a capable chef, accustomed to making dinner for large groups and confident in my ability to scale up recipes. If she was willing to be a part of this endeavor, I would buy all the food necessary to prepare and serve lunch to Jubilee's guests.

"How does that sound?" I asked.

Liguori stared at me for several moments, apparently trying to figure out if she trusted me or not. Then, from one side of her mouth, she hollered out, "BUTCH!"

"Yes'm," a man's voice answered from below.

"Get up here, and bring Sean!" Liguori yelled. For a sickly looking woman, she had an astonishing set of pipes.

There was double-time thumping on the stairs, and two men arrived, both of them panting and out of breath. Clearly, a call from on high was not to be taken lightly. I jumped up from my seat to greet these guys, which seemed to annoy Liguori. "Sit down, sit down," she said to me impatiently. "Butch, you stand. Sean, on the floor!" The men immediately did as they were told. Butch was broad-shouldered and looked very strong. I guessed he was forty-five. Sean, no more than thirty, was tall, lanky, and missing a front tooth.

Liguori waved her hand at me. "Tell 'em what you want," she said.

Self-conscious about repeating my story word for word, I abbreviated the narrative too much for Liguori's taste.

"Wait a minute! Wait just a minute! Tell 'em where else you've been."

As I mentioned cooking in India, Iran, and Japan, Liguori smiled in a proprietary way, as if to say, "See, boys? I caught us a live one!"

Sean's eyes widened as if I were describing a long-ago summer I had spent flipping burgers on Mars.

Butch was stone-faced. "What ya gonna make?" he asked, when I finished talking.

A fair question and one for which I should have had a ready answer. Stupidly, I thought I would figure this out tomorrow after I saw what was typically prepared at Jubilee. "Oh, a vegetarian curry? Some lentils. Rice. A green salad. An apple cobbler?"

"Our people like meat," Liguori said, matter-of-factly.

"Chicken curry?"

"Fine. And, the rest of it, too. It all sounds fine," she said. "I can't wait to try your cobbler."

Turning to Butch, I asked, "Do you have a rule of thumb to help me gauge how much food to prepare?"

"Naw," he said. "There ain't no rules. We just make a lot. If there's too much, we can serve it the next day. That ain't no problem. It's when there's not enough. Then, we got a problem."

Could I stop by tomorrow, I asked, and observe how Jubilee operated before attempting things on my own for the following day? Butch told me to come at 9:30 a.m. They would wait to start cooking until I arrived. Lunch was served at 11:00 a.m. An hour and a half to cook for 150 people? How was this possible?

Liguori had turned her attention back to her desk, where she was rifling through papers. From her posture, I understood that our meeting was over. A few moments later, I was blinking in the sunlight of a bright June morning.

I had been given what I begged for. I was thrilled. I was terrified.

AMY ACCOMPANIED ME later that afternoon to a grocery store in a Pittsburgh suburb called Shadyside. Based on Butch's advice, "just make a lot," I drew up a shopping list of what I might buy if hosting a dinner party for ten and multiplied everything by fifteen. Easy arithmetic, but I hadn't reckoned on how much space this amount of food would take up or what a commotion making such a purchase could create. Most customers were holding adorable hand baskets, apparently subsisting on Smart Water and bagel chips. By way of contrast, before my niece and I left the produce section, our two carts were full.

With each errand I dispatched her on, Amy always asked for confirmation that she'd heard me correctly: "Really, Uncle Steve? You think we need thirty cans of coconut milk?" And every time, her incredulity gave me a fresh attack of nerves. I had made exquisite entrées for a lot of dinner parties and holiday hors d'oeuvres for hundreds but not a complete dinner for a crowd this large. What was I thinking?

Soon we'd filled three carts and half of a fourth. People began to stop us in the aisles. Did we know something they didn't? Was a tornado about to hit Pittsburgh? I made the mistake of answering these first few inquiries honestly. A few minutes later, a woman laid her hand gently on my forearm. "Excuse me, dear, but did I hear you say you were going to bring all this food to the Jubilee Kitchen?"

I nodded.

"Well, praise the Lord! Folks tomorrow are going to have a fine, fine lunch thanks to you. You are a saint."

I looked down, feeling terribly ashamed, knowing all too well that I was anything but saintly. The lady still had me in a firm grasp; her eyes were sparkling.

"I'm not sure what I've gotten myself into," I replied.

"Don't worry. You will have all the help you need. God bless you!"

Shaken by this interchange and not wanting to risk anything like it happening again, I decided that if someone else asked me what I was doing with this food, I would lie.

"I've never rung up so large a single transaction before," a girl at the checkout counter announced. A few moments later, she summoned the store's manager. These employees, plus three packers busily putting the stuff into paper bags, were eyeing the cash register warily, as if it might catch fire.

It was taking a long time, and I felt bad about holding up everyone in line. Not knowing what else to do, I turned around and apologized to a couple of twenty-somethings who stood behind me. They were dressed head to toe in black, with multiple facial piercings and flamboyant tattoos.

"No problem, dude, but whassup? Is World War III about to start or some shit?"

"No," I replied. "We're having a party."

Only now did I notice that the woman I'd spoken with earlier was standing behind the goth couple. She gave me a complicit smile, as if my evasive reply was further proof of my holiness. This made me feel even worse and more of a phony.

In bed later that evening, I couldn't sleep and stared at the ceiling of a guest room in Amy's apartment. How would I ever cook all that food? I was attempting my version of a nazr, the Iranian custom of bargaining with God, when I wasn't fully convinced that there was a capital-G God up there, or out there, or even dwelling in my heart.

Honestly? It felt a little lonely.

At Jubilee Soup Kitchen the next morning, things immediately went awry. Sister Liguori was arriving at the same time I did. While I greeted her and we chatted for a few minutes out on the sidewalk, men poured out of the kitchen to help unpack my car. In this well-meaning rush, many grocery bags ripped, and their contents spilled onto the street. Food was then collected up haphazardly and stowed away in a series of walk-in refrigerators with which I was unaccustomed. I would waste a frustrating hour searching for items later that afternoon.

For today's lunch, which was boiled sausages and Tater Tots, I wasn't in charge. Butch set me to work making a salad. I washed radishes and peeled carrots alongside a woman named Fran Patton who, as it turned out, was an old friend of Sister Liguori's from high school. With her teased hair and important jewelry, Patton didn't look like someone who spent three mornings a week at a soup kitchen.

"One reason I come is that I miss cooking," she explained. "My husband has cancer of the lower intestine. He can't stand the smell of food anymore, so I don't use my kitchen at home." She let out a grim laugh. Smiling at the horrors of life, we agreed, can sometimes be as sane a response as any.

Printed on a large sign hanging at one end of the dining area was a set of rules, though how much attention was paid to them is debatable:

RULES

No Guns / No Cursing / No Violence
No Standing Up While Eating

Jubilee's clientele was a tough bunch. I smelled liquor on some of the men; others were stoned. One guy jiggled and jerked around like his skin was falling off. Every so often he would begin screaming, sometimes about those "goddam Moose-lim tear-ists."

"There was a knife fight here last week, you know," Patton said, her voice no more disturbed than if she'd commented on the weather. "The whole place went crazy—people screaming, tables overturned—and I had a ringside seat. My husband says to me, 'Fran, what am I gonna do if they pull a knife on you?' I tell him not to worry. I'm back here behind the counter. No one's gonna mess with me, especially since everyone knows I am Sister's best friend."

Patton made a quick, conspiratorial glance over each shoulder and then turned to me with an "I'm gonna tell ya a secret" look.

"Sister's got a heart of mush, but you don't want to cross her," Patton continued. "All the people here are scared of her because they know she can close down this place anytime she wants, and they'll go hungry. She doesn't take any government money, you see. Every cent that comes in here she's raised herself. If Sister wants to cut off the spigot, that's her choice."

"Why would she do that?"

Patton laughed for a moment or two before answering.

"A few weeks ago, someone stole a computer from her office," she said. "Well, soon as Sister found out, she makes an announcement. 'Someone here knows where that computer is,' she says, 'and I want it back. And until I get it, there won't be so much as a cup of coffee served here.' We were just about to dish up lunch, but Sister had us put all the food back in the refrigerator. Jubilee was closed for three days until the computer reappeared."

"Wow! That's tough love."

"You have no idea. You know what her nickname is, don't you? Attila the Nun!"

I smiled, but my amusement was cut short by Sister Liguori's voice rumbling down from her office.

"Stephen! Get up here!"

"I hope I'm not in trouble," I said to Patton.

"I hope you're not, either," she agreed.

AFTER OUR BRIEF meeting the day before, I had asked Sister Liguori if we could speak for a few minutes more. I again found her at a desk, flipping through file folders. For most of our chat that followed, she kept her gaze down, still at work, instead of fully engaging in what she considered a most unpleasant task: talking about herself.

She was born in 1941 and grew up in Duquesne, Pennsylvania, a mining town outside of Pittsburgh. Her father was a self-employed contractor who built houses all around town. She went to Catholic parochial schools until her junior year of high school in 1959, when she entered into the care of a convent, the Sisters of the Divine Redeemer. At the time of entering her order she assumed the name of Sister Liguori, in honor of St. Alphonsus of Liguori, Italy, an eighteenth-century Catholic bishop, theologian, and author of over one hundred published works. St. Alphonsus is still remembered today for his ability to respond practically and nonjudgmentally to people's everyday problems.

In college at Duquesne University, Liguori studied education and history and went on to Carnegie Mellon for a master's degree in history. For the next fourteen years, she lived in the convent and taught history in parochial schools. Then in 1972, she was invited to attend a summer session where twenty-three nuns from sixteen different communities came together to discuss issues of peace and social justice.

"I had done a few things. I was opposed to the Vietnam War and went to demonstrations. I became active in boycotts when Cesar Chavez came to town. But that summer of '72 was a turning point for me," she said. "Here were these women, all ages, young and old, and we spent six weeks together hashing out our concerns and dreaming up things we could do. I made my best friends in the struggle that summer."

(The struggle! I hadn't heard the social justice movement called this in a long time.)

These nuns entered into a commitment together, founding the Sisters Council of Pittsburgh. "It was an exciting time," Liguori said. "We were really at the ramparts."

"So nuns were more in the vanguard on social issues than the priests?" I asked.

It was this question that finally caught her full attention. Liguori's glare, focused on me over the top of her reading glasses, was blazing with impatience. Was I really asking her something this stupid?

"Much more," she replied, flatly "The priests were too busy with . . ."

It seemed Liguori was about to make an off-color joke. If I stayed completely still, she might complete her thought. Instead, her unfinished sentence lay between us like a loaded gun.

Without a trace of self-pity, Liguori mentioned her physical condition for the first time. She had undergone over a dozen operations and had two artificial knees. Her lower arms and hands were withered into awkward angles, making it difficult for her to hold things. A rotating group of friends helped her get dressed each morning.

"My health was especially bad back then," she said. "I couldn't stand very long at these demonstrations. I knew I'd never be able to go abroad. But you turned on the television, and all you heard about was hunger. I decided to do something locally, here in Pittsburgh, and suddenly I had the idea to open a soup kitchen."

How did she know she could do this?

"I didn't," she replied with no hesitation. "Up to this point, I was still teaching at St. Bartholomew's Elementary School. When I decided to leave, Sister Cornelia Racs, who was the school's principal, joined me to become Jubilee's first chef. She had escaped from the Iron Curtain in 1948, walking through Brenner Pass between Italy and Austria. In comparison to this, opening a soup kitchen seemed easy."

Jubilee now has eight thousand people on its mailing list. Liguori sends out twice-yearly update letters on the kitchen's activities, and she estimates that nearly 60 percent of the letters' recipients respond with enough donations to meet her annual budget. From the beginning she decided not to take any government money, preferring to embrace the philosophy of people helping other people. It was, she explained, the "Dorothy Day model." Liguori also made a promise to herself: she wouldn't mix religion with food.

"People know when we pray. If they don't want to be here for that, they don't have to," she said. "I don't think you should have to take a dive for Jesus."

LUNCH WAS OVER and the kitchen was clean when I got back downstairs. All helpers were gone except for Butch, who could not leave until I did. It was about 1:00 p.m., and I thought that the next few hours would be plenty of time to prep everything for tomorrow.

Was I ever wrong.

For starters, it takes a long time to peel fifteen dozen apples. When I made a desperate call to them, Amy and her boyfriend, Roger, agreed to come help. Even so, things went slowly. Butch got out a boom box and cranked up a CD with some blues from the Mississippi Delta. These were raunchy, downbeat tunes, and I wondered if Sister Liguori would approve. Then again, she didn't seem much interested in conspicuous piety—something else she might have learned from her namesake, St. Alphonsus.

Finally, three huge pans were filled with cut-up apples, lemon juice, cranberries, walnuts, and topped with a crumbly oatmeal topping. After being drizzled with melted butter and dusted with cinnamon, they went into the oven. Butch looked at his watch. It was nearly 4:00 p.m., which is when I told him I would leave.

"I think I'll need until six o'clock. I promise I will be gone by then, Butch."

"It's all good," he said. "You take as long as you need, baby."

Cobbler in the oven, I got Amy busy slicing onions and Roger chopping garlic. I peeled a large pile of ginger root, a miserable task, and then began to cut all the chicken—seventy-five pounds!—into bite-size pieces. Before I had finished this chore there was a blister on my right hand, and the kitchen floor was slick with chicken blood. Slipping as I grabbed a soup pot off the floor, a sharp pain cut into my back.

"Goddamnit!" I hissed loudly.

Butch responded with a low grunt of laughter and pointed to the rules posted on the wall, among them "NO CURSING."

All eight burners on the kitchen's range were fired up. Amy had gone back to her office at Duquesne University, where she was scheduled to counsel one of her therapy clients. Roger agreed to stay on with me without my asking. He was sautéing chicken with the onions, garlic, green peppers, and ginger root. In my haste, all those careful "times fifteen" calculations were abandoned. I scattered whole jars of curry powder, turmeric, and cumin as well as handfuls of brown sugar and cinnamon sticks into Roger's fry pans.

"Do you know what you're doing?" he asked.

"Sure I do!" I bluffed as I dumped cans of coconut milk into a huge stock pot, then added what we had sautéed.

The cobblers came out of the oven. They were bubbling around their edges and, I was relieved to see, appetizingly golden on top.

"Smells good," Butch called out.

I dipped a spoon into the ocean of chicken curry and gave it a taste. I couldn't believe it! Even with these absurd ratios, the flavor was excellent—neither too sweet nor too salty; flavors of garlic and ginger were there, and the cinnamon sticks had done their magic. This curry gave a warm welcome.

It was 6:10.

Roger and I managed to scuttle the pot of curry—full to its tippy-top and sheathed in tin foil—along the kitchen floor and into a walk-in refrigerator.

"Goodnight, Butch! And thank you," I yelled, heading out the door.

AFTER ANOTHER NEARLY sleepless night, I arrived at Jubilee early the next morning. Fran Patton helped me make a fruit salad and coleslaw. Just before 11:00 a.m., Sean thrust a book into my hand. "Sister wants you to do the invocation. Read whatever you think is best. Then, you'll lead us in the Lord's Prayer."

What? Hadn't Sister Liguori said that no one should have to take a dive for Jesus? Why, then, was she pushing me into the deep end of the pool?

The Bible felt strangely heavy in my blistered hands. I didn't want to do this. Worst of all, my exhausted mind was a total blank. I could not think of a single passage I wanted to speak aloud. Those many years of attending Sunday school as a child and memorizing verses of scripture!

It's no exaggeration to say that my whole life was intimately, inextricably bound up with this book, yet it was nearly a foreign object to me at this moment.

Sister Liguori struggled up out of her desk chair and was standing by a window above, peering down at the lunchtime crowd, all waiting to be fed. I was about to place the Bible down on a counter in front of me and simply speak a few thoughts of my own. Then, I remembered something. Rifling through the pages, I found my way to First Corinthians 13 with some words I do believe and, I trust, always will.

"Love suffers long, and is kind," I read, aloud. (The Bible I'd been handed was the King James Version.) "Love does not behave unseemly, seeks not its own, is not easily provoked, thinks no evil. Love rejoices not in iniquity, but rejoices in truth. Love bears all things, believes all things, hopes all things, endures all things."

I skipped down to the chapter's last verse: "Now abides faith, hope and love, but the greatest of these is . . ."

I looked up, thinking someone in the crowd might fill in the last word. The room was silent until, a few seconds later, when Sister Liguori sang out in her leather-lunged voice, "THE GREATEST OF THESE IS LOVE!"

Sean and I set about serving the meal. At first, it wasn't a disaster, but certainly not a hit. People asked for comparatively small portions, based on what I saw consumed of the boiled sausages and Tater Tots served the day before.

"I don't eat fruit," one woman announced, sounding aggrieved, as if I should have known.

"Ain't it got no mayonnaise?" another guy asked, grimacing at the "Asian" coleslaw made with an orange raspberry vinaigrette.

I greeted these comments with an abundantly fake smile, trying not to take them personally. This was difficult, since as a chef to have one's cooking rejected is very personal.

"Where the cake at?" a bearded guy demanded.

"Please try the apple cobbler, won't you?" I said. "You'll like it, trust me."

He refused my offer and walked away, his face scrunched up with distaste. Feeling like I was sucker-punched, I looked up at Sister Liguori, who was still standing at her office window above. She caught my eye and smiled.

I imagined her riding those office building elevators back in the 1970s, dressed in her nun's habit, not being a bit embarrassed to plead for what she did not yet have. My situation here in Pittsburgh was exactly reversed. I was perched behind piles of what I knew to be excellent food and pleading for it to be eaten. Well, if that's what I needed to do, I should get busy.

"The green stuff on top of the curry is cilantro," I explained to a suspicious woman. "It's fresh-tasting and zippy. Try it!"

To someone else I said, "Those are kiwi in the fruit salad. They taste a little like strawberries. How do you know you don't like them? Taste some, pretty please?"

My cajoling began to have some effect. Something happened, oh so gradually, as people kept moving through the serving line. The first eaters apparently gave some sort of approving signal. I could hear mumbled words of surprise being passed between diners. Men began gesturing with their forks, pointing to their plates.

A secret communications system exists within this community that allowed Sister Liguori's stolen computer to be returned. Now, that same network seemed to spread the news of good eats at Jubilee Soup Kitchen. More guests began to stream in, men and women I had not seen yesterday, new faces. People came back for seconds. Even the jittery guy who hated "Moose-lims" appeared slightly calmer when he showed up in the serving line for a third time.

Another gentleman, giggling to himself as he pored over a book with photographs taken in America's national parks, kept coming back so often that I lost count. As he finally left the dining room, he showed me a picture of Niagara Falls and shook my hand. He didn't say a word.

It was just a lunch, not the end of war, sickness, and poverty, nor the beginning of a new golden age. Chicken curry can only accomplish so much. Still, as I scooped out the last of the fruit salad, explaining for the umpteenth time that what made it taste so good was its mixture of lemon juice and honey, I felt glad. A whole lot of people ate a nice meal, and I had discovered something important—so important that it might even change my life.

I learned how to beg.

7

PAYING OUT THE YIN-YANG

A s I promised my niece—and God—during each of the four years Amy worked toward getting her PhD in psychology, I made an annual visit to Pittsburgh. Before each trip, I located and volunteered my services at a different soup kitchen, where I worked on developing skills in mass cookery.

I'd had beginner's luck with my chicken curry at Jubilee Soup Kitchen. I wasn't quite as successful when I cooked spaghetti Bolognese for the East End Cooperative Ministry the next year. Wasting too much effort on blanching tomatoes to more easily peel their skins, I didn't leave nearly enough time for the sauce to cook down into something rich and satisfying. The Bolognese wasn't bad, but it wasn't as delicious as I'd hoped.

Best of all was my third trip to Pittsburgh. I made Mexican pot roast in which the beef is slowly braised in tomatillo, jalapenos, and oodles of garlic. It turned out beautifully—so much so, one of the female guests that day pronounced it "better than sex."

I thought this was high praise.

Cooking for large crowds, I continued to learn, requires calculations beyond mere multiplication. Even with a forgiving recipe that's designed to feed six, when you multiply all ingredients by fifty, you don't automatically end up with something edible for three hundred. When scaling up, you constantly have to adjust, usually by subtracting here and there—less fluid, fewer chiles, and never as much salt. Even when a chef develops this instinct for jiggering flavors in mass quantities, there's still the problem of portion control. Have I cooked too much food, or too little?

When James and I entertain at home, I often prepare two entrées—one is usually vegetarian and/or gluten-free—along with several side dishes, making enough to offer guests their choice of everything even though I know that no one is going to eat a whole serving of each. As a result, I frequently have leftovers, sometimes lots of leftovers, and end up pushing Ziploc bags of food onto friends when they leave. There are worse problems to have, but if I was going to continue cooking meals at soup kitchens, I probably needed to figure out how to estimate quantities more accurately.

With this goal in mind, I started assembling a new library of books such as *Meals for Many: For School, Camp and Community*, by Katharine W. Harris and Marion A. Wood; *Recipes for Large Numbers*, by Stephen Ashley and Sean Anderson; and *Cooking for Crowds for Dummies*, by Dawn and Curt Simmons. I had to memorize the rules of "allowances" to make sense of a recipe such as "Cowboy Beans with Beer and Bacon for 25, 50, 100, or 200."

For instance, if a meal had a starch such as mashed potatoes or rice, each serving, or allowance, should be no larger than a computer mouse. A standard serving for steamed broccoli was the size of a baseball. Cooked beef, in its three-ounce allowance, resembled a deck of cards. Such comparisons really bugged me. They seemed stingy and mean. I didn't want to merely *allow* my guests to eat; I wanted to indulge and lavish them with food! Every chef does.

I kept at it, reading about "overcomplicated recipe syndrome," whereby you attempt too many "ooh la la" items on your menu; "Super-man syndrome," which is thinking that no one is as strong or fast a cook as you, so you attempt to prepare a meal for a hundred people all by yourself; and "Ohmigod, where did the time go? syndrome," a failure to realize that when tripling a recipe, the number of minutes it takes to cook the ingredients must also be multiplied by three.

I would repeatedly fall victim to all these problems and more. Even so, I struggled forward and eventually mastered "Pork Vindaloo for 6,

12, 25 and 50," "Artichoke and Chickpea Vinaigrette for 30, 50, 100," and "South of the Border Burgers for 100, 200, 500." The recipes varied, but all my new cookbooks agreed on one thing: better to have too much food than to run out.

IMMERSING MYSELF IN this research, I quickly found I wasn't the only self-proclaimed chef with no professional training who was interested in learning new ways to feed large numbers of people. Many groups across the United States were devising their own ingenious schemes for charitable cookery.

Loaves & Fishes, for instance, is a volunteer-driven agency serving the hungry in Minneapolis–Saint Paul. This organization's name alludes to a famous passage in the Bible's New Testament where Jesus got long-winded while preaching to a group gathered near the Sea of Galilee. When his disciples finally informed him that the crowd was weak from hunger, Jesus's response was to pray over a small collection of two fishes and five loaves of bread. *Shazam!* There was now food to feed five thousand people, with many baskets of leftovers. How the needy are nourished in the Twin Cities is only slightly less mind-boggling.

Since its founding in 1982, Loaves & Fishes has organized volunteers into serving teams who provide hot meals for more than 350,000 people each year. Sometimes a circle of friends, a family, or a book club will gather to make dinner. There are groups convened by schools, churches, and foundations as well as corporations such as Pillsbury, 3M, and Target. One gentleman left money in his will so surviving relatives could buy ingredients for the meals they make together several times a year in his honor. Currently, there are over 270 different volunteer teams who meet regularly to cook for others.

This sounded a little too good to be true, so I traveled to Minnesota to see for myself how it worked. I assisted a volunteer group one evening and then, at Hope Presbyterian Church in Richfield, cooked my own meal the next evening. This was a neighborhood south of downtown but near enough to the Minneapolis–Saint Paul International Airport that jets roared overhead every few minutes. The church's name, I decided, was a good sign. Everybody needs hope. It would be a pleasure to serve up heaping plates of hope. But to whom? What sort of people came to a soup kitchen in what appeared to be a middle-class neighborhood of ranch houses, all with neatly mowed lawns and American flags flying by their front doors? When I talked to Beth Ann Dodds, a coordinator for Loaves & Fishes who supervised at this location, she explained.

"Usually soup kitchens are very local, and poor people walk in, their belongings on their back. Not us. What we've got is primarily an elderly crowd, and they drive here, sometimes from great distances, even fifteen, twenty miles or more, which is a little freaky."

I agreed this sounded odd.

"Yeah, but it also makes a sad sort of sense," Dodds said. "Elderly people on fixed incomes might own their own homes, but they are paying out the yin-yang for prescription medicine. With a lot of our guests, they're either going to have their meds or they are going to eat. They can't afford both."

She continued: "I've worked at other sites that are more inner city, with transient folks, and you never know who you are going to see each day. But, it's very different with us. Of the hundred or so guests we usually have, I'd guess three-quarters are here every single evening. We've got a lot of husbands and wives. They sit at their own places, and they come to think of those seats as 'theirs.' They get pissy when someone sits at their table who they don't know or, for whatever reason, they don't like. It's kinda similar to teenagers in a high school cafeteria. Actually, the teenagers I've seen behave a lot better than some of our elderly folks."

The idea was vaguely humorous. I envisioned a rowdy food fight where, after throwing hot dog buns at each other, the senior citizens tossed their dentures or walking sticks.

Dodds warned me about one woman, Louella, who was a well-known troublemaker. "She's forever sneaking into the kitchen ahead of time to see what's cooking; then, she likes to cut in line to get second helpings before everyone else has even had their first plate of food. I say to her, 'It's about love, Louella. Be nice, Louella.' I just keep saying these words, and gradually she calms down. We're born as babies, and I guess we die as babies too."

Andrea Kish-Bailey arrived. She was the program manager for all eight dining sites that Loaves & Fishes operated across Minneapolis–Saint Paul from which a combined total of 1,500 meals were served each weeknight. Although most of these meals were prepared in churches, Loaves & Fishes still had to pay rent to use these facilities. At Hope Presbyterian, the fee to use the kitchen and fellowship hall four nights a week was $2,000 a month. Volunteer groups paid for their own food, Kish-Bailey noted, so they were free to serve whatever they liked. The atmosphere at dinner changed from evening to evening based on who was doing the cooking.

"Some groups see it as an expression of their love for God, and that's fine. But a lot of times, corporations will want to make sure nothing religious is going on. It's like I always say, 'Charity is not a faith-based impulse.'"

Kish-Bailey checked her schedule. "You're in for a treat tonight; the Band of Brothers is cooking."

"Oh, Lord," Dodds groaned, rolling her eyes. "It's always something with them!"

THE BAND OF Brothers was a group of former alcoholics and drug addicts. They met five years ago at a twelve-step sobriety group convening at Eden House, an organization in downtown Minneapolis that encouraged its members to find altruistic, or "pro-social," ways of using their time.

A group of at least half a dozen men, sometimes more, the Brothers, as they liked to call themselves, were not biologically related and functioned as their own nonprofit group. They were able to accept donations to supplement the costs of food, much of which they still bought themselves, and cooked together at different Loaves & Fishes sites an average of twice each month, or at least twenty times a year. Renowned for their ability to make a heart-warming meal (the Brothers' ribs were legendary), they exhibited the bonhomie of middle-aged guys playing a pickup game of basketball. They constantly teased each other and hurled about affectionate insults.

The Brothers were unofficially led by Tom Belting and Ezell Moore. Belting, who looked to be in his early fifties, had the manner of a born salesman. When he smiled, which was nearly always, the dimples on his cheeks drilled in. A loudmouth, he would have no trouble being heard over the din of a noisy bar. In conversation, Belting had the unnerving habit of edging right up to sincerity, then taking a 180-degree swerve away into the hoariest of jokes. The evening we met, he wore a polo shirt that had an eye-searing pattern of purple and blue.

"We can serve one hell of a meal, because in treatment you'll always find a couple guys who know how to cook," Belting said. "They might have been professional chefs or worked on the line at some restaurant, and this is how they got into booze and pot in the first place, because they needed to calm down after a hard night of slinging hash."

Belting, who was president of Dean Johnson Exteriors, a Twin Cities construction firm, described himself as a middle-class white kid who grew up in the suburbs and never knew much about poverty or the less fortunate until he found himself with an out-of-control drinking problem.

"I saw a lot, and I learned a lot about who I was during treatment. I was in for a year and a half. Tell you what. As a Republican, I turned into an Independent really quick!"

"Most of us were selfish pricks during the time we were using," Belting continued. "It really is an ongoing revelation to not only think of ourselves. There's just something about doing a random act of kindness—and when you see that smiling face . . ." He paused. Belting's voice had started to get a little thick with emotion. He took a couple of deep breaths. "I've had to pull guys off the serving line because they became too upset."

Screech! Here came the Belting U-turn.

"But, hell, we are not saints!" He then roared with a honking fit of laughter. "Sure, we like to cook, but we also get together and play cards once a week, and we like that fine too!" Belting hopped up from the table where we were sitting together. He banged his hands down on its top with such force that coffee splashed out of my cup. Belting didn't notice.

"I want you to meet Ezell! We call ourselves salt and pepper. He's my gangbanger brother, and he's the real deal. He learned how to cook in jail! He's got two bullets left in him!" Belting rushed off to the kitchen, returning a few moments later with his partner.

Ezell Moore carried his enormous belly with dignity. He had a full lower row of golden teeth and a baseball cap worn perpetually sideways. Salt and pepper was right! Moore was not only a different skin color than Belting but also an altogether different flavor. While Belting was a walking megaphone, Moore's manner was halting and taciturn. As Moore talked, he looked at his hands. I noticed that he wore rings on every one of his fingers, including his thumbs. Alexis Soyer was known to do the same thing.

"First of all, I have to set one thing straight," Moore said. "Tom likes to call me his gangbanger brother. I ain't never gang-banged no one, no how. I don't know where he gets this nonsense, but it ain't true."

When speaking about his past, Moore spoke tentatively, taking the occasional peek upward to make sure I wasn't bored. Originally from Missouri, he came to Minneapolis in 1999 and soon "fell in with the wrong crowd."

"When I was out there, I got in touch with God. He told me himself that I best leave them drugs alone."

On the day Moore graduated from his treatment program at Eden House, Belting was the guest speaker. After they met, Belting got Moore involved with the Brothers. "I did it once, and I just loved it," he explained. "It's great for guys in treatment. In all these years, I've never had to raise my voice; I've never heard a cross word. And, we is dealing with hard-core drug addicts and criminals here. I mean, some of these guys? They was bad!"

I asked Moore about the elderly crowd he would feed tonight.

"They're like my grandmother," Moore said. "They don't want to be here. It's a pride thing. I remember when I was on that side of the table."

He pointed to where the dinner buffet would soon be set up. "I always said to myself that when I got straight, I would give back. When you're high, you get a rush, you know? Well, now I get that rush when I'm cooking. Speaking of which, I'd best be getting back to work."

Moore walked off with his stomach-first waddle. As I followed him into the kitchen, I saw that his shorts—which were more like culottes, their hem grazing his lower calf—had one of the back pockets embroidered with an image of the Virgin Mary. Instead of the Virgin's customary beatific face, there was a grinning skull, and her halo was made of barbed wire.

It was nearly half past four, and dinner was nowhere close to being ready. Tom Belting found this unacceptable. "We're an hour behind schedule, and we've still got frozen chicken!" he screamed. "Come on, people! Get it together! We want all the legs turned to the left, and all the wings to the right. How often do I have to tell you this shit?"

None of the Brothers were paying him much attention, so Belting located another target for his bombastic energy when Beth Ann Dodds came into the kitchen carrying an orange three-ring binder. She'd shown it to me earlier, explaining that to qualify for donations from Minneapolis's city-run food bank, exact portion allowances and calorie counts for every meal served by Loaves & Fishes must be annotated in this binder. Belting knew this better than anyone, yet at this moment he found it convenient to act as if he didn't.

"Don't even start with me," he said, swatting Dodds away like she was a mosquito. "We got sixty pounds of potato salad, seventy-five pounds of chicken, fourteen pounds of rice, and fifteen boxes of stuffing. You figure out how that all breaks down into flippin' allowances, okay? I don't have time right now."

Ezell Moore emptied box after box of stuffing mix into stainless steel pans, then dumped in hot water and many sticks of margarine. The odor of sage bloomed across the kitchen, which suddenly smelled like Thanksgiving morning.

Outside, dinner guests started arriving at 5:00 p.m. on the dot. It was a mostly Caucasian crowd and quite old. I guessed these were people accustomed to sitting in rooms with window shades pulled tight and watching television in the middle of the day. Many had rolling walkers or toted along portable oxygen units, with clear plastic tubing snaking up their nostrils. The majority of guests I had seen at other soup kitchens were disheveled; when you got close to them, they exuded a ripe odor of dirt and sweat. This crowd was well scrubbed, with their hair brushed neatly into place.

As the guests found their way to tables, the room began to Balkanize. Some tables filled up immediately while others were occupied by a lone person, almost as if there were assigned seats. One of the volunteers rolled around a cart, offering hot cups of "Swedish gasoline." Frail hands shook as these elderly folks struggled to get the brims of coffee cups to their lips without burning themselves. Steam wafted up around their faces and fogged their eyeglasses.

Back in the kitchen, pots were banging, blasts of water rinsed off dirty pans in the enormous sinks, and the Brothers laughed together over a joke that was incomprehensible to anyone outside their fraternity.

"Fifteen minutes to kickoff," someone shouted.

"We're gonna be late, but it's gonna be good," Belting added.

At the peak of this pre-dinner insanity, a dozen teenagers arrived. They were sunburned and had wet hair, looking like they'd just come from swimming in a local lake. Most were girls and wore spaghetti-strap tops and blue jeans shorts cut high enough to expose half their buttocks. They were parishioners at a United Methodist church in Rockbrook, Nebraska, a suburb of Omaha, and were visiting Minneapolis on a missions trip. I was accustomed to hearing about teenagers heading off to Costa Rica or Haiti for such altruism. But Minnesota?

"We're from Youth Works!" announced a cocky boy. "We're here to help!"

"So? Do you want a friggin' medal?" Belting snapped. He was joking—sort of—but his humor was utterly lost on these kids, who looked scared.

Moore salvaged this awkward moment. Since there were extra volunteers this evening, he decided that guests would be given a special bonus of table service. "Why don't you go get on aprons and plastic gloves and join us back here in a few minutes for our group prayer?" Moore said to the teenagers, who scattered like sparrows.

Frantic food preparation continued. I don't know how these men did it, but they somehow managed to cook frozen chicken, slathered with barbecue sauce, in less than half an hour. It wasn't burned either, but looked both juicy and crisp. As food miracles go, this was not quite biblical in scale, but for a Minnesota Monday, it was startling nonetheless.

It was now time for the group prayer—something that is not obligatory for all groups but is a cherished part of the Band of Brothers' routine. They gathered in a circle and held hands. As Belting hollered out the "blessing," it appeared that even the Almighty was not safe from his incessant joking. "Dear God," he began, "Brother Ezell told me that you were the one who forgot to defrost the chicken, but I am pretty sure it was his fault, not yours. I'll forgive him if you can, Lord."

As I looked about, I saw that the Nebraska kids were shocked to hear God talked to with such impertinence. Their faces grew still more quizzical when the Brothers launched into their Serenity Prayer. "God, grant me the serenity to accept the things I cannot change, the courage to change the things I can, and the wisdom to know the difference. Amen!"

The Youth Works kids lined up and began to carry trays of food out to the seated diners. I got a plate for myself and sat alone in the room's farthest corner. Moments later I was joined by Dean Weigel, the executive director of Loaves & Fishes, who talked with me about his elderly clientele.

"Yes, they are on fixed incomes, and their pinched budgets need the help they get by receiving free meals," he said. As important, Weigel believed, is the social aspect of coming together this way. "These people mostly live alone or with their longtime husband or wife. They may not see anyone else all day until they come to Loaves & Fishes."

A few minutes later as I walked past the kitchen, I saw Tom Belting. He grabbed me into a violent hug, nearly squeezing the breath out of my lungs, while pummeling me on the back.

"Make sure you say goodnight to Ezell, my gangbanger brother," he said.

WHEN I RETURNED to Hope Presbyterian Church the following morning, I was skittish. Before we'd parted company the previous evening, Weigel told me he'd booked three of his very best kitchen volunteers—Sally, Bonnie, and Jan—to help me prepare my dinner that evening.

Gulp! Still new to this enterprise of mass cookery, I felt like a fraud. The prospect of three highly capable Minnesota women "assisting" me, when I imagined that they could bone and filet me, made me feel faint. You'd think that the disorderly way the Band of Brothers pulled their meal together might have allowed me to feel slightly reassured—I at least knew to defrost frozen meat—but it didn't. I grew up in church kitchens and was always intimidated by the unquestioned authority that women commanded as they churned out lunches at Vacation Bible School, or Thanksgiving and Christmas banquets. I feared Jan, Bonnie, and Sally would see through me right away.

To my immense relief, they were lovely. We jumped right in together—a band of sisters, if you will—and got to work on the menu I chose: couscous with chicken and roasted vegetables and a Greek salad with tomatoes, cucumbers, feta cheese, red onion, and black olives. These women followed my lead, even when it was fairly obvious I didn't know exactly what I was doing. Fact is, I was making up one of these recipes. I have eaten Greek salad many times but couldn't recall if I had ever prepared one myself.

Showing Bonnie how I seed a cucumber—peeling off the skin, cutting the vegetable lengthwise, and then scooping out its innards with a teaspoon—she protested, "But you lose half the cuke that way!"

"I know, but the seeds make people burp, and they're ugly, don't you think?"

I immediately regretted this somewhat fey question, as unattractive cucumber seeds were probably not high on Bonnie's list of things to worry about. She didn't dis me, though. Instead, she smiled. "If you think they're ugly, let's get rid of 'em."

Though I later learned that Sally was a strict vegetarian, she had diced nearly fifty pounds of boneless chicken breasts without a word of complaint.

"Why didn't you say something to me? You could have worked on something else," I said.

"Oh, it wasn't a problem," she replied. "I cook meat for my dogs."

Before roasting zucchini, acorn squash, and red peppers, I first smeared the empty pans with olive oil and placed them in the oven to heat. Why did I do that, Jan wanted to know. If the oil wasn't already hot before adding the vegetables, I explained, they would stick to the pan and burn.

"Would you marry me?" she joked. "If you did the cooking, I'd do all the dishes, I promise."

Our kitchen's mood, in other words, was altogether different from the night before. We worked quietly, doing our jobs and trading tips. This collegiality was slightly marred by a few factors beyond our control. It had been a swelteringly hot day; thunderstorms were predicted but had not yet materialized. By later afternoon, Minnesota's meteorologists were issuing tornado warnings.

"No one will come out in this weather," Weigel warned as he stopped by the kitchen shortly after four o'clock. "I hope all this food will last overnight in the refrigerator."

As if a twister headed our way wasn't dispiriting enough, an elevator that brought most guests to the basement dining room decided this was the perfect moment to start malfunctioning. "Our elderly folks can't handle the stairs. I don't know what we'll do, even if they do show up," Weigel said, thereby creating further stress.

Finally, as the cherry on this sundae, a fire alarm kept going off with a rapid series of piercing bleats. Each time this happened, Weigel would order Sally, Bonnie, Jan, and me to evacuate the kitchen. After the third time, I told him I wasn't leaving. "If the church is truly on fire, call me on my cell phone, okay?"

Just before 5:00 p.m., the Youth Works kids from Nebraska showed up again. They arrived with good news: the tornado had blown over, and the elevator was working again. If I had felt condescending toward them yesterday, these teenagers were now my saviors!

While the meal was served, I mostly stayed back in the kitchen. When things were nearly finished, I poked my head out.

"Young man, young man!" an old lady called out, her voice high and sharp as she beckoned me over to her table. "Did I hear that you cooked all this food?"

I was fifty-three years old at the time. Anyone who called me "young man" was going to get a friendly response. "Well, yes, but with a lot of help," I said.

She pointed at her plate. "What in the good Lord's name is that?"

"You mean the couscous?"

"Kookoo?"

"Couscous," I repeated, stressing the sibilant consonants.

She frowned. "Is it some type of pasta?"

"Similar, but different. It's made from durum wheat and is popular in the Mediterranean region. They're crazy for couscous in Morocco." I had provided too much information. In response, the woman stared at me.

"Do you like it?" I asked.

"Well, I can't rightly say. It needs salt, I'll tell you that much." She turned to the man next to her who I assumed was her husband. "Darling, did we ever go to Morocco?" she asked him.

He smiled but didn't answer.

"He's deaf as a doorknob. Can't hear a goddamn thing, can you, sweetheart?" She stroked a loose wisp of hair back behind one of his ears. "I believe we went to Morocco. Then again, I think we went to lots of places my daughter says we never did."

The woman once more pointed accusingly at her plate. "What's it called again?"

"Couscous."

"Is there any left?"

"Sure, shall I bring you some more?"

"If you wouldn't mind, sweetie. But make sure to put a good shake of salt on it, won't you? And can you bring me a few more of those raspberries?"

As I returned to the buffet table, I saw that Jan, Bonnie, and Sally were elated. "It's almost all gone!" Jan said. "People are loving the food you made."

"The food *we* made," I said, correcting her. "Well, I'm glad some people are pleased. Me? I've got a customer who isn't sure she likes the couscous but wants more anyway."

I tilted an ear back over my shoulder to indicate where the old lady was sitting. Sally and Bonnie both laughed.

"Oh, that's Louella," Bonnie explained. "She's a handful, that one. She's already been scolded twice for picking all the raspberries out of the fruit salad."

8

GOOD THINGS COME
IN SMALL PACKAGES

O VER THE YEARS, I'VE TRAVELED OFTEN TO MEXICO AND frequently been amazed by the hospitality shown there to strangers. The notion of *mi casa es su casa* easily expands from shelter to food, with Mexican hosts offering to prepare something delicious to eat for even their most casual of visitors or, at the very least, serve a cool drink.

However, it was not until I visited Xochimilco, a neighborhood to the south of sprawling Mexico City, that I experienced Mexican gastrophilanthropy on a truly fantastic scale. I was in search of the Niño Pa, a 450-year-old wooden statue depicting the infant Jesus that's much beloved in these parts. The way people show their love for the Niño Pa is through charitable cookery—and lots of it!

When I asked a few of my Mexican friends for help in locating this ancient religious icon, their advice was frustratingly vague. Don't worry, they promised, the statue is easy to find. Because the Niño Pa is watched over lovingly by one family for a year at a time, their house becomes a well-known pilgrimage site. Upon arriving in Xochimilco, I could ask anyone where the baby lived, and I'd be given directions instantly.

I was skeptical. Mexico City has over twenty million people, and Xochimilco, in the city's south, is one of its most populous neighborhoods. How could all of these people know the precise whereabouts of a centuries-old chunk of painted wood?

As I stepped out of the taxi I'd taken from the Centro Historico, an elderly woman who was selling Mexican breakfast pastries waved me over to her sidewalk kiosk. Asking the taxi to wait, I bought a churro. Then, feeling ridiculous, I haltingly inquired, "Por favor, Señora. A donde vive el Niño Pa?"

Well! It was as if I'd mentioned a favorite movie star, soccer player, or, better still, a child of her own. A smile spread across this woman's face, and her eyes lifted toward the heavens as if she was overcome with joy.

Turns out her mother was guardian to the statue back in the 1960s, and she herself watched over the Niño Pa thirty years ago. Although the statue lives with one family, she explained, and is under their official guardianship for a full year, this is primarily a nighttime job. The Niño Pa has a busy social schedule during the day as well and several times a week is carried forth to visit other homes, hospitals, schools, and churches. Not only is his primary caregiver expected to feed anyone who comes to see the Niño Pa each evening, but the family who assumes daily custody must also offer a meal to all those who encounter the baby while he's under their temporary watch.

The woman was speaking quickly, and my Spanish-to-English translations can sometimes err in a fanciful way, creating more poetry than was perhaps intended. Still, I was pretty sure she concluded her remarkably enthusiastic speech with the phrase "Everywhere the blessed baby goes, he floats on a cloud of love."

She then gave a shout to a teenaged boy who was lingering across the street. He quickly pedaled over on a bicycle rickshaw. Hesitant about this means of conveyance, I suggested that I'd prefer to take my taxi, which was still waiting for me at the curb. The woman laughed. Where I was going, she informed me, was impossible to access by car.

It was?

"Adelante, adelante!" she said, pointing toward the rickshaw. As I climbed in, she tugged on my sleeve. It was considered polite to bring the baby a gift, she whispered, and she was certain the Niño Pa liked nothing better than a bag of crispy churros.

Call me a jaded New Yorker, but I immediately assumed everything the lady told me up to this point was a sales ploy. Be that as it may, I bought what was left of her morning's inventory. Prices are cheap in Mexico; it's easy to be a hero in pesos.

"Vaya con Dios!" she cried, patting me on the shoulder, as the bicyclist took off.

My driver was a young man with earbuds jammed into each side of his head; I could hear the tinny blare of music blasting into his brain. I couldn't expect much in the way of conversation from him, so I sat back and tried to recall some of what I'd read about the Niño Pa and Xochimilco.

IN PRE-HISPANIC TIMES, Mexico City existed as an archipelago of a few inhabited islands set in the midst of a vast mountain lake. The biggest island, which today is the Centro Historico, was known as Tenochtitlan. To the south, Xochimilco was an agricultural center where mud was dredged up from the lake bed and placed on floating gardens called chinampas that were made of wattle and reeds. Farmers planted these fertile areas with corn, beans, chiles, squash, and other vegetables as well as fruits and flowers. Crop yields were high, with three harvests a year, so Xochimilco was a place of great wealth and abundance. In fact, as a precautionary measure before vanquishing the Aztec king Montezuma, Hernán Cortés thought it prudent to first conquer Xochimilco, which he did in April of 1521.

As for the Niño Pa, it is sometimes said that this carved figurine of the baby Jesus originally belonged to Martin Cortés, son of Hernán and the Indian woman (always called "La Malinche") who acted as Hernán's adviser, interpreter, and lover.

Today, Xochimilco contains seventeen different subsections, or barrios—Parroquia San Bernardino, La Assunciation, Tlacoapa, San Juan, San Antonio, Jaltocan, Belén, San Cristobal, Caltango, San Esteban, El Rosario, San Marcos, La Guadalupita, La Santisima, San Lorenzo, Santa Crucito, and San Pedro—and each of these barrios has its own Catholic church. A community-wide celebration of the Niño Pa occurs in Xochimilco every April 30 on what's called El Día de Los

Niños. Another highlight of the year is the arrullada, which happens on December 24. Arrullar is a Spanish word that means "to whisper sweet nothings; to coo." On Christmas Eve, there is a mass at which the Niño Pa is placed in a crèche at one of Xochimilco's churches, and the whole congregation (as well as those crowded together on the surrounding streets for many blocks around) quietly sing lullabies until it is decided the baby has gone to sleep.

In addition to his countless public appearances, some people believe the Niño Pa also miraculously travels about on his own each night visiting people in their dreams, watching over them and their houses, maybe even blessing crops that are still planted on the few remaining chinampas. Some of his guardians claim to have found mud on the statue's shoes in the morning as proof of these nocturnal travels.

My RICKSHAW DRIVER pedaled me into a labyrinth of Xochimilco's side streets and narrow alleyways. I thought of Hansel and Gretel, half-wishing I'd left a trail of crumbled churros to find my way out. At this moment, though, as we passed underneath a gaily decorated trellis over the street (with the words "Bienvenidos Niño Pa!" surrounded by large plastic flowers), I realized we must be getting close. Soon we arrived at a still more grandiose arch over the front gate of one particular home. A sign on a wall proclaimed this to be La Casa de Familia Guerra Ramirez.

Doña Antonia Guerra Ramirez was the lady of the house. Wearing jeans and a black T-shirt, her dark hair dyed a luminous shade of orange-yellow, Doña Ramirez looked younger than her forty-six years. She welcomed me with elaborate courtesy, and it was with some difficulty that I managed to decline her repeated offers of a plate of huevos revueltos or a cup of hot chocolate. Ramirez told me it was twenty-eight years ago, when she was still a teenager, that she first applied for the honor of taking care of the Niño Pa. While she waited nearly three decades, she saved her money and planned. Eventually, she felt it necessary to build an entirely new wing onto one side of her house and put a roof over her courtyard—thus making a dry, airy outdoor space for the many people who come every day to see the statue. She also modernized and expanded her kitchen, making it easier for her to serve food to whoever arrives at her door no matter what time of day.

"Won't you have a cup of chocolate?" Ramirez asked again. Once more I declined, but her offer reminded me of my little gift, and I handed over the bag of churros.

"Por el niño," I mumbled.

Ramirez was on a committee that maintained up-to-date requirements for those who hope to have the statue live in their house at some point in the future. Of the many stipulations to be followed, the most important are you have to be from Xochimilco, be Catholic, and be able to prove your absolute devotion to the Niño Pa, as he is never to be left alone.

Caring for the baby as well as welcoming and feeding his many visitors was Ramirez's full-time job. She'd worked for the federal government in an administrative post for Mexico City's police force but was given a year's leave of absence so she could devote herself completely to the Niño Pa. Amazed by this, I tried to imagine how the higher-ups at the New York City Police Department would react if one of its cops made such a request.

"It is a beautiful experience, but it is also a big responsibility," Ramirez said.

While we talked, I became increasingly curious about why I was the only one visiting here today. My eyes wandered about as I tried to get my first glimpse of the Niño Pa. I'd seen pictures and knew he was a small statue, so he might have been obscured by all the gifts brought by his worshippers. The courtyard where Ramirez and I were standing was filled with masses of flower arrangements and many dozens of mylar balloons decorated with images of SpongeBob SquarePants, El Dia de Los Muertos skeletons, pop-eyed little angels, and, of course, the Virgin of Guadalupe.

"Es possible lo veo?" I asked.

Yes, Ramirez replied, I could see the Niño Pa, but not until later. At this exact moment, the statue was in Jaltocan, another neighborhood of

Xochimilco, where a party in his honor was being arranged. She expected the Niño Pa to return home by 8:00 p.m., at which time Ramirez would lead a Rosary and offer coffee and pastries to everyone who accompanied him. Her manner was nonchalant, as if she were detailing the much-repeated schedule of her son or younger brother: "Let's see. He's got school until 3:00 p.m., followed by band rehearsal, then soccer practice."

What is the difference between magic and mysticism? Some people truly believe in the life-preserving power of certain rituals, such as crossing themselves before stepping onto an airplane. Others act by unconscious reflex, sidestepping to avoid walking under a ladder. To wait nearly three decades, to scrimp, save, and deny herself in preparation for this statue to reside at her house—thereby, she explained, forgoing the opportunity to have a husband or family of her own—Doña Antonia Guerra Ramirez must be of the first order of faith.

Rather than wait around, I decided to continue my search for the Niño Pa at today's fiesta. About to bid farewell to this gracious woman, I had one more question. Ramirez considered my inquiry with a thin smile. No, she replied, in the time she'd had the Niño Pa in her house, she had not experienced anything miraculous herself. She'd seen no mud on his shoes, she volunteered. However, Ramirez knows the statue has worked miracles for other people, and this is enough for her. The selflessness of her reply struck me as hauntingly poignant.

Outside, I climbed back into the bicycle rickshaw. Before I could say where I wanted to go, the young driver turned to me, yanked out one of his earbuds, and inquired, "Jaltocan?"

Even he knew where the Niño Pa was visiting today. Unbelievable!

We traveled down more alleys and crossed bridges over narrow canals of slowly drifting water. After another twenty minutes, off in the distance, I began to hear cohetes—firecrackers! Emerging from shady residential streets onto a busy, wide thoroughfare, I saw a crowd walking on the avenue, a helium-filled balloon tied to each of their wrists. This was a Wednesday, a few minutes before noon, yet there were at least three hundred people on parade. Didn't they have to be at work? Or, like

Ramirez's sabbatical from the police department, does a request to spend the day with the Niño Pa immediately and unquestionably allow you a day off?

A mariachi band wound its way alongside and through the crowd. Composed of three trumpets, two drums, one tuba, two trombones, two clarinets, and two saxophones, they were playing traditional Mexican music: up-tempo, brassy, and wildly alive. It is impossible to be in a bad mood when you are within earshot of mariachis. Their music grabs you by the heart and hips, shaking you free from life's small worries.

Adding to the revelry was a group of several dozen dancers, called chinelos, who were dressed in black velvet costumes accessorized with feathered scarves in vibrant shades of pink, yellow, and turquoise. They wore carved wooden masks with Caucasian features: white skin, blue eyes, and beards jutting out to a sharp point from their chins. On their heads were large hats that resembled upside-down lampshades with dangling fringe all about their top. The chinelos danced and spun about like a New Orleans krewe during Mardi Gras. Different groups of women had set up folding tables on the sidewalk, where they were squeezing oranges and handing out free glasses of juice to passersby.

Not surprisingly, the Niño Pa led the festivities. I spied him off in the distance being carried by the family who was hosting him that day. He was shielded from the sun under an enormous blue beach umbrella. The statue moved ahead haltingly, as nearly every step of the way someone came forward, carefully lifted the hem of his gown, and gave it a kiss.

The entire barrio had come to a standstill to accommodate this pageantry. Roads were blocked, with long lines of cars waiting at intersections, yet there was no honking or any obvious signs of impatience as the costumed dancers, the mariachi band, and a steadily growing crowd of people meandered slowly past. Bottle rockets continued to shoot off above our heads, streaking the blue sky with wispy trails of smoke before exploding in exceptionally percussive booms.

Someone handed me a balloon. I joined the procession and, strolling along, learned a few things from an older gentleman walking beside me. The name Niño Pa combines the Spanish word for "boy" with a word from Nahuatl (the ancient Aztec language) that means "place," meaning the Niño Pa is a boy from this place, Xochimilco. The register book of families waiting to take annual care of the baby is full until 2042. Around December 28 of every year, you can try to be granted the chance to host a daily parade such as this, and there is always a long line of people hoping to secure a spot before the calendar fills up.

My companion asked if I would like to get a better look at the baby. This new friend led me forward through the marchers until we were walking alongside the blue umbrella and I could look underneath.

The Niño Pa wore a diadem of three golden beams shooting forth like antennae from his sculpted brunette hair. He had dark, wide-open eyes, a high forehead, and pale pink skin, though his cheeks were painted a blushing fuchsia. His small lips, pursed into a tentative grin, were red as cherries. For today's outing, the Niño Pa was dressed in an all-white gown; its profusion of satin and lace looked like a meringue. He sat in a little wooden chair and was tied to it with a burgundy cord to prevent him from slipping off. A woman who carried the Niño Pa had a white towel tossed over one of her shoulders as if he were a real baby who might at any moment spit up.

After walking for a half hour longer, the parade arrived at Jaltocan's Catholic church. The chinelos lined up in two rows, making a passageway to the front door through which the family holding the Niño Pa proceeded. The old man and I followed sneakily in their wake. Inside, the church's aisles and pews were tightly packed with still more people— young and old, men and women, boys and girls—all holding balloons that bobbed above their heads. Several women wore their hair woven into braids that snaked down their backs, reaching nearly to their ankles. The old priest who presided over the service was unsteady on his feet. He was gently guided about by a lone acolyte, a stout young girl who wore a track suit in a glowing shade of chartreuse.

AFTER THE MASS, there was a slow procession from the church to the house of Don Martin Salas. He and his wife were the couple who carried the Niño Pa in the parade and would now be everyone's host for lunch. The Salas family lived near a dock where colorfully painted barges take off to transport tourists along Xochimilco's canals. These are the last vestiges of many, many miles of waterways that once crisscrossed the entire valley of Mexico during Aztec times.

A large tent was set up, its fabric thickly striped with green and yellow. The green blocked the sun's glare, but the yellow diffused it into golden bands of light. Crepe paper swags were hanging everywhere, stenciled with either the words "Bienvenidos Niño Pa" or "Gracias Niño Pa." Still more helium balloons fluttered about rectangular tables and chairs stretching the length of several football fields. Each table had a flower arrangement made from day lilies and zinnias. It looked as if our hosts were prepared to feed at least five hundred, maybe more. There was no check-in area, nor did I sense an invitation was required to take a place at any of these tables. Dozens of waiters in white shirts, black vests, and bow ties rushed about shouldering large platters of food with accompanying sauces offered from terra-cotta bowls called cazuelas. There was an empty chair next to a group of women who were quietly talking to each other. When I asked if this seat was free, they nodded, and wished me "buenas tardes."

One of the ladies informed me that she was a sister to a good friend of Doña Salas, our hostess. Some might consider this a tenuous connection, but this woman felt enough kinship that when the waiters lagged slightly in their service, she got up from our table and hurried off to help move things along. I soon saw her ferrying about baskets of fresh tortillas.

"This kind of community, a feeling of solidarity, is deep inside the mentality of the Mexican people," another woman said to me. "It is not lost, but it is forever hidden under the earth."

I wanted to talk about this further but wondered yet again if my Spanish-to-English translation had rendered her statement more soulful than she'd intended. Besides, the smells rising from the platters and cazuelas were too distracting. I loaded up my plate and began to eat.

There was rice, turned a dull red by being cooked with carrots and tomato juice; nopales (paddle cactus), which were boiled and then fried with chiles and onions; black beans in a thick garlic-laced broth; and a green salad with radishes and avocado. Finally there were carnitas, which are savory hunks of pork, slow-cooked in garlic, orange juice, and peppers and then grilled over a wood fire. There were no knives or forks; we ate with tortillas and our fingers. The food was marvelous, and I consumed two full plates and then half of a third, goaded on by the appreciative smiles of my table mates. They seemed to be personally gratified by my gluttony. I washed it all down with many glasses of a purple-red punch made from dried hibiscus flowers steeped in honeyed water.

Completely sated, nearly full to bursting, I asked about the logistics of such a meal. I'd seen our host and hostess passing by several times throughout lunch greeting friends, never pausing or sitting themselves, so focused were they on the comfort of their guests. It was astounding and humbling to be a participant in hospitality on this scale. How did one family make all this food? How long had they been cooking? How many people, other than all these waiters, were required to help?

"I'm exhausted just looking at them," I concluded.

From their quizzical reactions, I sensed they'd been to enough parties thrown in this baby's honor—and doubtless they'd cooked meals of their own, just like this one—that a gathering such as today's no longer struck them as unusual. For these women of Xochimilco, hosting a lunch for hundreds of strangers was altogether natural.

One of them finally spoke. "You've seen the Niño Pa?" she asked.

"Si, señora," I replied.

"Well, try to imagine this doll is actually a little piece of God. When you are around it, you are in the presence of God. If this were so, whatever you could do, you would do. And no matter how much you do, it still wouldn't be enough if you truly believe you are in the presence of God, right?"

I didn't know how to respond other than by bowing my head in silent agreement.

The ladies went back to talking among themselves.

After a while, I slipped away from the tent and began to amble slowly along the canals of Xochimilco in the warmth of a late afternoon's sunshine. I had a blessedly guilt-free sensation of being overfed that I usually only experience on Thanksgiving. How weird and wonderful this day had been! Though a foreign visitor, I was warmly welcomed into Doña Ramirez's home and then invited to an incredible feast.

I don't believe the Niño Pa is a little piece of God, yet I understood what the woman whom I'd dined with earlier meant. Blessed by the gastrophilanthropy of Señor and Señora Salas, my faith was restored in the importance of cooking for others and the possibility of improving lives— one plate at a time. I felt light, as if I were floating on a cloud of love.

9

THE NIGHT SPIDER-MAN
SAVED MY LIFE

Los Angeles Youth Network (LAYN) is a constellation of shelters that care for adolescents and teenagers, many of whom were kicked out of their childhood homes because they are gay. My friend Hope Biller is on its board.

Nearly thirty years ago, Hope was my assistant when we worked together at the New York office of Edelman Worldwide, a public relations agency. Since that time, she had become a reality TV casting director and now lived with her husband, Ken, a television show runner, and their two children, Sofia and Sam, in Los Feliz, a neighborhood below Griffith Park in East Los Angeles.

One afternoon when we were talking on the phone, Hope suggested that the next time I was out West, I might like to prepare a dinner at a LAYN house in Hollywood. What's more, she and her kids would love to help me cook. I immediately agreed this sounded like a terrific idea, and she supplied me with a name and telephone number for LAYN's head of volunteer efforts.

My husband James's sister, Jane, lives in Orange County; he and I usually go to California a couple times a year. A few months later when it came time for us to make our next trip, I gave Hope's contact person at LAYN a call and explained my idea. In addition to making dinner for youngsters who lived at a group house, I could also provide a few cooking lessons—demonstrating how easy it was to stir-fry spinach with garlic, or make a quick tomato sauce.

"Don't expect too much from these kids," he said after I suggested this possibility. "Many of them have been very brutalized by their up-bringing. They are angry and closed down. It's not like everyone sits together, holds hands for prayer, and eats family-style. It's great what you want to do, but I hope you don't think this is going to be like *The Brady Bunch*."

I was put off by his sarcasm. "Fine, I completely understand," I said, though I didn't really. "I guess I was getting ahead of myself with the idea of cooking lessons. Could you suggest some types of food the kids especially like to eat?"

There was an uncomfortable delay before he answered.

"It's anyone's guess what they'll want on a given night, but if they like it, they'll eat like wolves. Especially the boys. If you're confident of your cooking, I'd say you should make twice as much as you'd normally prepare."

OVER THE NEXT few days, I began to daydream about possible menus. Mac 'n cheese? Fried chicken? Sloppy Joes? I also tried to imagine who these girls and boys in Los Angeles might be.

Public perception has shifted over time, and today the media is much likelier to fuel fears of abducted children or those who are coerced into sex trafficking than to highlight the plight of homeless teenagers. As a result, the idea of runaways seemed anachronistic to me, a throw-back to the era of hippies and Woodstock. What I would soon enough learn, though, is the phenomenon of children fleeing from home is still a very serious problem in America—especially when they are gay or transgender.

The National Runaway Switchboard, an organization based in Chi-cago, maintains a toll-free number (1-800-RUNAWAY) to help children who've left, or are thinking of leaving, places in which they no longer feel welcome. This organization claims that 15 percent of American children will make at least one attempt to run away between the ages of ten and eighteen. It's also estimated that there may be between one million and three million homeless children currently living on the streets in the United States.

A twenty-first-century shelter such as LAYN is still heavily influenced by public policy decisions made decades ago, when runaways first became a national problem. Such, at least, is the theory of Karen M. Staller, an associate professor of social work at the University of Michigan in Ann Arbor. In her book *Runaways: How the Sixties Counterculture Shaped Today's Practices and Policies*, Staller explains how until the early 1960s there was a tendency to think of runaway youths as modern-day Huckleberry Finns—on a lark, their belongings in a kerchief that dangled at the end of a stick. When waves of teenagers began bolting from their parents' homes in unprecedented numbers around the time of the Vietnam War, public attitudes quickly changed. In response, elected officials began tinkering with rules governing when and how to regulate America's youngsters. In 1971, for example, the Twenty-Sixth Amendment to the U.S. Constitution lowered the voting age from twenty-one to eighteen.

Staller's book reexamines 1967 and its so-called Summer of Love, which brought thousands of runaways to San Francisco's Haight-Ashbury neighborhood. It was here that a counterculture group called the Diggers organized help for this influx of homeless young people, providing free places to sleep, health clinics, food, and telephone lines. When Huckleberry House opened in San Francisco, it was the first in what would become a nationwide movement of alternative service providers for runaway children. Other shelters began to open around the country, such as Covenant House in New York City, Ozone House in Ann Arbor, and Looking Glass in Chicago.

These places were not part of the traditional child welfare or juvenile justice systems. At them, teenagers could ask for help directly instead of being ordered into treatment by judges or other authorities, and care providers would not call either the parents or police against a teenager's wishes. While this was groundbreaking in the 1960s, a "children first" ideal is still the prevailing ethos at a place such as LAYN.

A FEW DAYS after I contacted the organization, someone called with a more specific food suggestion. At the West Hollywood group house, a girl named Cindy asked for chiles rellenos. Because she'd done well on a recent school test, Cindy hoped that life would reward her with this dish, one she remembered her Mexican grandmother making.

Now, I agreed with Cindy. Chiles rellenos are a special treat, but what makes them unusually good is a time-consuming and labor-intensive recipe—not exactly the sort of meal you want to make for twenty-five children who, I was told, should be counted as fifty because of their wolfish appetites. Though I knew better, I suppose I was still dazzled by the feats of Mexican gastrophilanthropy I had recently witnessed in honor of the Niño Pa. Unwisely, then, I claimed that making chiles rellenos would be a snap for me. *No hay problema*. Well, they were a problem, a huge problem if you must know, both for me and for my friend Hope, who offered me the full run of her kitchen.

Some meals come together easily, nearly as if an unseen hand is stirring the sauce. Others feel jinxed from the start. Unfortunately, Cindy's dinner fell into this latter category, beginning with the fact that all of Los Angeles's grocery store chains I visited—Gelson's, Pavilions, and Albertson's—either did not carry poblano peppers or were sold out of them. I had to scour half a dozen Hispanic grocery stores east of downtown to find fifty plump peppers. Then there was the searing and de-seeding of the poblanos, making a meat stuffing, dipping the prepared peppers in an egg white batter, and frying them until they were golden brown. *Ay, Dios mio!*

Back in the days when Hope was my assistant, she saw me spend inordinate amounts of time fussing over wacky projects such as a man-ufacture of the "world's biggest chocolate chip," then arranging for it to be blasted apart with a jackhammer at a press event for Nestlé Toll House morsels. I'm guessing these earlier feats seemed less strange than the sight of me hovering over a pot of frijoles negros that simmered on the back of her stove for most of two days.

Finally the food was ready, and on a rainy night in September, which felt more like an evening in Maine than California, we loaded up

Hope's car, and she, Sofia, Sam, and I drove over to Hollywood. When we arrived at the LAYN house, we rang the front doorbell and waited. No response. We tapped on the front door. Nothing. Ring-ring! Knock-knock-knock! Bang-bang! Eventually, a young man opened the door for us but turned away without any greeting and wandered back to the living room. A dozen kids were sprawled here on sofas, chairs, and the floor watching a Vin Diesel movie. They had the television cranked to such an incredible volume, I felt as if my own body, not Vin Diesel's, was being pummeled by each punch thrown on-screen.

Thinking some superheroic action of my own was required, I shouted, "Hola, amigos! We've brought you an incredible feast of Mexican food! Donde esta Cindy?"

No one returned my greeting or even took their eyes off the screen. Instead, as Hope and I repeatedly struggled through the living room, hauling in foil-wrapped pans and hampers full of food, we would occasionally hear little groans of exasperation when we'd momentarily block the television.

In the kitchen, we found two boys about to dig into a cardboard box recently delivered from Pizza Hut. The sharp stench of this nearly made me gag. "You guys! Don't eat that!" I commanded. "Didn't anyone tell you we're serving something special tonight?" They both looked at me as if I were a cop, which under the circumstances I sort of was.

"Give me fifteen minutes, please? If you don't like what I've made, you can eat the pizza, okay?"

Without answering, they shuffled away.

Hurrying to get things ready, I was glad to have cooked everything at Hope's house and not relied on this kitchen. There were no pots bigger than what's necessary to boil an egg in, and—as a suicide attempt precaution—no knives whatsoever and only plastic eating utensils. Juggling pans between what little fire I could muster, I heated up the chiles rellenos, rice, black beans, and a zucchini, tomato, and corn casserole. As the scent of these various dishes wafted out into the living room, a few kids managed to drag themselves away from the sofa long enough to peek into the kitchen.

"Where is Cindy?" I asked again, this time in English. I thought she'd be ecstatic to see what was going on in honor of her good test score and might act as some sort of emissary to the others.

"She ain't here," a young man with a thick mop of black hair told me. "No one's heard from her in, I dunno, like, a week."

What? I felt defeated that all my efforts on her behalf would not be noticed. But then, I gave my ego a much-needed kick in the ass. Get over yourself, Stephen! The important thing to focus on was that a child such as Cindy, wherever she was, had been kicked out of her own house and ended up here at LAYN. Then, for whatever reason, she'd felt compelled to leave here as well. This was the tragedy, not that my guest of honor was a no-show.

Children need to be shown love, I thought, not judgment. Well, a little begging might also work. I went out into the living room and placed myself squarely in front of the enormous TV. The sound of cars crashing and shattering glass boomed forth from behind me; I could feel the backs of my thighs trembling, as vibrations from the speakers were so powerful.

"Could someone hit the mute button for just a second?" I yelled. "MUTE BUTTON? PLEASE?" One of the kids picked up a remote control, and the room fell silent—shatteringly, apocalyptically silent.

"Okay, you guys. I know you don't know me, but I have cooked for two days, making some really good Mexican food just for you. Will you please come into the kitchen and at least look at it?"

No one moved.

"Por favor? I promise, you'll be glad you did."

Each child appeared drugged, as if in private orbit around a distant star. No one shifted position by even a fraction of an inch.

Thinking I would have to win them over one by one, I walked into another room where I saw a young man sitting next to a square table above which were hung heat lamps. I thought he was tending a terrarium, or trying to harvest bean sprouts. Nope. It was his collection of arachnids, aka spiders. Creepy-crawly things aren't my favorites. It took nearly all that was left of my goodwill to sit with this teenager while he introduced me to his friends, the tarantulas, brown recluses, and long-legged spiders.

"Oh, a daddy longlegs!" I said. "We have those back in New York!"

My outburst elicited a smirk from the boy. There are at least fifty thousand species of spiders, he said. Most spend their entire life capturing and eating other insects. "Spiders are killed only because they scare people, not because they are dangerous to humans," he concluded, his voice doleful.

It occurred to me there was some sort of comparison to be made between homophobia and arachnophobia. To wit: Wouldn't it be nice if we could learn to love everyone equally, gay or straight, human or spider, eight-legged or two-legged? But the sentiment was convoluted, and I couldn't get it phrased in my mind.

When he demonstrated how a spider can stun a fly and suck it in whole for later digestion, however, I asked if he would like to do the same to a chile relleno. He laughed, which was the first moment of genuine merriment I had seen since entering this bleak house. Happily, Spider-Man had some credibility among his peers. When he accompanied me back to the kitchen, others followed.

Dear readers, let me go on record as saying that I now believe in transubstantiation. No, not the Catholic dogma about the body and blood of Jesus Christ. What I saw in Los Angeles over the next hour was how a home-cooked meal can transform a roomful of sullen teenagers into a group of cheerful children.

A girl who had been weeping, alone, in the corner of the living room was eating frijoles negros and asking why she could taste lemons. She seemed genuinely interested as I explained the concept of zesting to her.

When I'd arrived at the house earlier, one guy, who was wearing lipstick and false eyelashes, looked me up and down like I was a used car. Now, dipping a tortilla chip into salsa, he inquired if I'd ever heard of the Fashion Institute of Design and Technology in New York City. Yes, I told him. I can see it from my office window. What did he want to know?

Finally, there was a husky boy whose lank hair hung across his face nearly as a shield. He'd sulked after I begged him not to eat that Pizza Hut delivery. After consuming two or three helpings of the zucchini and corn casserole, he pulled Hope's son, Sam, into his lap and was tickling him without mercy. Sam was laughing himself sick, giving as good as he got and twisting the kid's nose ring.

The Brady Bunch? Not exactly. But at least for one night these kids got to experience what it's like to eat family-style.

10

THE WEARY WORLD REJOICES

KILLIAN NOE AND I ATTENDED YALE DIVINITY SCHOOL together in the mid-1980s and became fast friends early in our religious studies. Part of what drew us together was that we'd both fled from our upbringing in fundamentalist Christianity. Like most refugees, though, Killian and I still liked to occasionally reminisce about the "old country."

She regaled me with tales of her brother-in-law, who was a minister of music at a Baptist megachurch in South Carolina. Killian described the Christmas pageant he produced each year as so lavish that it nearly put to shame Radio City Music Hall's "The Living Nativity," which always concludes their annual Christmas Spectacular. In addition to a full-scale re-creation of the stable at Bethlehem, complete with live camels and sheep, Killian's brother-in-law's version of Christ's birth featured a formation of U.S. soldiers marching through the church's aisles, weapons brandished. As if this melding of church and state weren't jarring enough, at the show's finale a cross rose up at the stage's rear, and a young man portraying Jesus was shown "nailed" to its beams. Let's keep Christ in Christmas, and God bless America!

When Killian heard through mutual friends what I'd been up to lately, she asked me if I would organize a special holiday meal—our own Christmas pageant—for guests at the Recovery Café. She founded this light-filled space in downtown Seattle, where poor, addicted, and lonely people come for comfort. At the Recovery Café's center, both architecturally and philosophically, is a coffee bar with dedicated baristas who make a mighty fine latte. There were no religious observances at Recovery Café because Killian had no patience for what she called a "pray to play" atmosphere.

One story might help you understand a bit more about this excellent woman.

A few years ago, Killian suffered a freak accident while trekking with friends through the jungle of Papua New Guinea. There she was, following the same path as everyone else, when suddenly the ground beneath her gave way. Killian fell nearly forty feet, straight down into a hidden pit, landing in a small patch of sand surrounded by sharp rocks. Had her descent deviated by even a few inches, she would have been killed instantly. Instead, the sand provided enough of a cushioned landing that she "only" broke both legs and had to be medically evacuated for immediate surgery.

When Killian told me about this, my out-and-proud agnosticism teetered a bit. I suggested it seemed somehow . . . miraculous. Didn't she think, I asked, that some supernatural force might have protected her so she could continue her charitable work in Seattle?

"No," Killian instantly replied. "Not for a minute can I allow myself to think that. Why would God, or any 'supernatural force,' as you put it, decide to make an exception for me, but not for the hundreds and thousands of other people who are killed every day? Besides, I don't want to believe in a God who would be so unfair."

ON MY FIRST morning at the Recovery Café, Killian introduced me to a regular visitor named Levon. In his early fifties, he was smartly dressed in a yellow polo shirt and blue jeans, the latter ironed with a front crease. Killian asked if he'd be willing to tell me something about his life. Levon nodded and began to talk in his low, resonant voice. An incident he described after a few minutes really got my attention.

"I guess I was about nineteen," Levon began. "By this time, I had a good job—good enough at least that I could afford to send my wife on a winter's vacation with some of her girlfriends to Cancun for ten days. It gets awful cold up there in Milwaukee, that's for damn sure."

I smiled. James grew up in Green Bay. We've often gone out to visit his family, and I knew exactly how miserable a Wisconsin winter can be.

"Well, the ladies was on an early flight from O'Hare to Mexico," Levon continued, "so early it seemed like a good idea that they should gather over at our apartment, and we'd stay up all night partying. Then they wouldn't have to worry about oversleeping and missing their flight."

An excellent plan, I concurred.

"So, I lays in the supplies. Cocaine, of course, and reefer. And naturally, there was plenty of liquor."

"Naturally," I agreed.

As Levon told it, the ladies and he had a "good ol' time," and sometime before dawn he helped them all into a shuttle van, whose driver he entrusted to take them safely to the airport. He went back inside the house, and the next thing Levon remembers, his wife was banging on the door and screaming his name.

"I thought you was going to Mexico," he called out.

"You fool! I done gone to Cancun," she screamed back at him. "Now get your ass to this door and let me in!"

Levon shook his head, smiling at the memory.

"So?" I asked, thinking I had missed something. "What happened to you for those ten days? How did you eat? Did people come visit you?"

Levon lifted his hands and shrugged. "I have no idea what I got up to. My neighbors say they heard me playing my trumpet once in a while. And, I found I wrote a song or two. All I know for sure is every last speck of them party supplies was gone!"

Levon had begun drinking heavily and doing drugs while still a child, he told me. Once, he got pistol-whipped by a boyfriend of his mother's because he'd knocked over the guy's bong. Because his father was in prison, Levon learned how to live from watching the other men in his neighborhood.

"The thing is, they all had jobs," he said. "They'd go to the factory or the shop. They work all day; they do their time. But after punching out? They'd get fucked up! It just seemed completely normal to me. It's all I saw; I thought that's what being a man was. I'm little, but I want to be a man, so I start getting stoned."

Levon said he became sober at age twenty, or a year before he was legally allowed to consume alcohol in the state of Wisconsin. We sat together, silent for a moment, both of us aware how unusual this fact was. I felt honored he'd taken me into his confidence this way.

My way of saying thank you for Levon's candor, and to the other women and men whose stories I heard in Seattle, was to cook them a truly special holiday meal. I devised a menu of Brazilian seafood stew, which was loaded with shrimp, chorizo, tomatoes, and red peppers, and a chocolate bread pudding for dessert.

THE MAIN CHEF at Recovery Café was a tough-looking guy named Jeff. He wore his T-shirt sleeves rolled up high, the better to reveal his massively muscular biceps as well as tattoos that covered both his arms. He appeared like a member of the Hell's Angels motorcycle gang, which back in his drinking days he had been. However, don't judge a book by its cover or a man by his ink. Within half an hour of cooking alongside Jeff, I discovered he had a ready smile and a boyishly goofy sense of humor. He didn't treat my arrival in his kitchen as a hassle, but as a welcome diversion from his usual routine.

When Jeff helped me unpack the many bags of groceries I bought the night before, I saw his apprehension at some of the price tags. There was several hundred dollars' worth of shrimp and two jars of saffron that each cost plenty.

"If we are going to use such fancy ingredients, let's get the most out of them," Jeff said, and he set about making a stock from the shrimp shells, which I was about to throw away. He also corrected me as I was busily de-crusting loaves of sourdough bread for the dessert. "That's the best part! The crusts will soak up the chocolate and become crunchy and sweet."

Finally, he taught me the fastest and best way to dice a bell pepper, a technique I use to this day, thinking of Jeff when I do so.

It's funny, this. My repertoire of cooking techniques is often an aide-mémoire, reminding me of the person who taught me a certain thing. There's my friend Todd Gribbin, who showed me how to cut up a head of cauliflower (slide a knife blade in around the stalk to gently pry away each separate floret). Or, Hope Biller's simple vinaigrette, its secret elements being raw garlic, a drop of honey, and crushed red pepper. And Rick Livingston's roasted bluefish recipe—with fresh sage snipped on top, and a drizzle of olive oil. I treasure these mental associations, as they make certain foods taste like friendship.

The Brazilian stew Jeff and I were making was a recipe adapted from Elisabeth Luard, a British chef and journalist I met once on a press trip to Puglia, Italy. Luard wrote a fascinating book titled *Sacred Food: Cooking for Spiritual Nourishment*, and I remembered her not only for this seafood recipe but also because of a fascinating story she told me about Aztecs in Mexico and their culture of blood sacrifice.

I thought Jeff might be intrigued by the story, so I shared with him that, according to Luard, a special ball game was played by Aztec men, and scholars believed it was the winning team who were slaughtered to celebrate their victory. For a particularly beloved player, a life-size effigy might then be created from a "clay" formed by mixing the blood of this sacrificed man with amaranth seed. His statue would be paraded through town, and fans of the slain player would break off bits and consume it in honor to their dead hero. When the Catholic priests first arrived in Mexico, then called "New Spain," they put an immediate stop to this post-game tradition. Most likely, the padres were upset by how much this Aztec custom resembled their own Eucharist service in which they believed they ate Christ's body and drank his blood.

When I finished this story, Jeff let out a low whistle of disbelief, and muttered, "You have got to be shitting me."

"No, I'm serious," I replied, "though I guess you could say the Aztecs ended up shitting their favorite ball players."

Jeff screamed with laughter over this.

He and I had a great time cooking together that afternoon, our collaboration disturbed by only one thing. At some point, the jars of saffron disappeared. I looked everywhere, certain I had put them on a shelf above the counter where we were working. It was bizarre. Who would be enterprising enough to understand how expensive this ingredient was, or to think they could potentially exchange it for cash?

Jeff was furious. He loudly proclaimed his intention to "kick some serious ass" and find out who was responsible. I thought of Sister Liguori, or Attila the Nun, back in Pittsburgh. She would have shut down the whole meal until the saffron was returned. But this was not my kitchen, nor was I that courageous. Instead, I opened my wallet and asked Jeff if we could send someone out to buy more.

WHEN WE SERVED the meal later that evening, did anyone truly notice the inclusion of saffron, the shrimp stock, or crusts left on the bread in the chocolate pudding? Probably not, but at least Jeff and I knew we'd done our best to make something scrumptious. Alas, my normal tendency to make way too much food utterly failed me in Seattle. Each of the two hundred or so guests had at least two full plates of seafood stew served over rice, but I spotted people running their fingers around the empty serving trays. They were hungry for more.

No one, I noticed, had a heartier appetite than Victoria, a full-figured drag queen who was the "guest star" at our dinner's close. To delight our guests and doubtless for Killian to amuse herself by arranging an entertainment altogether different from her brother-in-law's "Praise the Lord and pass the ammunition" Christmas extravaganza, she'd arranged for Victoria to perform a few songs.

When I met him earlier that day, out of his wig and makeup, the man who transformed himself into Victoria assured me that he had "complete mastery" of the entire songbooks of both Bette Midler and Mariah Carey.

"It's up to you to decide," he said. "Which diva do you prefer?"

"Couldn't you just surprise me, Victoria?"

"Girl! You bet your tits I'll surprise you," he replied.

While the dinner wound down and someone licked the last smidgen of chocolate bread pudding off a serving spoon, Victoria emerged from one of the Recovery Café's counseling rooms and signaled a sound guy to start playing a compact disc she'd queued up to the song required. She strolled majestically toward a microphone, set up beside a Christmas tree draped with a meager quantity of lights. That sad shrub looked still more wan in contrast to Victoria, a shimmering vision in high heels made of plexiglass and a black and silver sequined minidress.

She began her act with Mariah Carey's 1991 blockbuster hit "Emotions." This tune was written, Victoria told me earlier, as a showcase for Carey's command of a stratospheric octave range called the "whistle register."

Watching this performance unfold at the Recovery Café made me nervous. It's my sense that camp humor is an acquired taste, as is enthusiasm for drag performers. As such, a campy joke is much funnier the tenth, rather than the first, time you hear it; your love for drag grows the more you are exposed to it.

Despite the profusion of posters taped up showing humanitarian heroes—Rosa Parks, Mahatma Gandhi, and Martin Luther King Jr.—Seattle's Recovery Café was still a tough room to work. Most of the evening's dinner guests were hard-worn older men and women, some muttering to themselves or brushing imaginary insects off their shoulders. Many stared vacantly off into the distance as if both the room and their future were a shadowy fog. That is, they were until Victoria popped up before their eyes, an apparition formed not of blood and amaranth, but from guts and glitter.

A talented mimic, Victoria had every note, gesture, and inflection down cold. She quivered her cheeks comically to burlesque Carey's penchant for melisma, and as Carey's voice soared up-up-upward, Victoria would cup her ear, as does the diva herself, to "sound-check" her warbling. I have seen many drag queens, but Victoria was easily in the top five. Still, I couldn't accurately gauge how her act was going over.

To my astonishment, when "Emotions" ended, the crowd went wild. People were cheering, yelling, and forcefully punching the second syllable of the star's name: "Vic-*TOE*-ria! Vic-*TOE*-ria!" Exulting in the applause, she scampered about through the audience rubbing her chest in men's faces and hissing while baring her painted fingernails at the women. This got the crowd even more fired up. "Vic-*TOE*-ria!" they screamed.

What happened next was truly the Christmas miracle. With a flick of her wrist, Victoria gave another signal to the sound guy. She then walked back to her microphone and launched into lip-syncing Mariah Carey's rendition of "O, Holy Night"—in my opinion, the most poignant of all Christmas carols. Its melody has such swelling grandeur that even an atheist might be moved. Little known fact: "O, Holy Night" was among the earliest pieces of music ever heard on the radio when, on December 24, 1906, a Canadian inventor, Reginald Fessenden, broadcast the very first AM radio program and included this song on his playlist.

What Fessenden would have made of Carey's melodramatic version, much less Victoria's impersonation of it, I can scarcely say. The effect it had on this crowd in Seattle, though, was stirring to see. Grown men, myself included, had tears running openly down their cheeks as she sang the words:

> A thrill of hope; the weary world rejoices,
> For yonder breaks a new and glorious morn.
> Fall on your knees! O hear the angel voices!
> O night divine, the night when Christ was Born;
> O night, O holy night, O night divine!

It was truly a night divine at the Recovery Café, where something unexpectedly transcendent had occurred. For at least a few hours, a plate of seafood stew and a bawdy drag queen had given the weary world a thrill of hope.

Baking cookies for US soldiers in Iraq was an initial foray into gastrophilanthropy.

The Gurdwara Bangla Sahib in Delhi, India, feeds 20,000 people a day.

Muslim women in Iran practice a form of charitable cookery called a "nazr."

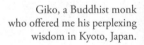

Giko, a Buddhist monk who offered me his perplexing wisdom in Kyoto, Japan.

Sister Liguori (a.k.a. "Attila the Nun") founded Pittsburgh's Jubilee soup kitchen.

Serving up boeuf bourguignon at St. Patrick's soup kitchen in St. Louis.

In Mexico City, the Nino Pa inspires tremendous feats of gastrophilanthropy.

Loaves and Fishes mobile food trucks bring comfort to Austin's hungriest citizens.

Shopping for produce at an open-air market in La Grama, Peru.

Aryeh Cohen runs
the Meir Panim free
kitchen in Jerusalem.

Rice, and lots of it, is spooned out for the needy in Busan, South Korea.

The Sauce Boss likes to say he preaches the "gospel of gumbo."

Making meatballs for a Dia de Los Muertos dinner in Guadalajara, Mexico.

The Midnight Mission
cares for the homeless
living on Los Angeles's
skid row.

Stirring a big batch of plov (rice with lamb) in Bukhara, Uzbekistan.

Cooking my weekly Tuesday lunch at a Salvation Army soup kitchen in Hudson, New York.

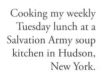

11

THAT TIME AIN'T YET COME

"THIS IS AMERICA!"

Alan Graham hollered this as we stood together below an elevated section of Interstate 35, a few miles south of downtown in Austin, Texas. Interstate 35 stretches from Mexico all the way to Canada, but its single busiest section is between San Antonio and Austin. More than half a million cars zoom by here every day on eight lanes of traffic that were now just above my head. The noise was cacophonous, as if we were at the edge of a cyclone with a whirring-sucking force so powerful it could easily hurl us up and away.

I was in Texas to learn more about Mobile Loaves & Fishes (MLF), a fleet of catering trucks that Graham established and operates for delivering meals to Austin's poor. MLF has a fleet of seventeen vehicles in six cities and five states. Every afternoon, dozens of volunteers drive them to street corners, parking lots, and highway overpasses. Food sufficient to nourish one hundred people at a time is loaded onto one side of the truck; on the other is stowed a collection of used running shoes, miniature bottles of shampoo, soap packets, tampons, combs, and a lot of socks.

"Socks are a whopper for homeless people," Graham explained. "A new, clean pair can brighten up your day—hell, your month!"

Graham, age fifty-five, had an optimistic personality that was contagious. He wore a downy white mustache and beard, spoke in a smooth drawl, and liked to utter wisecracks from the corners of his mouth; his zingers truly did come out sideways. Graham referred to his mobile trucks as "miracles on wheels," and he'd displayed nearly supernatural driving skills as he'd maneuvered one onto a sidewalk beneath the overpass a few minutes earlier.

When we arrived, I saw movement within the shadows under this enormous concrete structure. Six or eight men came creeping forward, blinking as they encountered sunlight.

"People live here, if you can imagine," Graham said. "Sleep deprivation is a constant problem when you're homeless."

On this scorching July afternoon—the hottest time of day in Austin is between 3:00 and 6:00 p.m.—Graham treated this pocket of poverty under Interstate 35 as if it were a secret fishing hole that only he knew about. Instead of nabbing sea bass or trout, Graham was a fisher of men. Grabbing hold of the wobbly-looking souls who emerged from the dark, he pumped their hands, clapped them on the back, and combined fraternal camaraderie with no-nonsense honesty.

One guy had a frayed and foul-smelling ace bandage wrapped around his left foot, which was massively swollen. Graham asked how long it had been like this. Was it sprained or broken? Could it be infected? These rapid questions were too much for this man to follow. Graham let the matter drop after making sure the guy was given a new pair of socks.

"Can you eat an apple?" he asked another man. "Smile and let me see."

What happened next was awful to witness. The man grinned, and he didn't possess any teeth, only gums that were blotched with bloody scabs. Graham was unfazed. "You'd better stick with a banana," he shouted and gave the guy a hug.

THE IMPORTANCE OF clean socks is a stark reality Alan Graham might easily never have learned. For most of his life, he not only had plenty of footwear but also loads of cash. He was a successful real estate developer who specialized in the construction of air cargo hangars at airports around the United States.

"I loved my business. We were making pots of money," he said. "The company I founded now has expanded worldwide. I was building huge storage facilities all over the place, but my biggest, my baby, was right here in Austin!"

In 1996, Graham was talking to a friend who lived in Corpus Christi. She mentioned a group of people who'd pooled their resources to start a soup kitchen there. While listening to her, Graham claims he suddenly saw a vision of a catering truck—one of those vehicles with quilted stainless steel sides you imagine pulling up to a factory gate and selling donuts—as a means of food distribution. "I had this radical thought we could go to where hungry people are, not force them to arrive at some centralized, downtown location," he said. "There's nothing particularly efficient about it, but the idea of a catering truck just grabbed me by the throat!"

Hearing Graham say this, I was reminded that Alexis Soyer, a century and a half earlier, had a similar idea when he decided to create a mobile kitchen and roll it into Spitalfields, a downtrodden neighborhood in mid-nineteenth-century London.

Before Graham could bring this idea to fruition, he and a group of his buddies began heading out to look for hungry people in one of their own minivans. "We called ourselves the 'Six Pack' because there were six of us but also because after we did one of our food drop-offs, we'd all go chug a few beers," he explained.

Graham quickly realized they didn't know what they were doing. Most members of the Six Pack attended Austin's St. John Neumann Catholic Church, located in one of the city's wealthiest neighborhoods. "We have billionaires, some really brilliant guys, but they don't know jack shit about serving the needy," Graham observed.

Willing to learn, the men started talking to St. John Neumann's custodian, a gentleman named Houston Flake. Born to homeless parents, Flake was a former drug addict who had spent time in prison.

"Houston was our eyes on the street. He'd lived out there; he knew where folks set up their camps and where they gathered," Graham told me. "With Houston's help, we identified one hundred and twenty locations across Austin where we could drive up and find hungry people any night of the week."

Then as now, a typical meal served from an MLF truck is a peanut butter and jelly sandwich, a hard-boiled egg, potato chips, and a piece of fruit.

I HAVE MENTIONED some zigzags in my life, yes? Well, this trip to Austin was a doozy! The reason I went to Texas was to write a story for *T*, a glossy magazine that is a periodic supplement to the *New York Times*. I'd been assigned a piece about a former ballerina named Julie Thornton who married a venture capitalist named John and turned them both into world-class patrons of the arts. Julie had recently built a new dining room in their vast, art-filled mansion. To differentiate this fourth dining room from the other three, she commissioned a site-specific work by a couple of Dutch artists, named collectively Maarten Baas, who burned wooden objects to the point of their nearly becoming embers. Then, through an infusion of polymer gel, they would stabilize the wood before it crumpled into ash. I know what you're wondering. No, it does not smell. Somehow this gel also seals in any burnt odor.

At the Thornton house, hardwood paneling was designed, milled, and installed in the dining room, whereupon it was removed and taken to an industrial park. The Dutch boys went at it with huge flame-throwing "cactus burner" torches in one hand, and a garden hose dribbling water (to control the burn) in the other. They worked at it for six weeks, living in a trailer and drinking beer at night in Austin's live music clubs. All their hot and dirty labor had created something incredible; the paneling now looked like a crocodile skin purse, all crackled, shiny, and brownish-black. When I asked, the Thorntons declined to say how much this artwork had cost.

After several days of interviewing Maarten Baas and the Thorntons, I was invited to a dinner party that Julie and John hosted to unveil their glamorously scorched dining room. They assembled a haughty crowd of artists and collectors from New York, Los Angeles, various cities in

Europe, as well as Texas friends who turned out to be some of Barack Obama's biggest financial supporters in the Lone Star State. Most of them had hosted fundraising dinners for him in their houses and were full of talk about what he was "really like" in person: charming and elegantly mannered with a sharp sense of humor.

One guy stopped conversation cold during the cocktail hour with his Obama story.

"When he was at my house," this man began, "I decided that everyone was constantly buttonholing Barack about their pet causes and bending his ear with really, really serious stuff. So, when I had a moment alone with him, I leaned into his shoulder and whispered that I'd just seen Michelle sticking some of our silverware in her purse. Should she really need it, she was welcome, I told him, but it was antique and difficult to replace. If she'd just like the cash value instead, I'd be happy to write Michelle a check. It didn't take Barack even a second to catch onto the joke, and he immediately took it a step further, pulling me closer to him and urging me not to tell anyone that his wife had this little problem with kleptomania, because if it got out to the media . . ."

The Texans adored this story.

"Barack is so goddam cool!" They all kept saying phrases like this. "You just can't believe how great he is. He is so fucking, fucking cool!"

It was the morning after this dinner party that I stood with Alan Graham under Interstate 35.

SHORTLY BEFORE TRAVELING to Austin, I spoke by telephone with Graham's wife, Tricia. She was delighted by my offer to come cook for a few days at the MLF kitchens and said I should feel free to make whatever I wanted. How about meat loaf sandwiches, I suggested, and a green bean salad with avocado and roasted red peppers?

"Oooo," Tricia said. "That sounds yummy!"

"And German potato salad, you know, the kind that's really vinegary and mustardy?" I continued.

"Oh, Lordy-Lord Jesus!"

"How 'bout some homemade chocolate chip cookies?"

"Bring it on, Daddy!" Tricia was shrieking by now. "Bring it on!"

It was like we were having phone sex—an observation I later made to Tricia that she found enormously entertaining. Both Alan and Tricia Graham were perfectly down-to-earth and able to enjoy salty humor.

At MLF headquarters, the kitchen had an oversized work island at its center. Metal shelves lined the room on either side, and a large portion of this storage space was devoted to five-gallon plastic tubs full of peanut butter and glass jars of Concord grape jelly. There were also countless boxes of plastic food-storage bags. Everything edible that went out on an MLF truck was pre-portioned and enclosed in one of these Ziploc pouches. This would soon include the meat loaf sandwiches I made.

Combining beef, veal, pork, diced onion, garlic, parsley, bread crumbs, egg, and milk—especially if cooking enough to feed two hundred people—is nearly impossible to do with a spoon. Using my hands to mix it up, I formed the sticky mess into smoothed-over mounds and wrapped them in bacon. When twenty of these loaves were lined up on baking sheets and spread out across the big island, it felt like a major accomplishment. As they cooked, the aroma enticed people from other parts of the MLF facility: secretaries from the front office and auto repair guys who kept the mobile trucks operational. I made sure to feed them crispy bits when the meat came out of the oven.

Then I got busy making the potato and green bean salads. Tricia pitched in, and while we cooked together she spoke openly about how unsettling it initially was to have her "high-rollin' business tycoon" of a husband abruptly decide to devote himself to helping the homeless. His gung-ho attitude was not easy for Tricia, and at first she resisted.

"Alan is much better about throwing things away than I am. He wanted to get rid of our wedding china at one point, claiming we didn't use it enough. I told him he could just forget it! I wasn't ready to do that." She looked up at me and asked, "Was I being unreasonable?"

"Not at all," I replied.

I sensed this was the wrong answer, because as she finished her story, Tricia explained that she didn't require as many "creature comforts" once she adjusted to the new reality. Instead, her life of caring for others was much more rewarding than what she'd known before. "I've still got my wedding china, and I still don't use it," she laughed.

People in charge of that evening's delivery began to show up. What a science they'd turned making a peanut butter and jelly sandwich into! Their secret was to fill a gallon-size plastic bag with grape jelly and cut a small hole in one of its bottom corners, creating a sack similar to what pastry chefs use. This allowed one person to squeeze out a blob of grape jelly at lightning speed onto bread that someone else had smeared with peanut butter. Thanks to this assembly-line process, a mother and her two teenage daughters made two hundred sandwiches in less than an hour.

Impressed by the diligent demeanor of these young women, I remarked to the mom how good it was of them to tag along with her and be such team players. Yes, it was, she agreed. She then slightly trimmed the wingspan of her angels by explaining that most of Austin's junior high and high schools have a community service requirement, whereby it is mandatory for all students to volunteer a few hours a week at a local nonprofit organization. More than a few teenagers decide making peanut butter and jelly sandwiches is a relatively painless way to do their "C.S.R."

Mandatory volunteerism—my new favorite oxymoron!

Around 5:00 p.m., Alan Graham showed up in the kitchen and punched me on the shoulder. It was time for a food delivery. I had cooked all day in an unventilated kitchen but this was a cool breeze in comparison to being outside on a summer afternoon in Austin.

Four of us piled into a catering truck. I was up front in the passenger seat next to the driver, Bruk Keener. In the back were Alan and his daughter, Taylor. She was a junior at the University of Texas who hoped someday to work in journalism.

Rush-hour traffic was heavy. As we slowly moved forward, I chatted with Bruk, who described himself as the "official grunt" of MLF and spoke freely of his many years of living on the streets. Oddly, he even smiled at these recollections as if he were reliving the night of his high school prom, or a trip he once took to Disney World.

When I asked how he'd ended up homeless, Bruk didn't flinch or pause. "I made poor choices," he instantly replied. "I started hanging out with the wrong sorts of people. I was pretty bad. Both me and my wife was. She had a reputation for being crazy-wild when she was drunk. There was many a time when I sat up all night, smokin' crack and chuggin' beer, right there in that park."

I looked at Bruk's outstretched finger. He'd pointed to a field surrounded by a chain-link fence. At its center was a rusted-out swing set tilted at such a precarious angle it appeared ready to topple over.

Bruk, whom I guessed might be thirty-five, had shaggy brown hair and a seductive grin. He had turned himself into something of a motivational speaker who addressed churches and other gatherings around Austin to raise awareness and money for MLF.

"Me and my wife, we mingle with the crowd beforehand, like we're invited guests. Then I get up and say, 'you know that guy who you used to pass by on the sidewalk, the one with the matted and dirty hair, the one who was drinkin' and stinkin'? Well, folks, that was me.'"

"Sometimes, people say to me, 'Oh, you were a hobo!'," he continued. "I tell them I don't like that word. I prefer to say 'feral human.'"

A short time later, we pulled up outside a subsidized housing development. It was a U-shaped configuration of low buildings and looked like it once had been a budget motel. Before we'd rolled to a stop, a line of thirty or forty people had gathered, the majority of them children.

Most of their mothers were sitting inside their apartments, watching TV, Graham suggested. They'd sent the kids out to act as their personal delivery service.

These youngsters were fairly well behaved. It was the grown-ups who gave us trouble. They'd pout and linger until I usually relented and gave them an extra meat loaf sandwich or another cookie.

After we made one more stop, at a corner near an abandoned gas station, our truck was cleaned out. I stood by Bruk, eavesdropping while he chatted with an unnervingly skinny man named Edwin. He was hollow-cheeked, with eyes that were buzzing black dots. Edwin, I realized, was high as a kite. He was making a great effort to speak, as if shouting from the bottom of a deep hole. I heard him say, "No matter what our circumstances in life, the only real question is, are we ready to learn something from it?"

Then, knowingly or not, Edwin invoked Charles Dickens's *A Tale of Two Cities*.

"To be homeless, in Austin, is the best of times and the worst of times. You find your people out there on the streets, you really do," he said. "If someone's got something and someone don't, well, they give it away. This is very common in the homeless community. It ain't no thang."

A teenage girl arrived. Upset to learn there was no food left, she appeared to be at her breaking point over this deprivation. She dropped her face into her palms and began to cry, her torso heaving with convulsive shudders.

"It's alright, sister. Here you go," Edwin said as he handed her a bag of food he'd collected for himself a few minutes earlier.

It was unbelievably hot. The sunblock I had hurriedly smeared on my face back at the MLF kitchen was melting and stung my eyes. I turned away from Edwin and the girl as I blinked back tears.

When we got back into the truck, Graham was driving, and Bruk, now in back, began to reminisce again. "Me and Edwin? When we was both on the street, we'd get stoned together. Somehow I got clean, but Edwin didn't." After a pause Bruk added, "Edwin had this ring, with Hebrew letters on it, that meant something like 'wherever you are, I will always be with you.' He sold it to me once for $5 so he could get a fix. I still have it, that ring. I've always thought I would give it back to him when he's no longer using. I guess that time ain't yet come."

We drove in silence for a few minutes.

"It used to be you would mostly see middle-aged people out on the street, but now there are also a lot of young people," Graham remarked. "These kids are disenfranchised. I mean, if you are smoking weed all the time—and believe me, I've smoked plenty of weed in my day—you are not terribly productive. I mean, let's face it, very little greatness comes out of drug use. Have you ever done anything particularly brilliant or that you wanted to hang your reputation on when you were stoned?"

Graham turned to stare at me. Apparently, this was not a rhetorical question.

"No," I replied.

"Damn right you haven't, and I haven't either. But just try to explain that to these kids!"

After we got back to MLF headquarters, I talked with Taylor Graham for a few minutes. Like her mother, she remembered the awkward transition her family went through as Alan Graham changed from being a rich businessman to a social worker.

"Omigod," Taylor said. "You have no idea! I would be at school, and it would be my dad's day to pick me up after classes. I'd see the Mobile Loaves & Fishes truck come rolling up in front of all my friends and it was, like, please just let me die right now! I mean, I was young and stupid. And selfish. Now, I'm proud of my parents. I brag to my friends in college about them and all the people they've helped. But, I'm not going to lie to you; I wasn't at this place back when I was in high school."

Finding ways to be generous is just like learning how to cook, Taylor assured me. "I always say to people, it takes practice, and you're gonna make mistakes. But gradually, you get better at it."

12

A GARDEN GROWS

I WAS HAVING A DRINK WITH A FRIEND WHEN SHE PIPED UP with this question: "How's it going with your magical misery tours?"

Her implication was that my attempts at charitable cookery were "slumming" or, even worse, an indulgence in schadenfreude. There was no good response. If I took the bait and tried to defend myself, she could always claim, "I was just teasing!" By keeping silent, I allowed her charge to stand.

This was not an isolated instance, either. Through the grapevine, I learned one of my friends was calling me "His Holiness" behind my back. Another sent an email saying I was quite the "inspo," her abbreviation for "inspiration," which I thought suggested a certain degree of mockery. Finally, someone I approached for help in setting up a trip huffily informed me that what I was doing was "obscene." Why was I getting on an airplane to feed people when there were plenty of homeless and hungry on any block in New York City?

Hearing these comments hurt, but such sniping didn't altogether surprise me. I knew what I was doing raised uncomfortable questions of power and privilege. In my parents' time, foreign aid workers and missionaries who traveled abroad to help other people were given unquestioned respect; now, individuals or groups who engaged in similar efforts were often viewed as culturally insensitive if not imperialist.

What most struck me, though, was that I had traveled all over the world—and often to impoverished Third World places—for many years without these journeys attracting any particular criticism. "Where are you off to next?" my friends always asked me. As long as I was going somewhere to write about art, food, or decorating, preferably for the *New York Times,* they were approving, even envious. But to add a few days, staying on in these same places to learn how Hindus, Muslims, or even Texans feed their poor people, left me open to accusations of misery tourism and "virtue signaling."

Volunteering to cook for others is a ticklish matter. There seems to be no perfectly correct way to go about it, but infinite ways to get it wrong. Making a meal is, after all, an imposition of your taste onto someone else. What I may think of as gastrophilanthropy, someone else might consider gastrocolonialism. Did the folks at Jubilee Soup Kitchen in Pittsburgh really need to be introduced to kiwi fruit? Might not the elderly of Minneapolis have been just fine without my pushing couscous onto their plates?

None other than Jacques Derrida, the French philosopher whose writings were my torture in graduate school, suggests to love your neighbor as yourself is a fantasy. That's because, as Derrida explains in his book *Of Hospitality,* charity is based on income inequity. To be charitable, one must be rich enough to possess more than what is necessary to meet one's own immediate needs for food, clothing, and shelter. In this view, hospitality is not a gift, but an assertion of private property ownership as well as a desire to control others. First, the host establishes sovereignty over the domain in which his or her "generosity" is to be shown—this is *my* house, *my* table, *my* meat loaf sandwiches. Then, a host limits the freedom of her or his beneficiaries by setting boundaries: what time to show up at my house, where to sit at my table, how much meat loaf is served. Follow Derrida's thinking to its natural conclusion, and generosity becomes an affront; to regard others as needy is cruel, as it forces them to acknowledge your superiority.

There you have it: a clever intellectual's rationale for doing nothing. Sigh! No wonder I dropped out of Yale.

What would Alexis do?

No one knew this tension around charity better than Alexis Soyer did. He endured the jeers of both friends and strangers when he began his efforts to feed the poor. His wealthy and spoiled clientele at London's Reform Club loved nothing more than to ridicule Soyer behind his back. "Who does he think he is?" they must have asked. "How dare this preposterous man in his cocked beret and patent leather boots imagine himself to be the Good Samaritan!"

That Soyer could ignore this derision is yet another reason he's such a compelling figure to me. His example gave me the courage to do the same.

AND SO, I found myself arriving in La Grama, a remote town nestled inside a mountain valley of northern Peru. It was yet another of my "robbing Peter to pay Paul" schemes. I had agreed to write a magazine story about taking a three-day excursion on the Peruvian Amazon aboard *Aria*, a luxury all-suites cruise ship with only thirty passengers. This paid my way to then rendezvous with my friend Jordan Mallah, who a decade earlier had been a Peace Corps worker in Peru. Every few years since, Jordan had arranged a trip and invited a group from the United States to meet him at La Grama, where they helped build a library, or assisted on a town-wide water project. When I went, Jordan's idea was to plant an organic vegetable garden behind the local elementary school.

La Grama can only be reached by a road called Trenta Tres Curvas (Thirty-Three Curves), a dizzying series of hairpin turns winding down through the Andes until the road terminates in a rural village with erratic electricity, no mail service, and what appears to be more dogs than humans. La Grama is about four city blocks square where a population of three hundred live in one-story mud-brick homes. What few roads exist are made of nutmeg-colored dirt that's pocked with large holes. It rains frequently in the Andean highlands, and this precipitation melts these streets into the consistency of pudding.

The people who live in La Grama subsist primarily on potatoes and *cuy*, or guinea pig. Hordes of these cute but clueless-looking creatures scurry about the dirt floors of most houses. When it's dinnertime, people clonk a cuy on the head and shuck off its fur. A quick chop, and into a fry pan the pieces go. Head, tail, claws—every part of the animal is consumed. A guinea pig tastes like the dark meat of a not very flavorful chicken. Jordan's goal was to help people supplement this diet with green beans or Swiss chard, hence the organic garden project.

When I first heard of this plan, even I balked. With the "His Holiness" flak I was taking lately, I worried how this sounded: know-it-all Americans imposing their culinary values on the Third World. Zucchini, good. Guinea pig, bad. After Jordan and I had a long talk, though, and he explained to me how desperately poor La Grama was, I set my hesitations aside. I agreed to join the trip and offered to cook lunch and dinner every day for a week, feeding a dozen people from the United States who would help build the garden as well as an equal number of Peruvians who'd assist with planting.

My BASE OF operations was the small but cheerful house of Jordan's friend Nattie. Her home was a logical choice, as Nattie's kitchen was more modern than any other I saw in La Grama. She had a refrigerator, a cooktop with four burners, and an oven. These last two appliances could not be operated simultaneously, however, as each ran from the same propane tank. On a previous visit, Jordan convinced Nattie to stop breeding guinea pigs and instead plant vegetables in her backyard. When I arrived at her house, Nattie immediately dragged me outside and gave me a tour of this Eden. Beets, peppers, tomatoes, pumpkins, lettuces, celery, and strawberries, among many other plants, were thriving and freely available to be used in meals I cooked.

Nattie is the unofficial mayor of La Grama. Everyone knows her, since she runs a Movistar franchise, one of Latin and South America's major telecommunications companies, from her kitchen. When not selling time for cellular phones, she's also a part-time baker of cakes, which she makes for birthday parties and other celebrations. From dawn to dusk, five minutes do not pass without someone showing up at her door. Nattie is a combination of life coach, therapist, and matchmaker for the village's residents. Nothing happens in La Grama without her hearing about it minutes later. Rarely have I met someone so irrepressibly generous. To have a group of Americans descend on her house for a week, with me turning her kitchen upside down as I cooked, appeared not to bother Nattie in the least.

The day we landed, I was impressed by how quickly she threw together a Peruvian lunch. Nattie served papas alla huancaina, or potatoes, smothered in a rich sauce made of milk, cheese, crackers, and yellow peppers. Then, a spaghetti with a pesto made of spinach, basil, and soy milk. Not only did she cook enough food to satisfy the appetites of twenty-five people in well under an hour (a time period that included her picking and washing vegetables from her garden), but she did so while continuing to attend to her never-ending stream of Movistar customers and other people needing help or advice. Everyone was greeted with a smile and a lilting chorus of "Que linda! Que linda! Que linda!" as if they were best friends Nattie was hoping would stop by.

ONCE WE WERE well fed and curious about our job ahead, Jordan led everyone in the group off to a plot of land behind the grammar school. Resembling a town dump, the field was ankle-deep with garbage. As we surveyed this desolate spot, there was much discussion about rocky soil and the ground's steep incline. "What about water?" many asked. During the rainy season there would be plenty, we learned. For the dry months, Jordan had petitioned some of his pals at the Peace Corps to donate money for a pump, which would keep the ground moist. (Other gardens in La Grama had jury-rigged an "irrigation" system by burying empty plastic bottles among the plants, each with a pinhole at the bottom, so water inside would seep more slowly into the dirt.)

An hour later, the school principal arrived. He was accompanied by a few other men who had wheelbarrows, shovels, and pickaxes. Jordan distributed these tools and assigned tasks. We got to work tilling the land, breaking up hard clods of earth into a more malleable layer of topsoil. There was an incredible amount of junk to be removed. Apparently, many generations of La Grama's schoolchildren had hung out back here snacking on candy and other treats, then simply dropped their foil wrappers and plastic spoons when they were done eating.

Working behind us, an old woman gathered up weeds that we unearthed. She carefully arranged them into neat bundles, which she would allow to dry before turning them into brooms. Several girls from the school had shown up too. Their idea of work outfits was halter tops, tight jeans, and flip-flops. When talking with them, I struggled to make the most of my Spanish. This was only moderately successful. Our shared smiles and laboring together side by side were better forms of communication.

Before I made dinner that first evening, I showed up at Nattie's house with presents. Jordan had alerted me that Nattie's cooking equipment was limited. Any pots, pans, or cooking tools I brought along would be very much appreciated—both by her and me. I gave much thought to what kitchen components were indispensable and now offered Nattie several chef's knives, paring knives, high-quality cookie sheets, and many jars of spices—turmeric, cumin, bay leaves, curry powder, tarragon, and oregano. She was thrilled.

The biggest challenge to cooking in La Grama, I soon understood, was water that's not potable. Jordan was something of a nag on this point, constantly reminding us to wash our hands and making everyone crazy with fear that any exposure to either guinea pig or cow droppings would invariably lead to a disastrous case of food poisoning. To be doubly safe, he mandated that produce must first be washed in tap water to get off the dirt and then again with purified water, which was stored in unwieldy 10-liter jugs. I was being assisted by one of Nattie's friends, a young woman named Fanny, who was put in charge of washing all fruits and vegetables, an onerous job she undertook with unfailing good humor.

I gradually began to take charge, with Nattie and Fanny as my helpers. Nattie stood by my shoulder, watching and asking questions about everything. She didn't know, for instance, that removing the seeds from chile peppers makes them less spicy, or herbs are best de-stemmed from their branches, as leaves alone provide a much fresher flavor. Nattie had never roasted vegetables in her oven or thickened a sauce with an egg. She had surprises for me as well. I discovered the mangoes growing on her backyard tree were about half the size of those I was used to, but twice as flavorful.

It became apparent Nattie and I had a different sense of time as well as what constitutes drudgery. For instance, when she cooked with garlic, she laboriously peeled every clove with a paring knife, then mashed it into a fine paste under a smooth river stone. I showed Nattie how easy it was to crush a garlic clove with the side of a chef's knife so the papery husk simply fell off. She feigned interest about my quick-and-dirty method but continued to prepare garlic in her own painstaking way. She felt no need to hurry; there was nothing but time in La Grama.

The village was impoverished, but also oddly beautiful. I could see this as I looked out upon the rushing river, sun-dappled fields, and the big sky with clouds drifting over the Andes, whose lower slopes were covered with squares of different farm fields, like a patchwork quilt. But La Grama was static. So little occurred here, after a few days I could not only recognize all the town's inhabitants but was also familiar with their animals. Women led their few cows out to the same pastures each morning and home at dusk. Certain pigs were always tied to certain trees. Hens and turkeys pecked away at the dirt, only a few inches from where they'd be tomorrow. For a week, this sort of daily consistency was calming. Any longer, and I would go bonkers. My mind and body are far too urbanized for such tranquility.

I made friends with Cruz, a woman who lived in a mud-brick house next door to mine. While sipping my first cup of coffee each morning, I liked to sit on the front step with my bare feet in the warm dirt road before me. When Cruz saw me she always said hello, and we'd carry on simple conversations in Spanish, mostly about the weather. One day, she came out of her house and gave me a bag full of lemons. After I thanked her profusely, we attempted a longer chat. I learned the house I was temporarily living in was Cruz's son's, and he'd rented it to Jordan for the week.

Working up my nerve, I asked if Cruz would show me her guinea pigs. I could hear them squeaking in the middle of the night when I wasn't able to sleep. She escorted me to a back room of her dark and airless house where there must have been fifty or more cuy capering on the dirt floor. A few were pure white, others pale brown, but most a mottled mix of colors. There was a low stone wall bisecting the room. Cruz explained the guinea pigs were not smart enough to figure out how to climb over this barrier, no more than eight inches high, so it prevented them from crawling all over her family, who slept on the floor on the other side of this miniature blockade. Why her husband and she were not kept awake by the squeaking and constant commotion of these animals was what most baffled me.

THE ORGANIC GARDEN was taking shape, while Nattie and I grew ever more compatible in combining our different ways of cooking. Not that there weren't bumps along the way.

One afternoon when I went to Nattie's house, I saw she was busy making a cake for one of her clients. Some flour had spilled onto her painted concrete floor, and as Nattie moved about her kitchen, she'd begun to track white footprints all over. I went to find a broom and began sweeping up. When she saw what I was doing, Nattie asked why I was cleaning while she was still cooking. If we don't get up the flour now, I said, other people would come in and out of the kitchen, and flour would spread all over her house. Nattie stared at me as if I was spouting utter nonsense. It was a touchy moment, especially as I couldn't figure out what I did wrong.

When I asked Jordan about it later, he explained Nattie's is one of the very few houses in La Grama that has a concrete floor, and even hers is a recent improvement. When you are used to padding around on a dirt surface, sweeping up all the time is not part of your daily routine. Hearing this, I felt ashamed by my assumptions about "good housekeeping." No matter how poor I have been, I was always able to afford a high level of domestic hygiene. Nattie was new to this luxury.

Luckily, such misunderstandings between us were few. The unusual opportunity to step outside Nattie's kitchen and pull vegetables from her backyard garden inspired me to leave aside tried-and-true recipes and try new flavor combinations. How about squash roasted with apples and raisins? Lemongrass and thyme on the carrots? Beets with pomegranate seeds? As Nattie and Fanny assisted me with such experiments, they told me more about life in La Grama.

I asked about the guy with only one leg who hobbled about on crutches. They explained he was a farmer who had cut himself one day when out in his fields digging with a shovel. Badly gashed, his big toe was nearly severed from his left foot. Unable to surgically reattach it, a local doctor took off the toe. Unfortunately, this operation was done incorrectly, and the wound became infected. As a result, the man's entire left foot was severed. When the exposed ankle became gangrenous, more amputations resulted, first at the knee and then the whole leg up to his hip. Only during this last procedure were the proper amounts of antiseptic and suturing employed. When the man eventually recovered, he could no longer work as a farmer with only one leg. He spent most days shuffling about town begging for money so he could buy beer.

Another story Fanny told concerned a baby born at La Grama's pitifully ill-equipped medical clinic. Only after the infant was out of its mother's womb did the doctor realize there was no cloth to wrap it in. There was an old man waiting his turn for attention from the doctor. Shivering with cold, ill with some sort of influenza, his body was wracked with rumbling coughs. The man was wrapped in a dirty blanket. Without a moment's hesitation or even asking permission, the doctor snatched this covering from him and wrapped the baby up in its filthy folds. Somehow the infant survived. The old man did not; by the next morning he was dead.

ONE DAY, AS we were about to serve a meal, I said, "Nattie, tu necessitas una mesa mas grande en la cocina."

She regarded me with a perplexed smile.

I was winging it and frequently spoke the wrong words in Spanish. As far as I knew, though, I had correctly suggested Nattie needed to have a bigger kitchen table. The cooking area in her house was of an adequate size, but there was no wide counter, or island. It was making me nuts, trying to push out meals for several dozen people, three times a day, with no work surface larger than a narrow ledge by her sink. Showing Nattie what I meant, I got out a tape measure and drew a quick sketch of the table I thought she should have.

As she studied my drawing, her eyebrows clenched in concentration, I realized I'd done it again! Like my sweeping up her concrete floor, this declaration of the necessity of a large work table was altogether condescending. The reason Nattie did not have such a "mesa grande" wasn't because she'd never thought of such a thing. She could not afford one. Thankfully, I comprehended this obvious fact before she was required to spell it out for me. Saving us both from further embarrassment, I explained how grateful I was for the experience she'd given me of letting me play around in her kitchen. To show my appreciation, I told Nattie I wanted to buy this table for her. Before she could refuse, I suggested there was a guy doing carpentry work a few streets away. What about hiring him?

No, Nattie immediately said. He was too expensive and a drunk. Instead, she knew another carpenter over in the next town whom she trusted and liked. Nattie suggested we should go see him later that afternoon. It would be simple, she said—only a two-hour walk. Each way, that is.

Now it was my turn to have a perplexed smile. "Couldn't we call first to make sure he's there?" I asked.

"He doesn't have a phone," Nattie replied. "He'll be there," she insisted.

Setting off right after lunch, we walked at a brisk pace, covering what I estimated to be six or eight miles, until we arrived at the workshop of this carpenter, who was named Joel. I showed him my drawing. After thinking it over for a few minutes and scratching out some calculations in the dirt with a stick, Joel named a price, which was alarmingly low. I would have paid three times as much without hesitation and still considered it a great bargain.

Nattie saw things differently. She reacted with shrill anger, as if Joel had demanded both of my testicles. Nattie and Joel really went at it and argued heatedly, back and forth, for several long minutes. Finally, to make peace, I stepped in and tried to save face for everyone involved. I told Joel that I would pay his price, the equivalent of $80, and give him half the money up front. But he would only get the balance if he delivered the finished table on Friday morning. This was Tuesday afternoon.

The following Saturday would be December 25, which was also Nattie's birthday. A midnight dinner was planned on Christmas Eve, and dozens of townspeople had said they planned to drop by to wish Nattie both a *Feliz Navidad* and a *Feliz Cumpleaños*. Having a big table to work on would make all the difference in hosting a crowd this size.

Joel agreed to my terms. I gave him the $40 deposit. Our business settled, Nattie and I walked the two hours back to La Grama. I was feeling pretty damn cocky—that is, until I saw Jordan and told him what I had done.

"You just threw away your money," he said. "This is Peru, not Manhattan! I'd be amazed if someone in this country could make a table like that in three months, and you gave him less than three days? Are you smoking crack?"

"Joel said he could do it," I replied. Even to me, my voice sounded petulant and irritating.

Though I was crestfallen, Nattie kept the faith. I had redrawn my sketch to give a carefully ruled copy to Joel, but Nattie thumbtacked the first draft I made up on her kitchen wall, right next to a color illustration of the Blessed Virgin Mary. Other women began to drop by and gaze expectantly at the empty space in the center of Nattie's kitchen where the table would go. It seemed as if this was the most exciting thing that had happened in La Grama in months. I couldn't even look at Jordan. Trying to forget this mess I had created, I redoubled my efforts on the organic garden.

AFTER SEVERAL MORE days of preparatory work clearing away large rocks and creating a series of raised rectangular beds, it was time for seeds! Several dozen children showed up for planting day, and I asked three boys to help me: Carlos, Franklin, and Angel. They were thirteen years old and prone to fidgeting and making funny faces. Nearly everything I said caused them to react with exaggerated shock and then to collapse into fits of laughter. Angel, Franklin, and Carlos were clever young men, though. They took the seed packets from me and quickly showed me how it was done.

When we were ready to water our beds, the hydraulic pump was nowhere to be found. An improvised length of hoses was stretched from the garden back to the school building, where there was an outdoor spigot. These hoses were old, worn-out, and not affixed firmly with screw-together junctions. Instead, the sliced-off end of one hose was simply pinched and shoved into another. Unless this precarious daisy chain was moved with extreme care, different sections of hose would slide apart, and water gushed everywhere except into the garden. This comedy of errors caused still more shrieks of hilarity from the children and much head-scratching for the adults. All the time and effort we'd put into planting this garden, and now it would simply dry up?

Just then, dark clouds appeared on the horizon, rolling over the top of nearby hills. As the skies quickly changed from blue to gray to black, the air temperature dropped, and rain began rocketing down around us. The Peruvians scattered at the first drop, but we Americans were too grateful to move and stood there getting soaked. If there is a God, she or he seemed to be giving a green thumbs-up.

Back at Nattie's house, I discovered there was no electricity. This was a frequent enough occurrence in La Grama, and there could be no knowing when it might come back on. Blame it on the romance of cooking by candlelight, but I suddenly had the idea to make a carrot cake for Nattie's birthday. Some substitutions were required, since I couldn't just dash over to Whole Foods for a box of macadamia nuts or cream cheese. While I was out in the garden, flashlight in one hand and digging around for carrots with the other, Nattie came rushing out her back door.

"Ven aqui!" she cried. "Ven aqui, ven aqui!"

Said once, "ven aqui" means "come here!" When it's rapidly shouted three times, it translates as "Get your ass inside, NOW!"

Because I am a natural-born worrier, I immediately assumed the worst: some guy had been stabbed in a drunken brawl, or a girl was hemorrhaging from a botched abortion. For all the natural beauty of its location, ghastly things happened in La Grama—such as the farmer whose cut toe ended up costing him a whole leg. I had only lived there for one short week but already had ample opportunity to learn this.

I rushed into the house, and there was Joel, the carpenter, huffing and puffing his way through Nattie's front door with a big table on his back. I couldn't believe it. He'd finished a day early!

Even with the warm glow of a candle's flame, I saw this item of furniture I had commissioned was no artistic triumph. In fact, it looked strangely similar to the rough-hewn table my father used to stand behind when he officiated at holy Communion on Sunday mornings at Levittown Baptist Church. Beautiful, no, but the piece appeared solidly strong. Joel had even thought to give a wax finish to wide planks of wood on the table's surface to repel fluids and grease. I could tell it would serve Nattie well for many years to come. And so could she. The expression on her face was priceless! It was as if Nattie had just been informed she would never die, but would live forever in a perpetual state of youth and good health.

Having given up all hope for this moment, it felt nearly like a dream to help move the table into the kitchen where, I was relieved to see, it fit perfectly. I paid Joel the remainder of what I owed and then I made a pantomime, bowing to him as if he were a deity or king. Joel clutched my hand into a finger-crushing squeeze and pumped my arm up and down. In walked Jordan. We all began to laugh, scream, and hop about the kitchen in celebration.

On the face of it, the four of us were very different. Nattie and Joel are Roman Catholics, Jordan is a Jew, and I am a former Baptist turned agnostic. We were three men and a woman. Two Peruvians, two New Yorkers. English speakers, Spanish speakers. Straight and gay. Poor and relatively rich.

Was the sudden appearance of this table an act of gastroimperialism? The end of another magical misery tour?

These questions as well as our national and economic differences seemed very small, the mere squeak of a guinea pig, in comparison to this shared moment of tremendous joy.

13

TOUGH LOVE IN TIBERIAS

IT HAD BEEN A TENSE FIVE MINUTES. STANDING BY A DEPAR-ture gate at John F. Kennedy International Airport, I was being interrogated by a humorless security agent from El Al Airlines, and it seemed as if one wrong response might prevent my boarding the flight from New York to Tel Aviv.

When nervous, I will sometimes become flirtatious and try to lighten the mood by coaxing a laugh. Do not do this, I was warned earlier by a representative from the Israeli Tourism Board who had invited me to go on this trip. The El Al people are always on high alert for potential terrorists, he said, so don't screw around. Just answer all questions briefly and honestly. This is exactly what I had done up to this point, patiently outlining my proposed itinerary for the next couple of weeks, explaining why I had a copy of Leon Uris's novel *Exodus* in my backpack (I never learned why this, of all things, raised any suspicion), and belatedly realizing I needed to apologize profusely for having visited Iran after this country's stamp was spotted in my passport.

Now, the guard asked me yet again his most urgent question. "Why exactly do you want to visit Israel?"

This was something I could not exactly answer, as I was keeping a secret from my hosts at the Israeli Tourism Board. They had arranged a series of enviable experiences I could write up in another of my breezy travel stories. I'd soon be shown about the Presidential Suite at Jerusalem's five-star Mamilla Hotel, which, I was assured, was "Condoleeza Rice's favorite room." I'd sample crisp Sauvignon Blancs at a Golan

Heights vineyard and soak in a hot mineral-rich mud bath at a spa alongside the Dead Sea. The real reason I agreed to come on this trip, however, was a wish to spend time cooking in Israel's soup kitchens.

Of the world's seven billion people, roughly half are believers in two religions, Islam and Christianity, but both of these faith traditions trace their origins back to the Jewish patriarch Abraham. I had seen how much of charitable cookery in America is influenced by Christianity and that Iran's method for feeding its poor came from that country's Islamic heritage. I thought a pilgrimage to Israel might help me better understand the source of these gastrophilanthropic customs.

Not that I said any of this to the El Al security agent. I don't recall now what I answered, but he handed my passport back to me and allowed me to proceed.

Once on the plane, I found myself surrounded by a boisterous group of evangelical Christians from Chicago. Several of them were complaining about how narrow the coach seats were. "Let's not make this a problem, people," one guy loudly proclaimed. "We're too anointed to be disappointed!" This man, whom I overheard addressed as "Pastor Bob," turned out to be the tour group's leader, and he wedged himself into the seat in front of mine.

It takes a rare degree of insensitivity to proselytize for Christianity aboard an El Al flight, but Pastor Bob was up to the task. I soon was eavesdropping on his spirited conversation with a young yarmulke-wearing Israeli seated in the aisle across from him. This younger guy argued that Christianity violates the first of the Ten Commandments: "Thou shalt have no other gods before me."

"You Christians worship Jesus above your devotion to God," he said.

Good point, I thought.

Pastor Bob took this in stride. His reply, which had the well-polished delivery of a phrase said countless times before, likened God to an egg. The shell, white, and yolk were distinct, yet all three, "like the Holy Trinity—Father, Son, and Holy Ghost," weren't different eggs but instead were wrapped into one. "I don't worship Jesus above God," he continued, "any more than I worship a yolk above a shell. Actually, I couldn't if I tried, because it's impossible to separate them."

"I guess you've never eaten an egg white omelet?" the Israeli guy asked.

Ignoring this riposte, Pastor Bob drove his point home. "We worship the same God, you and I. We each have a covenant. I'm not saying yours and the Jewish people's covenant is bad. No. It's just the Christian covenant is newer. You don't take offense at this, do you, brother?"

It was this "brother" that nearly made me choke on my Diet Coke. I tensed up, certain the Israeli would give Pastor Bob a well-deserved tongue-lashing, but he didn't. Amazingly, he seemed to find Pastor Bob funny. But I didn't, and I couldn't endure hearing any more of their conversation. I put on headphones and opened up my copy of *Exodus*.

WHEN I ARRIVED at Ben Gurion Airport, the Israeli Tourism Board supplied me with a car and driver as well as an irascible guide named Moshe Takomi. He was both a retired cop and a psychoanalyst, or so Moshe assured me. In his early seventies, Moshe had his hair dyed a shade of red best described as "medium rare." He was solidly overweight, rounded but hard like a basketball. Moshe had the disconcerting habit of answering any question with "Whazzat?"—no matter how slowly, loudly, or articulately I phrased my query. This way, he bought more time to formulate his answer.

Moshe and I put in many miles together, traveling from Tel Aviv to Jerusalem, on to the Dead Sea and Golan Heights, across to Haifa and Caesarea, and back to Tel Aviv. Everywhere we went, he would flood me with stories, many of which, I subsequently learned, were true.

Toward the end of our week, Moshe and I arrived at Capernaum, located on the northern shore of the Sea of Galilee. The most significant landmarks here are the architectural remains of a magnificent synagogue that dates to the third century. These ruins are built on a still earlier site where it's thought Jesus may have come to preach after his miracle of feeding the five thousand. After finding us a shady spot to sit, Moshe launched into one of his epic anecdotes.

"Jesus came to this place from Nazareth, but why here?" he asked and, not waiting for any response from me, rushed on. "You're from New York, right? You like Broadway, right? Well, you know, then, that before a show opens in Manhattan, it sometimes gets an out-of-town tryout. Same thing with Jesus! He was polishing his act here in Capernaum before he went on to the main stage at Jerusalem's temple. Because he's working on his timing, still learning his best lines—*badda-bing!*—Jesus decides he needs a simple, trusting audience to practice on. Fishermen are simple. They fish all night, and in the morning they mend their nets. While they work, they're willing to listen. This, then, was the very spot where people got a sneak peek at Jesus. Capernaum was his big break, so to speak."

Moshe continued talking—not to me, but *at* me. In this respect, he reminded me of my father, whom I had thought of often since arriving in Israel. How Dad would have loved to be in Capernaum! Yet I was here instead—and, if you please, as an honored guest of the Israeli government.

"Bread of heaven, bread of heaven, feed me 'til I want no more; feed me 'til I want no more!"

Someone was singing this old gospel hymn aloud, and it wasn't Moshe. Looking up, I was gobsmacked to see Pastor Bob standing less than fifty feet away! Still leading his Chicago group, he was wearing a headset microphone, its black foam ball floating in front of his lips. He paused by a pile of crudely carved basalt rocks I had noticed earlier when Moshe and I walked past them. Pastor Bob now explained that these were massive mortars for the grinding of grain and olives.

"The Hebrew word for this type of stone is 'Cuisinart,'" he joked, and everyone in his audience gave a hearty chuckle. "Lots of people will tell you the big business around Capernaum back in Bible times was fishing, but it wasn't! It was the manufacture of food-processing equipment. The important thing to remember is this: as Jesus began to formulate his message, he spoke in a language the widest possible audience could understand. Everybody eats! So, he frequently used imagery of food. Jesus called himself the bread of heaven!"

Moshe noticed I was distracted and no longer listening to him.

"That guy was on my flight from New York," I explained.

"Whazzat?"

"Him," I said, pointing. "He was sitting right in front of me."

Not at all pleased by my divided attention, Moshe raised his voice. "Judaism began with Abraham, who lived in what we now call Iraq," he said. "Abraham was what we might call a pagan, because tradition has it that several thousand years passed before Moses would write the Torah. Have you ever read the Bible? There are spy stories and love stories and war stories. It's really wonderful!"

Have I ever read the Bible? Such a question, Moshe! I wanted to brag that, yes, I've read it straight through, cover to cover, thank you very much. But I was still straining to hear what Pastor Bob had to say about Jesus's fondness for food metaphors.

WHEN ISRAEL WAS founded as a nation in 1948, patriotic fervor created a belief that hard work would make this new country self-sufficient. This ambitious goal for Israel to feed itself would require making fertile even the Negev, a scorched desert wasteland that comprises much of Israel's southern half. As David Ben-Gurion, Israel's first prime minister, wrote in 1954 when he moved to the Negev himself, "For those who make the desert bloom there is room for hundreds, thousands, and even millions."

Such optimistic assurance caused incredible things to happen. By the early 1960s, Israelis had pioneered the use of drip irrigation, which delivers water straight to a plant's roots. Later innovations in desalination processes and water recycling drew the world's attention. An arid coastal plain between the Mediterranean Sea and the Dead Sea was alive with vast fields of watermelons, tomatoes, olive trees, and date palms.

Since then, however, the desert hasn't continued to bloom equally for all Israelis. According to the relief agency Meir Panim (Hebrew for "Lighting Up Faces"), a third of Israeli children suffer from hunger, and one-fifth of the elderly need assistance.

Founded in 2000 to help alleviate such suffering, Meir Panim operates over thirty food and social service centers throughout Israel, including nine free restaurants, which feed nearly five thousand people each day. Most of the funding for this nongovernmental organization comes from Jewish communities and wealthy individuals who live outside Israel.

"We serve people with dignity and respect," said David Birnbaum, the executive director of American Friends of Meir Panim, which is based in New York City. "It's not about a soup line and a piece of bread. We want our guests to feel like we really care for them. This will help them gain self-confidence."

Over the course of several weeks, I cooked at Meir Panim kitchens in central Jerusalem as well as in Dimona, which is in the south. My first stop, during a few steamy days at the beginning of August, was Tiberias, on the western shore of the Sea of Galilee bordering Syria.

Many ancient stone columns were erected here two thousand years ago by Roman pleasure-seekers who came to relax in the area's natural hot springs. Following the exile of Jews from Jerusalem in the first and second centuries, Tiberias became a center for Talmudic study. Today, it is considered one of Israel's holiest cities. While Orthodox Jews visit in honor of this history, groups of American evangelical Christians—such as the one being led by Pastor Bob—tend to congregate on Galilee's eastern shore, where Jesus preached his famous Sermon on the Mount.

It is also in Tiberias that Varda Sohan operates a soup kitchen under the auspices of Meir Panim. She'd agreed to let me cook with her, so after bidding a fond farewell to Moshe ("Whazzat?") Takomi, I went to meet with Sohan.

"THERE IS A myth all Jews are wealthy and every Israeli is a Rothschild," she observed on the morning we met. "To the contrary, many people in this country are in desperate straits."

Sohan informed me that a crowd of 400,000 people had gathered in Tel Aviv for a recent march to raise awareness of poverty. Angry protests have occurred in many other cities across Israel too. So thick was the despair at one of these rallies that two men—one of them a son of Holocaust survivors—set themselves on fire. Both men died from their injuries.

"A Buddhist monk in Saigon, maybe," Sohan said, shaking her head. "But for a Jew to pour gasoline on himself and light a match? It's unthinkable."

Age fifty-four, Sohan was a heavy smoker and had the scratchy voice to prove it. Her brown eyes were deep-set and nearly lost in shadows. A pile of gold bangles clattered about on one of her wrists. Sohan's parents immigrated to Israel in 1950 from Arbil, Iraq, which she told me has a history dating back to 6000 BCE and is considered one of the oldest continuously inhabited cities in the world.

"It is very hard in Israel now. The price of bread is up! Petrol, up! Alcohol, up! Cigarettes, up! It's all up, and up, and UP!" She pounded the table between us, and her bracelets rang like a dropped platter of silverware. This was one of her standard gestures of emphasis, yet in the two days I spent with Sohan, I never got used to it and flinched each time.

We were seated inside the Meir Panim restaurant, which has an all-glass facade overlooking Hagilil Street. One of downtown Tiberias's best addresses, Hagilil is handsomely landscaped with palm trees and well-tended flower beds. The restaurant's interior was a long, tall-ceilinged space, which for most of the day was filled with enough sunshine that no electric lights needed to be switched on. There was a breakfront cabinet stuffed with tchotchkes—stuffed animals, teapots, and other bric-a-brac—as well as vases full of silk flowers.

"When I first opened it, my idea was to make people feel happy, not like coming here to eat was something to be embarrassed about," she said. "We ask no questions. People show up by mistake sometimes, and I will have to explain what Meir Panim is. I am proud this place looks enough like a regular restaurant that people might not know the difference. We feed whoever comes in: Jews, Christians, Muslims. Everyone is welcome."

Nine years ago, Sohan was working as the manager of a food-storage facility that shipped ingredients to restaurants across northern Israel. When a friend in the local government of Tiberias asked her to open a soup kitchen, she agreed to take on the challenge. This site on Hagilil

Street was already a dining establishment, so her initial tasks were relatively easy. Attracting customers took more time and effort.

"At first, it was one by one. But pretty soon, we were a full house. The restaurant currently feeds between one hundred and fifty and two hundred and fifty people a day," Sohan said. "Some eat their food here; others, especially if they have kids, will bring some sort of plastic container, and we'll put food in that for them to take home. There are a few street people and a few who drink or take drugs, but most of our diners are old folks who don't have enough money to live on."

The food is free, but for those who can afford it, they are charged two shekels, about fifty cents, for an all-you-can-eat meal. "For some people, giving this money is a way of maintaining their dignity," Sohan explained.

Sohan has one paid employee, Ziva Sharon, a woman in her mid-sixties who was partial to wearing capri pants and gaily colored sandals. Sharon had a crooked smile, which caused any expression of happiness to appear more quizzical than truly pleased. These two women were assisted by a bunch of young men they called "the criminals."

Because Meir Panim is a kosher restaurant, a rabbi comes every few days to make sure Sohan is following rules as decreed by Kashrut (Jewish dietary laws). Of these, the most important is a prohibition against any mixture of milk and meat. Not only should these items never be combined in any recipe, but additional rules dictate how separate a person should keep them inside their own body. Those who eat meat must wait six hours before drinking any milk; conversely, milk drinkers can't eat meat for two hours.

"I'm not Orthodox, but I respect the idea of kosher," Sohan said. She knows all the rules—no pork, no shellfish—though there are some she doesn't completely understand but adheres to nonetheless. "For some reason, I can't serve cauliflower. I don't know why it's not kosher, but I don't cook it."

Sohan furthermore explained that there are various levels of Kashrut. "There's kosher, there's *kosher*, and there is KOSHER," she said, slicing her hand horizontally in ascending heights. "The top-top-top level of kosher is very expensive, and we can't afford to do that here."

The menu for that day included chicken drumsticks, schnitzel, rice, roasted potatoes, pumpkin soup, beet salad, carrot salad, bread, and water. If there was a piece of fruit for dessert, it was given by a local farmer. Israel's Upper Galilee is something like the Salinas Valley in California and has many farms growing vegetables and fruits, predominantly grapes for wine.

The morning sped by as I worked with Ziva Sharon and others on Meir Panim's staff to get these menu items ready. Lunchtime guests began to arrive. Sohan knew all their personal stories. She pointed out a woman whose hair was bundled up inside a knitted cloche, a popular head covering for Orthodox women.

"See her? She looks after herself. She's clean. But, she gets no more than one thousand three hundred shekels each month from the government [a little more than $300], and what sort of life can you have with that?" Sohan inclined herself toward me and lowered her voice. This conspiratorial posture caused me to lean in also. "This woman has one son, and her daughter-in-law doesn't like her and doesn't want her around," she whispered. "So, she has three grandchildren she's never even seen!"

A heavyset man walked in the front door. He was wearing the full garb of an Orthodox Jew: black overcoat, vest, pants, and broad-brimmed black hat. Without removing a cigarette from her lips, Sohan muttered, "Okay, let's see what this one wants."

Without so much as a word of greeting, he demanded to know exactly how kosher the food was. When Sohan told him, he left, apparently not satisfied.

"It's a funny thing," she said. "Some poor people try to maintain their self-esteem by being fussy eaters. You've heard the expression that beggars can't be choosers? Well, I see choosy beggars all the time! People will be hungry, but they claim to be unable to eat certain things—tomatoes, say, or onions—as it might upset their stomach. I tell them, what really upsets your stomach is when there's no food in it!"

She dropped her hand to the tabletop with a big bang of her bracelets.

As diners continued to arrive, Sohan jerked her head up each time the front door opened and glanced quickly at anyone who entered.

Someone who was a stranger to her wouldn't be for long. What is the secret of her rapport, I asked, that these people will easily share intimate details of their lives with her?

"It's pretty simple," she said. "If people look sad, I talk to them."

Lunch was served from 11:00 a.m. to 1:30 p.m., with diners arriving whenever they liked during this time. All the while, Sohan worked the room as if she were the hostess of an elegant salon. She gave hugs, rubbed shoulders, and offered words of support. Most often she merely listened, nodding her head with interest. Her cellular phone rang constantly, and several times the caller was her four-year-old daughter, Leah.

When the crowd began to thin, Sohan invited me to sit with her again. She lit yet another cigarette and explained how she became pregnant. "At a certain point, I said to myself, 'Okay, I guess I am not going to get married. I'll have to make a baby on my own.'" From the ages of thirty-nine to fifty, she underwent twenty-one different attempts at artificial insemination and endured twenty-one miscarriages. "I did not give up. I was going to be a mother! Finally, just as I was about to turn fifty, God says to me, 'Here is your birthday present!'"

Sohan showed me a picture of Leah. Twenty-one miscarriages! The story was beyond improbable, nearly into the realm of science fiction. I didn't know what to say.

Instead, I asked about the young men who were working as volunteers—serving food, washing dishes, and cleaning the kitchen. They kept to themselves, preferring to sit and talk only with each other. Sometimes they fooled around, zapping each other with dish towels; mostly, they stared at the floor with blank faces.

"They're criminals, all of them," Sohan said.

I laughed, again assuming this was just a figure of speech. But as it turned out, these guys had all been found guilty of some crime. Rather than being sent to prison, they were assigned lengths of service during which they must show up at Meir Panim, a hospital, or a senior citizens center, where they worked for seven hours each day.

"None of them is a murderer—at least not that I know of!" Sohan said with a throaty cackle. "They were driving without a license, or got into a fight with their parents or wife. A lot of them are married and have children."

If an Israeli youngster has any sort of police record, he or she is ineligible for mandatory draft into the Israel Defense Forces. This is a shortsighted rule of the government, Sohan said. She believes military service is a crucially important rite of passage for many Israeli youths because they are forced to become truly responsible for the first time. "We hand them guns. They are given the power of life or death. That makes you grow up pretty fast."

Her "criminals," as she insisted on always calling them, haven't been drilled with army discipline. It falls to Sohan and Sharon to help them straighten out their lives.

"I tell them it is shameful to steal. It is no shame to do dishes!" she said. "Their probation officers come every week, and we go over their cases. They each have a card. I make notes and record if they are late, don't show up, or are lazy. If they don't do their jobs—" Sohan clapped her hands together, wrists jangling—"then they're off to prison! Meir Panim is kind of like their jail too, but I always tell them, better to have me for their warden than what they'll get behind bars."

Again, Sohan allowed herself a raspy laugh. "Ziva and I care about this place and the people who eat here. We want to keep our restaurant very neat and tidy. We're always scared the criminals won't do things right but will take shortcuts. I scream at the boys and tell them that if one of our guests gets sick, it will be their fault. You'll see," Sohan said, with a wink. "Ziva and I scream at them a lot!"

THE NEXT MORNING, I found Sohan counting foil-wrapped trays of food in the Meir Panim kitchen. Someone had gone on a hotel run and returned with these donations.

Seeing this, I thought of something I learned from Rabbi Jeremy Kalmonofsky, who is the spiritual leader of Congregation Ansche Chesed on the Upper West Side of Manhattan. A few months earlier, while planning this trip to Israel, I met with him to ask about the role of charity in Judaism.

"What you need to understand," Rabbi Kalmonofsky told me, "is that for most of premodern Jewish history, until the twentieth century in some cases, Jews tended to live in near-complete isolation from the dominant culture, be it Christianity or Islam. Jews huddled together in shtetls, or ghettos, where they only associated with other Jews. These communities were almost like Indian reservations. They had their own elders and their own laws."

"An important part of this setup," Kalmonofsky elaborated, "was how the shtetl's governors acted as the police authority, or a parallel judicial system. They would visit each family regularly and place a charitable assessment on each household. Giving to the poor was not optional. Those who were richer were required to help support those less fortunate."

It seemed to me that a Meir Panim truck pulling up to a luxury hotel along Tiberias's waterfront was similar, a compulsory form of charity—something like those schoolchildren in Austin, making peanut butter and jelly sandwiches as part of their "mandatory volunteerism." Is doing a good deed less good if it is coerced? Or do the ends justify the arm-twisted means?

Doubting that Sohan would be in the mood to muse philosophically on such questions, I asked, "What are we making for lunch?"

"It's a little like Hanukkah every day," she replied. "We never know what we'll be given; it's always something of a surprise. I open all the packages first to see what we've got. If there is fish, this must be the first thing to go. Anything with tomatoes we can't keep for longer than a day; it goes sour too quickly."

Foil coverings removed, there were many trays of roasted potatoes, other trays containing green beans mixed with sliced carrots, and a few with pieces of poached salmon. Sohan bent over to smell the contents of every pan, taking a pinch of this, a nibble of that, to see how things had been spiced. A skilled hand when it comes to repurposing leftovers, she deployed ingenious tricks to refresh food that was a day or two old. She didn't deliberate long. The salmon went into a warming oven while she began sautéing a large pan full of turkey sausage to mix with the roasted potatoes.

I took this opportunity to speak with one of Sohan's workers and asked what crime he'd committed so that he was working here. He had long eyelashes and shining dark hair that curled gently around his ears.

"I did funny things with Visa, selling access to stolen credit card numbers over the Internet," he said. He then arched an eyebrow, as if to imply "you would have done the same if you were smart enough to know how."

He'd been in prison for three years in Tel Aviv but was serving the last six months of his sentence at Meir Panim. Which was harder, I asked, jail or the soup kitchen? He answered by darting glances at Ziva Sharon and Varda Sohan.

TEMPERATURES ROSE AS the day grew warmer. Sharon and I were arranging small plates of carrot salad to have them ready for the lunch rush. She told me that she's a second-generation Israeli; her parents came from Syria and Morocco. She'd formerly worked selling "natural" skin products at a hot springs resort a few miles farther down the beach. She'd also volunteer from time to time here at Meir Panim.

From these experiences, Sharon knew how hard her friend Varda Sohan worked and that it was difficult for her to be alone all day, surrounded by young men who were in trouble with the law. One day, Sohan's father asked Sharon if she would consider working full-time at the restaurant. "He said Varda and I were like sisters practically. Sisters will have fights, sure, but then they will make up. He convinced me to take this job. That was seven years ago."

Something about this explanation didn't add up. Why did Sharon come to work here, I asked. Wasn't it a much easier life when she was selling cosmetics?

Sharon answered by sharing more of her background. Born in 1950, she claimed there were far worse problems back then between Israel and its neighbors than those that exist today. The east side of the Sea of Galilee still belonged to Syria, and life around the lake, even over here in Tiberias, could be dangerous as a result. Her father was a naval policeman; one day, the other cop on his boat was shot and killed by a Syrian sniper. Sharon's mother insisted her husband quit and find some safer line of work. He tried various occupations, all relatively unsuccessfully, but to keep food on the table he occasionally worked as a fisherman.

"In April, St. Peter's fish, which is the most plentiful seafood in Galilee, go to the eastern shore to lay their eggs. They become scarce here on the west side, and prices go up. My dad had a friend who said to him, 'It's Passover. Early in the morning, we will go a little bit further out into the middle of the sea, closer to the east bank, throw one net, and come back. There won't be any problems.'"

Sharon paused and smiled one of her crooked grins.

"I was eight at the time. My dad and this other guy, they row out. They toss one net. Then, a Syrian shot my father right between the eyes," Sharon said while pointing a finger at her own forehead. "He fell into the boat. That was it. He was already dead."

Her mother was a widow with five young daughters. It was a struggle each day to keep the family clothed and fed. "The mentality then was that you didn't get remarried," Sharon said. "You must also realize, in those days the Israeli government didn't think of the person who killed my father as a 'terrorist.' It wasn't until 1973 that the government finally began to recognize the significance of deaths like my father's and started giving financial support to the survivors of people who died from terrorism."

Had this experience made her more sensitive to others in need, I asked Sharon.

If she was insulted by my armchair psychoanalysis, she didn't show it. "We take people in to work here that no one else will," she replied. "We try to help everyone. As you can see, we don't coddle these boys. We want them to understand they're here to WORK! For some, this message gets through. After they leave, they come back to see Varda and me. If they have a wedding, they call us and we go. For others, they can't learn to arrive on time or show up at all, and they are sent back to prison. I feel terrible for them."

"They are all so young!" I exclaimed.

"Yes, and that's when you usually make the biggest mistakes in your life—when you are young," she replied.

It was 11:00 a.m., and a few of the earliest diners had begun to arrive. Sharon started serving lunch from behind the counter. I was stationed a few feet away from her offering spoonfuls of the potato and turkey sausage dish, which was very popular. The next half hour went by in a blur of nonstop activity.

Then, completely without warning, a loud argument broke out between Sharon and a young woman who was putting out bowls of vegetable soup. Whatever caused this disagreement was unclear to me, as the women were screaming at each other in Hebrew. What I could understand was that once the altercation began, neither would back down. Both women kept trying to get the last word, which only started the argument up again. Sharon continued to hand out plates of food; the girl ladled bowls of soup. All the while, they took potshots at each other. Their bickering went on for many minutes. Finally, it died down. Then it reignited, flared up, and began to get really wild. Sharon and the girl were standing toe-to-toe, faces mere inches from each other, yelling at incredible volume.

One of the young men rushed over, trying to reestablish calm as he interposed himself between them. But the women simply screamed over, through, and around him. There was no hitting or slapping. It was strictly a battle of words. But what a war it was! By a wide margin this was the most full-throated fight I had ever witnessed, including the sight of rival gangs of teenagers threatening each other on the New York City subway system. This skirmish in Tiberias was much rawer.

A truce was finally established, but this felt fragile, like it might not last. I had the sharp pang of a tension headache caused by standing so close to this dispute. What amazed me was the non-reaction of other guests at Meir Panim. There must have been eighty or a hundred people eating lunch or waiting in line for food while this shouting match occurred, but no one took any notice of it.

When you live in Israel, you exist with the constant possibility of missile attacks, bus explosions, or sniper fire. Your house is legally required to have a bomb shelter equipped with water, tinned food, and an air-filtration system where you'll take cover if nuclear or biochemical weapons fall. You've seen worse, in other words, than a couple of women screeching at each other. I haven't, though. My life is largely free from overt hostility, and even being a bystander to it had unsettled me in a profound way.

Later, Sharon asked if I was ready to eat lunch. The salmon was very good, she suggested. I looked up at her. Only a few minutes ago her face was contorted in a purple rage, and she was producing sounds the likes of which I scarcely knew the human voice was capable. Now, she purred with the solicitous concern of a grandmother.

"Thanks," I said, "but I should go."

After giving her a kiss on the cheek, I went to say goodbye to Varda Sohan.

Then, I got in my rental car and drove off. Still shaken, I traveled for some distance, unaware of anything but my jangled thoughts. Gradually, I began to notice a bad smell. Sharon wouldn't take no for an answer and insisted that I take a plate of food before I left Meir Panim. Several hours had gone by, and the salmon's scent was making me nauseous. Spying a trash can, I pulled off the road and threw this free meal away.

14

BUT FOR THE GRACE OF GOD

GENTILE TRAVELERS, BEWARE! IN ISRAEL, IT SOMETIMES can feel like everything closes for Shabbat. From sundown on Friday until sunset on Saturday, whole parts of the country go on holy hiatus, including government offices, shops, restaurants, museums, and even soup kitchens.

This was particularly the case when visiting Tsfat, a small town in the country's north. On my way from Tiberias to Jerusalem, I made a stopover in this mountain village, a center for Jewish mysticism and study of the Kabbalah. Wandering about, I came upon Eshel Binyamin soup kitchen, a charitable spot mostly patronized by Tsfat's elderly citizens. A sign outside proclaimed that it was funded by a grant from the Conference on Jewish Material Claims against Germany. Intrigued, I wanted to learn more about this Claims Conference, but my visit was on a Saturday morning, and Eshel Binyamin was locked up tight. Jotting down the address, I noted this soup kitchen was adjacent to the Beirav Carlebach Synagogue.

"Tsfat is like a big circle. No matter where you start, you'll end up coming back to the same place."

My face had been turned into my notebook, so I was startled to hear a voice behind me. The person who spoke was a bearded man, and he was smiling. We shook hands while he introduced himself as Irving Ginsberg. "It's spelled like Allen Ginsberg," he said. "You've heard of him, the great American poet?"

In short order, Irving Ginsberg told me he'd grown up in New York City but is now the cantor and spiritual leader of the Beirav Carlebach

Synagogue. He pointedly demurred from calling himself "rabbi," because although Shlomo Carlebach had been dead for many years, Ginsberg hinted that, aided by prayers of the faithful, Carlebach's spirit still returned each Shabbat. Thus, Ginsberg considers Carlebach to still be this synagogue's official rabbi.

Endeared by his gregarious personality, I asked if he had another moment for a quick question.

"I have two moments! I have many more than two! Come into my office. Come! Come!" Ginsberg unlocked the temple's front door and gestured for me to go in before him.

We sat in his office, where I sketched a brief biography of Alexis Soyer, described my interest in gastrophilanthropy, and explained my wish to learn what was distinctive about how the poor are fed in Israel.

Biblical scholars, Ginsberg told me, agree what's most significant about Abraham is that his story represents the first time there's anything like a reciprocal relationship between man and God. Before Abraham, an all-powerful deity is shown to be oddly capricious in his dealings with humanity.

"When God is in a good mood, it's a lovefest, but when God is angry, watch out! Floods, plagues, and fireballs might be hurtling your way," Ginsberg said. "In his relationship with Abraham, though, God behaves in a more collegial manner. This God can be reasoned with; this God seems to listen to Abraham, opening up a possibility that God may heed our thoughts and prayers."

As a result, Ginsberg explained, human beings now live on a continuum: our behavior within the larger community determines how God will treat us. It's a slight tweak of the Golden Rule: do unto others as you would have God do unto you. In several passages in the Torah, God commands his people to perform acts of tzedakah, which is the Hebrew word for "justice" or "charitable behavior." Ginsberg wanted me to understand that even this definition somehow misses the mark, though, since charity is typically understood to be a spontaneous act of goodwill. In Judaism, tzedakah is not an "as the spirit moves you" whim but instead is an ethical obligation.

"If you have something, you are commanded to share it!" he cried, his voice getting very animated. "God says, 'If you are rich, it's only because I gave this to you. If you give it back to others, you prove to me I was correct to have entrusted it to you in the first place. If you don't, well, money comes, and money goes.'"

"Charity is something Jews are told to do every day," Ginsberg continued. "You can always find someone who needs something, even if it's as little as a dollar or a dime. And it doesn't have to be money! It could be a box of pasta or an old pair of shoes. In the unlikely circumstance you don't run into someone who needs your assistance on any given day, there is always the pushke!"

The what?

Ginsberg explained that pushke—which is pronounced variously as PUSH-kee, push-KUH, or PISH-kee—is a Yiddish word derived from Polish. It means a small can or box kept in the home, often in the kitchen, in which loose change is deposited. When your pushke is full, you give this money away to a charitable cause.

I mentioned my conversation with Rabbi Kalmonfsky back in New York and his idea of a "charity police" who could simply demand money from the more well-off citizens in a shtetl. Irving Ginsberg took some exception to this.

"It's not so much the giving was forced," he said. "Or, at least it's not that way now. No, the idea is something more like if you give and give big, you will be greatly blessed. You get a better seat at the shul. People recognize you for your generosity. There are worse things to be known for, yes?"

From Ginsberg's office, I went to a store in Tsfat that sold Judaica and bought two pushkes: one for my office and the other for my bedside table at home. All my stray pennies, nickels, dimes, and quarters would be donated to charitable causes, I vowed to myself. Admiring these small boxes, I noticed they each had a tiny padlock, a reminder that such altruistic vows are easily broken. Presumably, these little locks were to make it more difficult for someone (me?) to pinch from the poor.

Jerusalem's Meir Panim restaurant is located on Hatzvi Street near the city's Central Bus Station. Traffic in this part of town is thick, as every few minutes buses arrive in the capital from all over Israel. A few young men, nearly identical in age and demeanor to the "criminals" I met in Tiberias, were mopping the floor as I entered the soup kitchen. While they went about their work, they were singing, in heavily accented English, cadences of a U.S. Navy marching song, "I don't know, but I've been told: Navy wings are made of gold . . ."

I was a few minutes early for an appointment to meet David Roth, who is Meir Panim's national director. Approaching a couple of these workers, I said, "Excuse me. Is Mr. Roth here?"

They looked at me for a moment, then burst into rowdy laughter as they continued to practice their language skills by repeating some of what I just said.

"Egg-scooze meh!"

"Ek-coose mee!"

Let them have their fun. I backed away with a respectful bow and went to wait at one of the restaurant's empty tables. I saw a tremendous number of signs posted on the walls, their letters spelling out names of benefactors.

> Meir Panim is generously supported by the
> Iranian-American Jewish Federation of New York.

> Frances Frymet (Auschwitz Survivor) in memory of
> her family who perished in Treblinka, and her friend,
> Rosa Robate, who perished a martyr in Auschwitz.

> 250 meals at Meir Panim Free Restaurant were
> generously contributed by the Jewish Community
> Foundation of Los Angeles, California.

There were dozens more, all with messages worded similarly to these. So many acts of tzedakah for just one soup kitchen!

Only now did I notice an angry-looking man seated at a table in one corner. I guessed he was a probation officer checking up on the young lawbreakers working off their sentences here. When I attempted to photograph some of the benefactor signs on the wall, he'd thought I was trying to snap his picture. Leaping up, he sternly waved me off. He was equally brusque with the boys. As each sat before him, the man scowled mightily to demonstrate how extremely serious he was about this job.

A few more minutes passed before Roth arrived. He appeared harried and announced he had only a few minutes to spare. Once seated, however, he immediately started in on what I surmised to be his stump speech.

This began with a preamble about Dudi Zilberschlag, who founded Meir Panim fifteen years earlier. Because the two men were friends, Zilberschlag asked Roth if he would help run the organization. Roth was living in Brooklyn at the time with his Israeli-born wife, Esther, and had a thriving business selling electronic equipment such as televisions, stereos, and DVD players. "But we were not blessed with a family of our own," he said. "After years of not having children, Esther says to me one day, 'Let's go back to Israel.'"

Roth shook his head sadly. "We'd had twenty-one years of consultation with doctors, all ending in sorrow. There was no chance, no hope for us having children," he said. "So, after being in Israel for a couple of years, we were about to adopt, but my wife wondered if we shouldn't try once more for one of our own. Our doctor said it was a waste of time and money, but on Shabbat we finally found out the test results. A miracle had befallen us! My Esther was pregnant!"

Befallen? His archaic choice of word only increased how much Roth's story sounded like one from Hebrew scriptures—that of Abraham and Sarah. It was also eerily reminiscent of Varda Sohan's travails; Esther's twenty-one years of doctor visits compared to twenty-one miscarriages before Sohan finally gave birth to Leah.

"I thought all my prayers were answered, but then came the hardest part," Roth continued. "In September 2001, Esther was diagnosed with preeclampsia."

This, Roth explained, is when a pregnant woman develops high blood pressure and hypertension in her second or third trimester. Doctors said either the mother or child could die—or both. Faced with such dire alternatives, Esther Roth underwent a caesarean section in her twenty-fifth week of pregnancy. The baby girl weighed slightly more than one pound and was given only a 3 percent chance to live. She stayed in an intensive care unit at the hospital for six months, at the end of which the medical staff told Roth and his wife they shouldn't try to take care of the child at home.

"They said we wouldn't want her, she would be so deformed and mentally impaired. Yet, today she is eleven years old and is completely normal. She gets 90 to 100 on all her tests. She's smarter than her father. Her English is better'n mine, that's for sure! I don't speak so good, *cuz I'ze 'riginally from Brooklyn.*"

I suspected Roth had told this joke countless times, but I grinned obligingly.

"That is what made me get involved with Meir Panim. You see, we'd been blessed, Esther and I, but there are still many more children who need help, children who through no fault of their own are born into bad circumstances. I made a promise to help each child in Israel—whether they were Jewish, Christian, or Arab."

This promise, Roth acknowledged, has been hard to keep. With the Israeli economy in such bad shape, it was exceedingly difficult to raise money. "In Israel, people don't usually want to give shekels; they prefer to give value," he said. "For instance, restaurants intentionally cook too much food and donate the extra." Food is the least of his costs, though. What's more expensive is paying the rent and utility bills for the Meir Panim locations. "I can only do this if I have strong partners," he said, gesturing at the plaques I noticed earlier.

Aryeh Cohen arrived at our table. He managed this free restaurant in Jerusalem, and I could see the job exacted a heavy toll. Cohen had a fretful air, and his posture was bent forward as if by the psychological burdens he carried. His pants and topcoat—he was dressed in the same all-black ensemble as Roth—were splattered with food he'd been cooking that morning. Cohen had extra lustrous payes, which are the side curls of hair worn by Orthodox Jewish men. Cohen's dangled down to his waist. He'd immigrated to Israel, or made aliyah, from England nearly three decades earlier, though his speech still retained the lilt of his native Newcastle.

Cohen apologized that he would need to postpone our interview. Some of his workers today were "rough boys," he said, and they were overly stimulated by the presence of young women in the kitchen. As Cohen rushed off, Roth explained there was yet another problem this morning—namely, a surplus of volunteer workers. Two different families, one from Canada and another from the United States, would be showing up in an hour or so to serve lunch as part of celebrations surrounding both a bar mitzvah and a bat mitzvah.

Just as he finished telling me this, pandemonium erupted. The Straus family, all fifteen of them, had arrived early! They hailed from Kew Gardens Hills in Queens, New York, and had traveled to Israel in honor of a thirteen-year-old girl named Michal. Roth sprang into action, greeting these visitors and making them feel welcome.

"Have you ever been inside a soup kitchen?" he asked Michal. The girl blushed and smiled but didn't reply. Undeterred, Roth continued his banter. "Well, you are going to have to put on plastic gloves. I bet you've never done that before either, have you?"

We were joined by Aryeh Cohen, who pointed to a series of stainless steel sinks where many hundreds of potatoes were soaking in murky water. These needed to be peeled and chopped, a daunting task that the Straus family and I were told to tackle. While we worked, I talked with Avigail Straus, mother of Michal, the bat mitzvah celebrant. After Cohen handed her a vegetable peeler, Straus rubbed it back and forth across the potato like an emery board on a fingernail.

"I brought my children here so they could see life is not all 'No, I want sushi! We had Chinese last night!'" Straus said. "We don't see this sort of poverty in New York—not where we live, at least. I always say 'there but for the grace of God.'"

I have heard this expression my whole life and even used it a few times myself. Hearing it in this setting, though, it struck me as heartless.

How can we be so blasé in suggesting that God decides to treat some people better than others?

These troublesome thoughts were pushed aside by the work of the next hour. Lunch today was roasted chicken, lamb goulash, potatoes, and sautéed mushrooms, with plums for dessert. Cohen told me about an organization called Lekot that harvests any unpicked or surplus produce from various farms in Israel and then distributes it to places such as Meir Panim.

"Every Monday someone from Lekot will call and tell me what they've got, and it is delivered the next day," he said. "This week, I got plums. Lots and lots of plums. So many plums, I have no idea what I will do with them."

While speaking about this excess of fruit, Cohen's face was the very picture of worry.

JUST BEFORE NOON, people began to filter inside. They chose their tables, and groups of three or four senior citizens clustered together, kibitzing, as they waited to be served lunch. Because the restaurant's interior had no air-conditioning, the front door was wide open. An Israeli flag hanging beside this entrance fluttered in the commotion caused by the constant arrival and departure of buses at Jerusalem's Central Bus Station.

The dining area was small, seating around forty at once. There was no fixed time for lunch. Instead, people were free to come whenever they liked between noon and 2:00 p.m.

"I don't like it to be all in one 'go.' I could not handle the pressure of serving everyone if they came at once," Cohen admitted.

Like Varda Sohan in Tiberias, Cohen knew the personal history of all his regular clients.

"He's an *Arab*!" Cohen whispered to me, his voice quivery as if reluctant to speak the word. He was pointing at a very dark-skinned man who sat alone and was sweating profusely as he ate. After finishing his lunch, he pulled out plastic containers and asked if these could be filled.

"It's food for his kids," Cohen explained. "His wife used to come in here, but she was too picky and would only take the stuff she liked to eat. The children were starving!"

About another woman, Cohen observed, "She has three children, and all of them are autistic. Do you know what autism is in America?"

The food station was barely six feet wide. To prevent congestion, volunteers brought lunch to the assembled guests. In honor of her bat mitzvah, Michal Straus was allowed to deliver that day's first meal. Smiling shyly, she placed a tray down in front of an elderly gentleman. His hands shook badly; while maneuvering a fork up to his open mouth, much of what he'd lifted fell onto his shirt front.

During the next two hours, a steady stream of guests arrived. They shuffled into the restaurant, sat down, and plates of goulash were put in front of them by Michal, others of the Straus family, and me. People ate, either not noticing or having no interest that visitors were doing a mitzvah around them. I worried their lack of response would discourage Michal, but I was wrong. No sooner did she drop off one tray then she raced back to the serving line to pick up another. Cohen, observing her zeal, regarded the girl fondly.

Things turned briefly weird when a guy came in who looked both mentally ill and drunk. He was carrying many plastic bags, the rustling bustle of which created a swirl of chaos around him. His shirt was buttoned out of sequence and bunched up sideways across his chest. He smelled as if he'd urinated into the grimy pants he was wearing.

Dropping his bags at one of the tables, he brushed aside all offers of help, preferring to barge up to the serving line himself, where he grabbed two plates of stew and half a dozen slices of white bread. Returning to the table, he carefully picked the lamb chunks out of the gravy, made sandwiches, and smooshed them closed with such force that his dirty hand left a shadowy imprint on the bread. He then shoved these moist sandwiches down into the bottom of one of his bundles.

"Aryeh!" he yelled. "Aryeh! ARYEH!"

Hearing his name, Cohen rushed out from behind the serving counter, where he'd been plating food for others. A white plastic apron flew up about his waist, and his long side curls trailed aloft. By gently squeezing the man's arm and whispering into his ear, Cohen managed to placate this fellow. With exaggerated care, the man picked up his bags and slowly made his way out the front door.

"Dining with dignity" is a slogan often used to describe the distinctive sort of gastrophilanthropy practiced at Meir Panim's free restaurants. How difficult this is to achieve was powerfully shown by the gale force of hysteria caused by this one man.

When the lunch period ended, a few remaining diners came to the serving station, and Cohen scraped leftovers into their plastic containers. He had told me it pained him when anything went uneaten, and I could see this was true by how carefully he coaxed every last drop of food from each pan. Nearly three hundred people passed through today, Cohen told me as he stood over a garbage can, looking at what did not get eaten. For this large of a crowd, there were remarkably few plate scrapings except for the mushrooms, which were not to everyone's liking.

"I don't need compliments on my cooking. I just want people to eat everything on their plates," he said. "My father was from Poland; he was poorer than poor. Thinking of him, I can't stand to see any food go to waste."

Cohen said he needed to relax for a minute. Perfectly content, or unaware, that he was still wearing a plastic apron and rubberized gloves, he sipped a cup of tea while telling me some of his life story. He was fifty years old and had ten children, two of whom lived in the United States. Before coming to work at Meir Panim, he studied the Torah full-time and taught many students.

Cohen told me how easily discouraged his Torah students would become. "'I don't understand! I'll never understand,' they would cry." Cohen confessed it infuriated him how often he would have to stop his lessons and back up to the point where they'd become lost. "You get this, right?" he'd say before moving on. "And then, you understand this, yes?"

"Each step builds on the next," Cohen said. "It's about patience. If a child sees you are not being patient with them, they will never understand."

We heard a whoop of laughter from the kitchen. Cohen spun his head around and saw a pretty girl was again distracting some of his workers. He exhaled slowly. "These boys—they didn't get good treatment at home. They never learned how to keep themselves out of trouble."

Cohen then frowned and mentioned Avigail Straus, the mother from Queens, New York. Earlier he'd noticed, as had I, that she seemed unaware of how to use a vegetable peeler. "A woman her age does not know how to skin a potato?" he asked.

Before I could answer, Cohen offered his own theory. "I guess she's rich enough to have some machine that does it for her. Bzzzt! Bzzzzzzzzt!" Cohen was imitating the sound of whirring blades on his imagined appliance.

No, I told him. Other explanations were more likely. Straus might have a servant to peel her potatoes. Then again, she could be so worried about gaining weight that she never ate carbs.

"Carbs?" he asked, his eyebrows alert with foreboding. "What are those?"

"Carbohydrates. Like in pasta, bread, or potatoes."

"There are many Americans who never eat pasta or bread?"

"Many," I said. "Especially if they are rich."

Cohen stared at me. From his look of dismay, it was as if I had divulged that most affluent Americans live on a diet of human blood.

15

GIMME THE KIMCHI, BABY!

O N THANKSGIVING MORNING, ROAST TURKEY WASN'T ON the menu when I cooked for a group of hungry people in Busan, South Korea. Korean cuisine is famous for the abundance of side dishes that accompany a meal, however, so we were serving up plenty of trimmings, including several varieties of kimchi, or what's sometimes called "Korean ketchup."

After reporting for a story I'd write about the Busan Biennale, an international arts festival, I arranged to stay on for a few days longer to cook with Shon Gyu-Ho. Ten years earlier Mr. Shon founded an organization called Busan Baffer, which currently feeds an estimated three thousand people a day. He wears his long black hair pulled back into a ponytail and has a somber, scholarly air that's underscored by his customary attire: a black Mandarin collar jacket.

In addition to nourishing the body, Shon believes his organization must help heal minds. "The reason homeless people have trouble interacting with society is they think they're weak," he said. "We try to help people know they can do something with their lives."

We were standing together beside a truck retrofitted with immense cookers in which rice was steamed and a stainless steel cauldron where a small pond of soup simmered. Next to this mobile kitchen was parked another van holding a battered collection of folding card tables and stackable plastic stools. Because the weather was sunny and clear, these would soon be arranged on a cobblestone plaza in Hae-undae.

This is a wealthy neighborhood in Busan, a coastal city that is located nearly at the Korean Peninsula's southernmost tip. Hae-undae is known for its densely packed cluster of tall apartment buildings as well as its luxury hotels, the grandest of which is the Paradise Casino. Advertising posters for this casino were plastered all over Busan and displayed a photograph of the American movie star Robert De Niro, who looked especially cranky as he shuffled a deck of cards. If not quite a paradise for Busan's poor, Hae-undae nonetheless attracts the hungry, who come here to panhandle from rich tourists, paw about in dumpsters, or sit alone on concrete walls by the beach looking out across the South China Sea. Many of them also make their way to the Korail station to get a free lunch from Busan Baffer.

This gastrophilanthropic organization's name alludes to the fact that no Korean meal is complete without rice. Every Korean kitchen has an electric rice cooker, and it's always accessorized with a flat spoon made of bamboo or plastic that hangs on the cooker's side. Koreans prefer a short-grain rice, which clumps together as it absorbs moisture and is dished out in big blobs, like a generous scoop of ice cream. Both the action of serving rice and this special spatula are called *baffer*. In Korea, the word connotes abundance, similar to *smörgåsbord* for Swedes or "all you can eat" for English speakers.

I FIRST MET Shon earlier that morning at the Busan Baffer headquarters. Along with a dozen or so other men, he was sitting on the floor, at a low table, eating his breakfast of grilled fish, rice, and kimchi. It was barely 8:00 a.m., yet these men had already been working for several hours, loading up the truck with ingredients for today's lunch.

The room in which they huddled was chilly, and I couldn't figure out why everyone in this group appeared comfortable in shirtsleeves or T-shirts. As I took my place next to Shon, I found they were seated on an electrified plastic mat, which in most Korean homes replaces carpeting.

Shon offered me a cup of instant coffee, which I sipped while we talked. Noting that the weather was starting to get colder, he said Busan Baffer was gearing up for head counts to increase markedly in the months ahead. Similar to snowbirds—those elderly folks in the northern United States who relocate to sunny Florida for the winter—there's a migration of homeless men and women to Busan.

"It is much colder in Seoul than here," Shon said. "Starting at the end of November, homeless people, usually men, will get onto trains headed south. They don't have tickets, but the railroad conductors know these poor passengers will make a scene if they try to eject them. So, they ride for free."

This annual influx provides an eerie echo to how Busan was first populated. During the Korean War (which Koreans call their civil war) in the early 1950s, Seoul was relentlessly targeted with bombs from the north. Refugees by the tens of thousands abandoned South Korea's capital and fled to Busan. Most settled close to the water's edge in hovels and shacks around the city's main port. Busan was South Korea's only major town that never fell to communist rule, a fact the city's citizens still take pride in.

One often hears South Korea referred to as an economic "miracle." The seventh-largest exporter in the world, it is one of the planet's most technologically advanced societies. During the spectacular recovery South Korea made after its civil war, many parents focused obsessively on their children's educational and professional success, expecting their offspring's future wealth would eventually provide a cushion for them. In the Confucian ideal of filial piety, children must show unquestioned respect to their parents, so a nuclear family was the only source of social security. (South Korea neglected to create any sort of national welfare system until 1988.)

Things didn't work out as planned. The postwar shift from an agrarian to an industrial society scattered a younger generation to cities or abroad. These sons and daughters began to face problems of their own, especially during the Asian financial crisis of the late 1990s, making them less willing or able to care for their aged parents.

"Their children have all moved away and forgotten them," Shon said.

Today, South Korea's suicide rate is among the highest in the world, according to statistics released by the Organization for Economic Cooperation and Development. Measured by suicides per 100,000 people,

South Korea's numbers rose from 13.6 in 2001 to 31.2 in 2010. Most disturbingly, the suicide rate leapt from 35.5 per 100,000 people to 81.9 among those who are sixty-five and older. These figures suggest a near total collapse of South Korea's Confucian social contract and helps explain why elderly people make up the majority of those who eat meals provided by Busan Baffer.

When Shon was a child, he told me, he lived next door to an orphanage for disabled boys and girls. These youngsters became his friends. At age eighteen, however, they would be declared independent and summarily kicked out of the orphanage and put on the street.

"A lot of them could not adjust to society. Several people I knew committed suicide," he said. "This stuck with me even as I started my career and began to raise my family. I kept thinking that I have to do something for these poor people. Human beings have a right to eat, to be clothed, and to have a roof over their heads."

For many years, Shon taught computer skills to elementary school students in the fourth through sixth grades. All the while, he schemed and dreamed, until he finally figured out his system of two trucks that operate as a tag team to deliver hot meals. While Busan Baffer now looks to be a well-oiled machine, getting it operational wasn't easy. Pushing back against traditional values, which taught each family must take care of its own problems, Shon's efforts were viewed by some as meddling and intrusive. Only when the scourge of homelessness and hunger in South Korea grew to a point where it could no longer be ignored did donations and volunteers begin to come his way.

BAECHU IS SOUTH Korea's most popular form of kimchi and is made by combining cabbage, garlic, ginger, salt, and red pepper flakes, after which the mixture can be stored for months. Even when you wear rubber gloves while making baechu, the chili pepper eventually works its way through the plastic and begins to burn the flesh around your fingernails. It's a slowly escalating type of agony. I learned this the hard way when making tall piles of kimchi with Shon.

I also cut up many crates of persimmons, which are harvested in the fall and are to South Korea what apples are to America. Finally, I cooked vats of soup made with cabbage, onions, pork bones, potatoes, garlic, and sesame leaf. Its broth was loaded with a red chili powder called go-chugaru. Vigorously spicy in flavor, this soup's color was a fiery orange.

When lunch was ready, I would fall into line behind other volunteers and bring trays of food to our guests. This crowd in Busan, especially the women, were unusually old, many in their nineties, with faces deeply etched and creased by their years. The word for "grandmother" in Korean is halmune and is something of an honorific; that is, it's completely polite to use when greeting an elderly woman you've never met.

From the kitchen truck's window, I watched the halmunes arriving for lunch. They'd come hobbling into the plaza where folding tables and chairs would soon be set up. Bent low over canes, their torsos were nearly parallel to the ground. After finding a place in the sun, they'd sit, gossiping with their friends, while snacking on dried seaweed.

One day shortly before we were to serve up the soup, a woman wearing a celadon-colored sweater and skirt came bounding into the plaza. She was at least a generation younger than the other women. With remarkable charisma, she skipped about, screaming "Hallelujah!" while she passed out hard candies and pinched the cheeks of the halmunes.

When we'd had breakfast together, Shon mentioned in passing that he was a Christian. But he also wanted me to know Busan Baffer is a nonreligious organization, and he doesn't allow any preaching or prayer. Yet here was this woman, perpetrating an act of guerrilla evangelism. Once her candies were distributed throughout the crowd, she began to belt out a song. She had a strong alto voice, and though the words were Korean, I instantly recognized the melody, an old gospel tune called "What a Friend We Have in Jesus." She danced while she sang, doing jaunty pirouettes and sometimes wiggling her butt like a burlesque dancer.

"She must be a little crazy," I whispered to Shon.

He smiled. "No, she's just a little overly excited about her idea of God."

Other workers unloaded folding tables—each of which could seat four guests—and plastic chairs. This created a melee. The old ladies who'd been patiently waiting were roused into territorial skirmishes, trying to lay claim to tables in certain parts of the plaza. Spots under trees, where the midday light was dappled, were considered most desirable and worth fighting for. There was a lot of pushing and shoving, with some sharp elbows tossed. Who could have guessed these women still had so much fight left in them? Eventually everyone found a place, and tables were set up in a neat rectilinear pattern.

Before we servers could begin picking up trays, we were given a pep talk by a chic young woman wearing a beige cashmere overcoat. From her manner of crisp dispatch, it seemed like she was about to preside over a posh luncheon for the Junior League, not a crowd of impoverished grandmothers. She murmured into a microphone attached to an amplification system that hung from a strap over her shoulder and was no bigger than a purse. To my considerable alarm, I was now handed my uniform: a pink-and-white boldly checkered gingham smock—not a midriff apron tied at the waist, mind you, but a full-frontal affair with abundant ruffles from kneecaps to shoulders—which was accessorized with a poofy hat made from the same gingham fabric. I wasn't being singled out; all volunteers had to wear this cutesy costume, as if we were waitresses at a pie shop in Mississippi.

Portion control was strict. Every tray got precisely the same amount of food. It took three people to reassemble every serving of soup: one to place a spoonful of cabbage, another to add a few pieces of pork, and a third to spoon the bright orange broth over these first two items. Trays were only complete after they were further loaded down with a big baffer of rice and a splat of kimchi.

Alexis Soyer would have appreciated this exactitude of serving size, as he instituted a similar protocol during the Crimean War when he assisted Florence Nightingale in the care and feeding of the British Army. He would have admired my gingham flounces too, as Soyer understood how disarmingly powerful funny clothes can be. Our silly aprons certainly cheered our guests. These grandmothers would look up, then begin laughing and laughing until tears ran from their eyes. My pain was their gain.

Our hostess in the beige coat waved her arm in the air as a signal for where diners still needed to be served. We had to hustle, as there were only ten of us waiters to take care of fifty tables. When people finished eating, a new group of hungry diners sat down to take their place. As I was carefully coached to do, before placing food before a seated guest, I chanted "Ma shih ke du say yo!" This is a Korean way of saying "Bon appetit!"

THE FOLLOWING DAY, Busan Baffer served lunch from a canvas tent erected alongside an abandoned train station in a neighborhood called Busanjin. Situated at the base of the Sujeong mountains, this is one of Busan's poorest neighborhoods. That day's guests were primarily homeless men. Far less amiable than yesterday's chatty grannies, these guys sat alone and were mostly silent inside their private realms of misery.

Given this oppressive atmosphere, I was startled when one guy called out to me, "Hello, USA!"

When I returned his greeting, the man began to talk loudly in excellent and nearly perfect English, no doubt pleased at this opportunity to show off his language skills in front of other diners. Since smoking was forbidden inside the tent, he suggested heading outside where he could have a cigarette while we visited together.

"That's really what I do all day. Smoke and drink. Drink and smoke!" he said with a laugh, though his mirth quickly turned into a phlegmy cough. After he regained his composure, he told me his name was Tae Ha. His teeth were brown around their edges, stained by nicotine.

Part of the national psychology of Koreans is they prefer to cluster in groups and to socialize in packs, Tae Ha told me. But, it's hard for men living on the street to make friends with each other. Ultimately, they are competing for the same handouts of food, or the limited space over a subway grate on a chilly evening.

Tae Ha comes to this tent every Friday to eat; he recognized most of the other regulars. I began to understand there was a pecking order based on whose story was the most pathetic. "See that guy? He's an ex-marine, blinded in action. Him? One of his legs is shorter than the other, and he can't get around without those crutches. Oh, and that guy. He's a bully. Tries to control everyone and make them do what he wants. But, he's just furious because he has liver cancer."

Tae Ha snuffed a cigarette out under his heel and immediately lit another. "Unlike most of the guys you see here today, I can read and write in both Korean and English," he said. "I have nothing in common with them. They think I'm nuts. Me? I couldn't care less."

All he'd eaten since lunch yesterday, Tae Ha claimed, was half a chocolate bar and a bottle of shoju. This drink, distilled from rice, has a high alcohol content—some varieties up to a whopping 45 percent. When I asked Tae Ha how he could afford to buy shoju, he appeared insulted.

"I have a bank account!" he said indignantly. "When I need money, I call someone in my family, and they make a deposit. But I don't spend much, as the only things I ever have to buy are shoju and cigarettes."

More blustery declarations followed, the truth of which I could only wonder about. By his telling, Tae Ha's father was a foreign diplomat. Although he grew up in Iran, Tae Ha came back to South Korea when he was in his twenties and went to college for a couple years in Seoul. Not managing to finish his degree, instead he got a job working as a silkscreen artist at a plastics manufacturer. In the financial crisis of 1997, he was laid off and couldn't find another job. He said his lack of a bachelor's degree is the single biggest challenge he faces; many executive employers will not even consider hiring someone unless they are a college graduate. Another problem is that South Korea's white-collar economy is overwhelmingly centered in Seoul. Most of the work Tae Ha might find in Busan is characterized by one or more of the three Ds: dirty, dangerous, and difficult. Apparently, Tae Ha thinks well enough of himself not to accept such demeaning labor.

At this moment, stereo speakers crackled to life with the loud sound of K-pop music. The chirpy bounce of these melodies, so addictive to Korean adolescents, was in marked contrast to the mood inside the tent, where long rows of tables were set up and several hundred men had gathered. As Tae Ha and I moved to the entrance, I noticed Busan Baffer not only provided free food, but also screened the occasional movie.

I asked Tae Ha if he'd heard of the film that would be shown that evening. He had and told me that the title, translated from Korean, was *I Am King*. It starred a handsome young actor named Ju Ji-Hoon who is very popular in South Korea and told the story of a prince during the Joseon dynasty who does not want to become king, so he hires a beggar to take his place. Hearing this synopsis, I was startled. Wasn't it perverse to subject a crowd of homeless men to such a plot?

Teams of volunteers were lining up, almost all of them men. In place of the girly gingham of yesterday, these guys were mostly dressed in sober business suits over which they wore nylon vests emblazoned with the names and corporate logos of some of South Korea's largest corporations: Hyundai, Daewoo, and KEPCO, which is the country's leading provider of electricity. Evidently, today's acts of community service were also a public relations effort for their employers.

I was about to pick up a tray of food, but Shon pulled me aside. In what seemed an uncharacteristic moment of pessimism, he started to complain about the difficulty he'd had in finding a permanent home for these lunches in Busanjin to replace this dark and cold tent. His offers to refurbish an unused building or even a floor of office space were repeatedly ignored. Shon was particularly incensed that Busan could afford to organize a massive fireworks display each year, which was shot off from the city's main bridge. This money would be better used, he felt, to benefit the truly needy.

"Ah, but most of South Korea's elected officials are not really interested in social welfare," Shon said. "Politicians are much more willing to serve the rich than help the poor, because it is the wealthy who donate to their electoral campaigns."

Such corruption is indicative of what Shon believes is the growth of class consciousness in South Korea and the very deliberate creation of an elite, or what he called an "upper-crust" segment of society. "Our economic crisis is growing," he said, his voice weary. "The rich are richer;

the poor are poorer. The Korean government recognizes this but does not have any policies in place to counteract it."

With a pang of shame, I realized all these charges he'd made against South Korea could be leveled against the United States. I didn't think hearing this would make Shon feel any better, though.

After a moment, Shon shook off his pensive mood and looked at me with a grin. "Well, the soup will not serve itself, will it?" he said. "Let's get busy!"

16

LET THE BIG DOG EAT

BILL WHARTON IS A MUSICIAN WHO CALLS HIMSELF "SAUCE Boss." Wharton uses this stage name because when he's not playing classic blues songs, he is hawking "Liquid Summer," his signature recipe for a hot chili sauce, and cooking enormous pots of piquant soup, which he serves to concert audiences. More intriguing still, at least to me, is that on days off from his paying gigs, Wharton performs for free at soup kitchens, where he preaches what he half-jokingly calls "the gospel of gumbo."

As I'd cooked in charitable settings throughout the United States, I'd often heard about Sauce Boss. Several times, I arrived in a city he'd passed through a few weeks or even months earlier, but people were still talking about how fun and funky he was. Curious to witness one of his amazing feats of mass cookery, I eventually arranged to meet up with him in Manhattan.

Wharton was booked to appear at Terra Blues, a small, dimly lit bar that's a vestige of the dozens of live music clubs once operating on a stretch of Bleecker Street in Greenwich Village. Legends such as Lucky Peterson, Corey Harris, and Saron Crenshaw have all played at Terra, which advertises itself as the only place in New York City where you can hear the blues 365 days a year. On the night I was present, perhaps half of the club's seats were occupied, mostly by foreign tourists. At nearby tables, I heard people speaking Japanese, Russian, and Hebrew.

Finding my way backstage, where I was to meet Sauce Boss before his show, I found out that punctuality is not high on Wharton's list of priorities. While waiting for him to arrive, I passed the time by chatting with members of his two-man band: Justin Headley (drums), a big-bellied teddy bear of a man with bright pink cheeks, and John Hart, who plays bass and holds his lank dark hair off his forehead with a neatly folded bandana. Playing with Sauce Boss, these guys do over one hundred shows a year, often staying out on the road for a month at a time. In addition, they estimate they've fed several hundred thousand people at homeless shelters across America.

"Actually, the vibe at soup kitchens is a lot cooler," Hart told me. "It's not like a typical Friday night bar crowd where people will just show up to see whoever is playing. With homeless people, we come to them, which is so unusual they're genuinely excited to see us."

The blues is a feeling more than a style of music, added Headley. "The songs might be about not having any money, or you've lost your job, your ride, your phone—maybe your wife has left you. But it's more than that. It's uplifting too. Singing the blues is how you encourage yourself when you are going through a rough patch. Our soup kitchen crowds really respond to that."

Three-quarters of an hour late and only a few minutes before he was scheduled to go on, Wharton showed up. Slope-shouldered and slender, he sported a white goatee. He was outfitted in a chef's uniform of a white toque hat, white buttoned-up jacket, and checked pants—a look Wharton made his own by accessorizing it with black-and-white spectator shoes. Sauce Boss looked like a trimmer version of Colonel Sanders, the founder of Kentucky Fried Chicken.

Wharton was unclear who exactly I am or why I was here even though we'd spoken several times on the telephone over the past few days, including earlier that afternoon. I was fairly certain I smelled marijuana smoke on his clothes.

Hart and Headley went off to complete a sound check while Wharton fussed with his mise en place. There were plastic bags full of prepped ingredients for his gumbo (chopped onions, peppers, chicken stock, and shrimp), gallons of filtered water, and a portable cooktop with a propane tank—a setup nearly identical to a field stove that Alexis Soyer cooked on during the Crimean War of the 1850s. Wharton also checked the contents of a black suitcase where he stores Sauce Boss compact discs and bottles of Liquid Summer, which would be on sale after tonight's concert. Since I imagined he was in the midst of a pre-show ritual that shouldn't be disturbed, I watched all this quietly.

I was startled, then, when Wharton jerked his head up suddenly and looked at me with a piercing stare. "G'head. Talk to me, brother," he blurted out.

I asked how he describes his type of blues.

"I play a kind of bottleneck 'Delta Slide,'" he answered. "It's 'gut bucket' blues and very improvisational. I think of myself as someone who just plays what I'm feeling at the time."

Wharton showed me his slide, which is a metal cylinder similar in shape to foil wrapped around the neck of an uncorked wine bottle. He pressed down on this tube, worn on his left hand's index finger, as he rapidly maneuvered it up and down his guitar's fretboard. Delta Slide, he said, began in country music and blues but migrated into rock-and-roll bands ranging from the Doors to Metallica.

Wharton, who is sixty-five, grew up in Orlando, Florida. Even as a young child, he wanted to be a musician. He started performing professionally when he was fourteen. "I talked myself into a gig, and then I taught myself how to play," he explained.

As a teenager Wharton was in a band called the Sapphires, which performed covers of songs by Bob Dylan and the Byrds. Another band of his, the New Englanders, was a "Beatles knockoff." It wasn't until a friend gave him an electric guitar, however, that he found his way to the blues.

"The blues are incredibly poetic, yet they usually have the most basic lyrics," Wharton said. "Think of a phrase like 'I woke up this morning / I had two minds.' Not 'I woke up this morning / I felt schizophrenic' or 'I woke up this morning / I was filled with existential anxiety.' Just 'two minds.' It is simpler, and much better."

Wharton told me about the "Rosie," a work song that was once used to enliven the rhythmic labors of slaves and prisoners working on chain gangs. He thumped his chest with a fist, stomped his foot, and improvised a simple ditty: "Be my woman / [THUD!] / I be your man."

"The music was their meter," he continued. "Every time they pounded another spike in a railroad tie or cracked another rock for a highway, the downbeat was what kept them going. That's the thing about the blues; they're primal."

As a self-described "old white guy," Wharton allowed he's something of a rarity in a musical genre dominated by black men. "But I have an affinity, a true resonance with Africa," he said. "I know what it is to suffer. Things haven't always been easy for me. This is what allows me to righteously sing the blues. I know this life."

What did he mean by this, I asked. How has he suffered?

Wharton fixed me with a cold look. "Let me put it this way," he began. "There was a time when I was sitting in a jail on Good Friday, trying to figure out how to make a noose from a bedsheet, and—"

A stage manager appeared and asked Wharton if he was ready to go on.

I found a seat out front, and a few minutes later Sauce Boss bounded onstage. "We're gonna hang out, cook up a little food, and play some blues!" he shouted. "That sound okay with everybody?"

His audience reacted with tepid applause.

Undeterred, Wharton tore into "Let the Big Dog Eat," the closest thing he's had to a hit. Director Jonathan Demme included this song on the soundtrack of his 1986 film, *Something Wild*.

Wharton's music is fast; real toe-tapping, hip-shaking stuff with long riffs that are both muscular and agile. While he plays, he wears a startled expression on his face as if the melody and lyrics were spontaneously generated, not a well-rehearsed act he does hundreds of times every year.

Some of Sauce Boss's music taps into a rich vein of ribald sexual humor that runs through the blues. (Think of Dave Bartholomew's love song to his own penis "My Ding-a-Ling," a tune made famous by Chuck Berry, or "Ain't Got Nobody to Grind My Coffee," a number Bessie Smith used to feature in her act.) As he sings a risqué lyric such as "Big-legged woman / I can tell what you got cookin' / I want to stir your pot," Wharton rolls his eyes about to make sure his audience gets the double entendre.

Wharton played for a solid hour before he even cast so much as a glance at a large stock pot that was placed center stage. "I've just been having too much fun to start cookin'," he said with a chuckle. As he cranked open the propane tank and lit a flame under the pot, Headley banged the drum set with a mighty crash that made the whole audience jump. After adding chicken stock, onions, and peppers, Wharton popped the lid off a plastic bucket labeled "Savoie's Old-Fashioned Dark Roux." He scooped up a big brown hunk with a metal spoon and showed it to the audience.

"For those of y'all that don't know, roux is just oil and flour—oil and flour that's been all cooked down until it looks like this. Ain't it gorgeous? I think roux looks like molasses! Or chocolate! Roux looks like . . ." Darting his eyes in that berserk way he has, Wharton teased out the obvious response.

"Shit!" several people screamed.

"That's right, it looks like fudge!" he countered, laughing and snorting like he'd never done this gag before. He dropped the roux into the pot. As broth for the gumbo began to heat and thicken, Wharton took a huge gulp from a glass of red wine. "Look around you! Turn your head left, and turn right! Everyone around you looks a little bit different, right? Celebrating our differences is what it's all about! We can put them all in a pot, stir 'em up, and make something that tastes really, really good. And that, my friends, is the gospel of gumbo!"

I wasn't hungry when I'd arrived at Terra Blues, but as a spicy smell floated across the room, I was suddenly ravenous. It was well past 1:00 a.m., however, and Sauce Boss was still whaling away on his electric guitar, with no ladle in sight.

A FEW DAYS later I was upstate in Buffalo, New York, waiting for Wharton to arrive at the Matt Urban Hope Center, a soup kitchen on

Paderewski Street. I talked with Tom Acara, a sales manager for the Conference and Event Center of Niagara Falls, whose wife, Cynthia, had arranged for Sauce Boss to play a free concert here.

"This was never a rich neighborhood, but back in the day it was extremely well taken care of by the proud Polish people who lived here," Acara said. He reminded me that Ignacy Jan Paderewski was a Pole who in the 1920s and 1930s was a world-renowned pianist and composer.

Buffalo is laid out on a plan designed by Frederic Law Olmsted, Acara explained, and was the first place in America to have electric street-lights because city fathers could harness the hydroelectric power of nearby Niagara Falls. Bethlehem Steel once had 18,000 employees in Buffalo. General Motors, Ford, and Allied Chemicals, which made in-digo blue dye for denim jeans (Levi Strauss was Allied's biggest cus-tomer), had prospering factories here.

Those boom times are long gone. Paderewski Street now bisects a neighborhood in ruins, with many boarded-up homes and empty store fronts. The Matt Urban Hope Center typically feeds 150 people a day, though a slightly smaller crowd had shown up to see Sauce Boss, who was once again running behind schedule. Because Wharton was also not answering his cell phone or replying to any of her texts, Cynthia Acara was starting to get anxious.

An hour late, Sauce Boss sauntered in, moving with a confidence that suggested there was no need to rush. On the contrary, his band-mates, Headley and Hart, hurried to arrange their sound equipment as well as Wharton's cooking supplies. They set up in front of a brightly painted wall mural that proclaimed "PATHWAY TO PROSPERITY."

A few minutes later, Wharton launched into "Let the Big Dog Eat." As the song ended, a man in the audience shouted, "I'm the big dog 'round here, and I'm already eating!" He wore a filthy orange T-shirt, and a Styrofoam container full of spare ribs was open on the table before him.

"Okay, big dog," Wharton said to this guy.

Wharton played a few more tunes for this crowd, which was recep-tive to say the least. In fact, the bouncy rhythms and sheer volume of

Sauce Boss's music soon had everyone jacked up. One woman was busily shaking her hands with an imaginary pair of maracas. Another guy was loudly humming along with a tuneless backup vocal. Some people slapped their thighs and jiggled their feet; others tossed back their heads and hooted with pleasure. There was also a whole lot of heckling.

"Man? You only playing two drums?" one man called out to Justin Headley, the percussionist. "I got me a set with some thirty drums in it!"

"That sho' be a raggedy-ass lookin' guitar you got there," someone else yelled, pointing an accusing finger at Wharton's battered black Fender.

"You sho' 'nuf right there!" Wharton agreed.

As each song ended, one woman called out the same question: "When's you gonna start cookin'?"

Wharton was unfazed by this commotion; he seemed to thrive off it.

"I gotta tell y'all, I like to eat!" he said. "My idea of a good time is a big ole bowl of gumbo and a big ole plate of biscuits, each with a fat slice 'a butter on 'em and drippin' with Tupelo honey. Sounds mighty good, don't it?"

Wharton's audience at Terra Blues the other night was primarily young, affluent, and white, which caused him to use certain words and make particular jokes. Here in Buffalo the crowd was older, poorer, and almost completely African American. It was subtle, but Wharton's diction had become looser and lazier for this crowd; consonants were hit softer or disappeared altogether. Sometimes Wharton's patter became impressionistic, even surreal.

After dumping an entire bottle of Liquid Summer hot sauce into the stock pot, Wharton said, "We's a-gonna let it simmer down now into the primordial ooze that squishes between the toes of your taste buds."

Curious about the gumbo's progress, different men and women, sometimes in groups, got up and streamed forward in the middle of one of Wharton's songs to stare down into the bubbling fluid. In Greenwich Village, Wharton had to jump off the stage to interact with the crowd; here, people were coming to him.

When it was time to pray before the meal, Wharton did so in his own inimitable manner. "Can I get an 'Amen'?" he yelled at his prayer's conclusion. Unhappy with the mumbled response, he again shouted, "Is that all you got? Can I get an 'Amen'?"

This time, just about everyone bellowed out "AMEN!"

"Well, thank you, Jesus, and thank you, Leo Fender!" Wharton cried, thereby equating the son of God to Clarence Leonidas ("Leo") Fender, the son of orange grove owners in Anaheim, California, who in 1950 invented the first mass-produced electric guitar.

CYNTHIA AND TOM Acara served up lunch while Wharton sat down to talk with me. How does he keep track of the gumbo's recipe, I wondered aloud, such as when it's time to add new ingredients or if it's finished cooking?

There are occasional mishaps, Wharton admitted. There was a drunk guy in Chicago who cracked a glass beer bottle into the gumbo. And one time in Toronto when Wharton was playing for a crowd of nine thousand people, an enormous kettle slipped off its propane burner. "There was a gumbo tsunami all around the band! But these Canadian guys, they always have their snow shovels handy. They just squeegeed the whole mess off the front of the stage!"

Has cooking in soup kitchens changed him?

"Well, sure! I mean, before I was a pretty slick guy. I played a mean guitar. People wished they were me." Wharton paused and stuck out his tongue to make fun of what he'd just said. "But when I started cooking in soup kitchens, it was a reality check. Life is more than collecting accolades, you know, and getting applause. Now, my main thrill is looking people straight in the eye and giving them respect. It's been bad out there, and it's getting worse. Everyone has a story."

I reminded Wharton that he'd earlier mentioned a suicide attempt in prison—that bedsheet noose? I half-expected him to clam up or simply be evasive in what he said next. Instead, he flashed me a big smile and replied, "I like to smoke pot, okay? So, I was growing some for myself and maybe a little more that I'd share with friends."

He let out a deep sigh.

"What happened to me was a sting! Someone pretended to be a friend of a friend, and I got busted. In some ways, I think of myself as having been a political prisoner. Someone went out of their way to set me up, and I'm still not quite sure why."

Wharton was incarcerated for two months in 1983 and then put on three years' probation. He took his time in prison as an opportunity to start up a new band and spark some jailhouse rock. "We'd have concerts inside where all the players and all the audience were inmates," he said. "It was awesome!"

He then launched into a story about an inmate named Calvin Craddock who'd played bass guitar with him. Eventually this anecdote wound its way to Craddock's grandmother, who grew okra in her garden in Alabama.

"Now, 'round June, Grandma Craddock would go out to her backyard, and she'd cut herself a switch—a nice long and strong switch. Then, she'd go over to her okra plants and whip 'em, just whip 'em good. Well, dontcha' know, come August when she'd look at 'em again, them okra plants would be bushing out all over and just popping with okra!"

By now, Wharton's eyes were rolling around in his head, a visual cue to notice what comes next.

"Well, I think that's a little like you and me, ain't it? You can beat me up! You can whip me and try to keep me down. Maybe some parts of me will fall away, but those are my weakest bits. What's left is my human dignity. You can't take that away from me! And, long's as I got my human dignity, I can still blossom and grow!"

On the flight from Buffalo back to New York City, I looked out the plane's window and mulled over Sauce Boss's act. He'd laid on the corn pone routine pretty thick, which made certain details of his biography a bit difficult to believe. Then again, he told awfully good stories. Did it really matter whether or not they were true?

There was one thing I knew for certain, however. Sauce Boss was about as close to a reincarnation of Alexis Soyer as I was ever going to see.

Both Soyer and Wharton were gifted musicians and performers as well as highly theatrical chefs. Each had fashioned a sturdy public persona, complete with eye-catching costumes. Neither saw any reason not to enjoy attracting attention to themselves while in the process of helping others. No air of holiness hung about these two men's actions, so the recipients of their generosity never felt patronized or subjected to benevolent condescension. Finally, though all too aware of their own weaknesses, Wharton and Soyer didn't let their failings prevent them from attempting to do good.

Wharton was something of a pothead and had a frustrating tendency to inconvenience others with his inability to show up on time. What mattered more, though, is that he does always arrive, and he then puts on a supremely entertaining show for people who really need cheering up. Best of all, he feeds them a soul-stirring meal. Sauce Boss deeply enjoys what he is doing, and as a result you can taste this love in what he's cooking.

And that, my friends, is the gospel of gumbo.

17

PEOPLE DON'T PAY FOR FAT

Y OU'VE SEEN PICTURES OF HER. A DIGNIFIED OLDER WOMAN who always has on a broad-brimmed hat decorated with ostrich feathers. She wears a floor-length dress and carries a parasol to shield her skin from the sun. Correction: this lady has no skin. She's a living, breathing skeleton called La Catrina.

Christmas has Santa Claus for its popular mascot, and every Easter, out hops a bunny rabbit. But down Mexico way in late October when everyone celebrates El Dia de Los Muertos (The Day of the Dead), La Catrina is this holiday's icon as families and friends gather to celebrate the memory of those who've died.

El Dia de Los Muertos is not a sad time. It is a playful occasion when a comforting illusion is put forth that the dearly departed are not really gone, but can be summoned through stories told and parties arranged in their honor. So, it's fitting that La Catrina was my constant companion when I traveled to Guadalajara to cook a special dinner one October for a group of homeless street kids and transgendered sex workers.

This visit came about when a mutual friend put me in touch with Reverend David Kalke, a bishop in something called the Ecumenical Catholic Church. This church has nothing whatsoever to do with the Vatican or the pope. In fact, Kalke's work often pits him directly against the Roman Catholic Church, which at least in Guadalajara tends to address more diligently the needs of affluent people, not the pains of the poor. Relentless in his advocacy for the underprivileged, Kalke is one of the bravest and most progressively minded people I have ever met. He may have a weakness for stupid old jokes, but Reverend Kalke is no-body's fool.

This was immediately evident when we talked on the phone before I traveled south to be with him. Kalke said he would very much like to help me organize "una fiesta," but wanted to be realistic about difficulties we might face in getting a crowd to show up.

"I work with a community of outcasts," he explained. "These kids are not used to anyone doing something nice for them. A few will be suspicious of why you would cook a dinner in their honor. They may even imagine it is some sort of trap by the police. I don't think we have to be too terribly concerned about violence, but it's always good to be cautious. I'm willing to take the risk if you are. Why don't you think about it and call me back?"

Given the quantity and brutality of murders that Mexico's endless drug wars have caused in the past decade, I was unsettled by Kalke's casual mention of violence. After puzzling this over for a while, I decided to take my chances and arranged to spend a few days with him in Guadalajara.

THE WEEK BEFORE I left I was immersed in preparation for a dinner party James asked me to cook at our apartment for a client of his, Laura Alber. She was the CEO of Williams-Sonoma, a chain of retail stores selling high-end cookware and kitchen accessories. In the days leading up to this affair, James's assistant, Hillary, would regularly call me, nearly breathless with excitement, as she had news of yet another celebrity chef who'd responded "yes" to our invitation, a list that included Éric Ripert, Marcus Samuelsson, and Padma Lakshmi.

Among our circle of friends, James and I have a reputation for being attentive hosts. We work hard to make sure a good time is had by all. For this shindig, though, people were not excited to attend out of any love for us. These chefs and foodies had product lines such as pots, pans, dish towels, spice mixes, and cookbooks they hoped to sell at Williams-Sonoma. Dinner with Laura Alber was like asking a bunch of actors if they'd care to chow down with Steven Spielberg. Everyone—and I do mean *everyone*—we invited said yes. Then, the guest list kept growing due to the dreaded "plus one."

What to prepare for this group? Well, if Alexis Soyer could make his rich clientele from the Reform Club try a soup recipe he invented before bringing it to Dublin during the potato famine in the late 1840s, I decided I could use the best chefs in New York as taste-testers for entrées I'd soon cook for transgender prostitutes in Mexico.

A couple of nights later, our guests arrived—all sixty-five of them, including Dana Cowin, the editor of *Food and Wine* magazine; Melissa Clark, food columnist for the *New York Times*; and Pilar Guzman, who was editor of *Martha Stewart Living*. James and I have enough plates, cutlery, and wineglasses to accommodate this many, but we don't have five dozen chairs in our apartment. As a result, some guests sat, others stood, and still more plopped down on the floor around a coffee table in our living room. (I even found a giddy threesome sprawled across James's and my bed.) This sounds haphazard, but it kept things lively. It can be grim when you're trapped at a dinner table between two people who are not making any effort to be friendly. No one had to suffer such a fate at this party, which was freewheeling and loose.

At the end of the evening, a couple of nice things happened. Laura Alber sidled up to me and pressed an envelope into my hand. "Very few people have one of these," she said in a stage whisper. "Don't lose it."

The envelope contained what looked like a white plastic credit card. On its front was the Williams-Sonoma logo as well as the words "FOR PROFESSIONAL CHEFS." This card and its corresponding VIP number would give me a 25 percent discount on anything I bought at a Williams-Sonoma store. Wow! The discount was nice, but I mostly kept staring at the all-capital-lettered words as if I'd been magically anointed. Best of all was when Éric Ripert sought me out as he was leaving. A Frenchman, cookbook author, and television personality, Ripert is also the chef and co-owner of Le Bernadin, a seafood restaurant in Midtown Manhattan that's considered one of the finest dining establishments in the world. I told Ripert how much James and I had liked our meal at Le

Bernadin when we'd been there to celebrate our wedding anniversary a few months before. Ripert accepted my compliment before offering me one of his own.

"Thank you, but what *you* did tonight!" he said. "I would never attempt to cook for this many people in my own home. I respect your accomplishment."

Ripert didn't beg me to give him my recipe for shrimp with pumpkin seed sauce. Still, it was a great moment and empowered me to think I was ready for El Dia de Los Muertos.

THE SECOND-LARGEST METROPOLIS in Mexico, Guadalajara has a population of eight million people—about the same as New York City. Capitol of the state of Jalisco, this region was settled by Spaniards in the 1540s, only a few decades after Hernán Cortés first conquered Montezuma. Set in a region found to be extremely rich in both silver and gold, the city is surrounded by desert but has an unexpectedly robust water supply from a natural aquifer.

As we drove into town from the airport, Kalke told me about the first time he conducted a Eucharist liturgy here. Shortly before that morning's service began, he was alarmed to discover there was no Communion wine. He instructed an old man who was the church's caretaker to hurry off to the market and buy some vino. Unfortunately, Kalke was unaware that in Guadalajara's local dialect of Spanish, "vino" can refer to wine, but is more typically used to mean tequila. He was already standing at the altar when the caretaker brought him a chalice filled with potent juice from the blue agave plant. Flustered but unwilling to turn the Eucharist into Margaritaville, Kalke made the questionable decision to drain this entire chalice in one gulp while ordering the caretaker to go find some vino tinto (red wine).

"I don't remember much of the service after that," he admitted.

Kalke grew up on a farm in rural Iowa. He must come from hardy stock, as his mother was 101 and still healthy when I was visiting him. After college he spent several years in Chile, which was roiled by a bloody aftermath of the 1973 US-backed coup that deposed President Salvador Allende.

"There were human rights violations going on in Chile that no one has ever heard of," Kalke claimed.

Once back in America, Kalke tried to raise awareness of the political situation in Chile by going on a cross-country speaking tour under the auspices of the International Association against Torture. As a result of this work, he began to think about liberation theology. He attended both Union Theological Seminary in New York City and the Hamma School of Theology, an institution for the training of Lutheran ministers in Canton, Ohio. After graduating from Hamma, Kalke focused on work with refugees, spending a great deal of time traveling in Central and South America.

I asked what is his definition of "liberation theology"?

"You are involved in a political process, and this reflects on your actions, theologically," he replied. "You are in the streets, working with people who've been kidnapped, battered, or 'disappeared.' You're not sitting in your office, smoking a pipe, and writing books about the historical Jesus."

Kalke relished being in the streets. I also got the impression that he enjoyed being a thorn in the side of his bourgeois congregants a great deal more than they liked being pricked. Recounting his decades of parish ministry, Kalke acknowledged his activism often wore out its welcome. His career ended in San Bernardino, California, where, true to form, he was fired from his church job after devoting too much of his attention to building a community center for gang members.

Kalke moved to Mexico in 2009, ostensibly to retire. Instead, he started a social service agency called Comunidad de los Martines, which is named for St. Martin of Tours, Martin Luther, St. Martin of Porres, and Martin Luther King Jr.

By now, we'd arrived in downtown Guadalajara. Kalke took me to see Plaza Tapatia, a multi-tiered park with fountains and covered arcades, located directly behind the imposingly grand Catholic Cathedral. Plaza Tapatia is hub to most of the city's sex trade. As we walked about, Kalke explained that there are an estimated three thousand female prostitutes in Guadalajara and five hundred transgendered sex workers (individuals who were born male but identify and dress as women). Many of their customers are white American men who've come to Mexico as sex tourists, or to retire.

"I suppose I could have been one of those guys," Kalke said, with a sigh.

Seeing how blatantly these assignations were arranged in Plaza Tapatia—I noticed many portly gringos talking to young girls and boys—was incredible. Even with the low cost of living in Mexico, it was pitiful how little these prostitutes were paid for intimate acts. Oral sex earned the equivalent of six U.S. dollars, while the fee for vaginal or anal sex was somewhere around twenty dollars. Transgendered prostitutes, I was interested to learn, get paid more than other types of sex workers. One of Kalke's goals was to unionize all the prostitutes, as they are in Argentina and the Netherlands.

After this brief look at central Guadalajara, Kalke drove us about twenty minutes away to Polanco, the part of town where he lived. Polanco is a poor district settled by squatters who simply laid claim to this land; most of his neighbors do not have title deeds to their property or houses. Kalke opened a coffee shop here, Cafe Los Martines, that operates as a hangout spot for local kids where they can be shielded from drugs, gangs, and other dangerous temptations. Inside, there was a rack stocked with literature about safe sex and a box of free condoms that's always in need of refilling.

At the café I met two Mexican girls, Carla and Yvonne—Carla was a student in culinary school, and Yvonne was a single mother—as well as a young man named Benjamin. Kalke said these three would assist me in cooking for the next couple of days. I also was accompanied on this trip by two pals from New York, Mark and Katie, and had arranged to bring down my niece, Amy, as well as her friend Mia, from San Francisco.

The café's kitchen had a small oven with only one rack inside. Kalke had brought a four-cup food processor from his own kitchen as well as a couple of Pyrex pans. I was aghast at the prospect of preparing enough food for 150 people with this insufficient equipment but tried to hide my fears.

"Is everything what you expected?" Kalke asked.

"No, it's better!" I lied. "This will be terrific!"

Shopping in Guadalajara's sprawling open-air produce market, trying to convert my recipes into the metric system while speaking Spanish, was my first challenge. I had to keep repeating to myself "one kilo equals 2.2 pounds." Adding to the difficulty was that Kalke, in his well-meaning way, thwarted my plans at nearly every turn.

He had preordered a lot of groceries based on a tentative menu we'd discussed a few weeks earlier—this despite my specifically asking him not to shop for me, as every chef wants to choose the ingredients she or he is going to cook. I was woozy to see how much Kalke had bought. There were enormous mesh sacks holding onions, each the size of a grapefruit; dozens of heads of garlic; bunches of cilantro that resembled shrubbery; and woven baskets spilling over with tomatoes, avocados, and tomatillos. Clear plastic bags full of chicken, pork, and beef were so heavy I could barely lift them. By my hurried calculations, there was almost a pound of protein for each guest expected to attend our party, where the menu would also include rice, beans, and several salads. Seeing all this stuff piled up, even I, with my woefully deficient ability for portion control, knew there was way too much food.

Kalke refused to listen. Poor folks in Guadalajara eat very simply, he said, and are accustomed to having little more for dinner each night than a glass of milk and a piece of bread. If this was going to be una fiesta, we needed to really give them something to remember!

"Everything will get eaten, Stephen," he promised. "What's not consumed at the party will either go to a school for the blind or to my neighbors, who've never seen a buffet like you are going to make."

I wanted to believe him, but I also knew it would take an incredible amount of work—and time!—to prepare all these groceries in the tiny kitchen at Cafe Los Martines.

We worked like demons for two solid days. Knife cuts, steamy temperatures, buzzing flies, upset stomachs—nothing could stop us. Not that I didn't feel unhinged at times, swinging from euphoria ("these caper-stuffed meatballs are fabulous!") to an all-consuming rage ("this goddamn oven is killing me!").

Late on our first afternoon, Kalke showed up. He was accompanied by Pedro Chavez, who was his primary contact with the city's sex workers. Chavez was thirty-five years old, stocky and tall but going slightly wiggly at the waist. Training to be a lawyer, he also owned a funeral home in Compostela, a flyspeck of a village about an hour and a half outside of Guadalajara. Chavez suggested we head over to Doña Diabla, a gay bar downtown where our event would take place on the following evening.

Inside the bar, one wall was decorated with photographs of María Félix. She was Mexico's biggest movie star of the 1940s, what's often called the golden age of Mexican cinema, and *Doña Diabla (Madam Devil)* is her best-loved film. Along another wall was a painted mural where large hands were shown holding cigarettes or making the peace symbol. Several of the fingers had their flesh eaten away, with bare bones showing through. This death-in-life theme was also evident on a Dia de Los Muertos altar arranged near the bar's entrance. On it were placed candles, crucifixes, flowers, and skulls made from sugar candy as well as photographs of several transgendered sex workers who had died or were killed in the past few years.

As Kalke and I looked at this macabre display, he said, "Pedro was concerned I would disapprove of having images of Jesus on a Day of the Dead altar." He then shook his head and smiled. "I would think by now, Pedro would know I'm no fiend for doctrinal purity."

Chavez offered to take me on a tour of several neighborhoods where transgendered prostitutes—Chavez referred to them simply as "trans"— ply their trade. He knew several dozen locales around town, including storefronts that appear to be hair salons but are actually brothels.

Chavez hailed a taxi, and as we rode he explained that clients sometimes become furious when they discover they've ended up with something different than what they expected. "We've had trans murdered, and they're from out of state," he said. "Their families, even if we are able to contact them, sometimes refuse to claim the body." In several of these sad cases, Chavez had arranged for a funeral and burial at his own expense from his Compostela mortuary.

We eventually ended up at the Posada San Juan, a hotel where accommodations can be had for the "Happy Time Rate" of twelve U.S. dollars for three hours. Rooms are also rented for considerably shorter amounts of time—twenty or even ten minutes.

Despite this, Chavez wanted me to know that Posada San Juan was a "respectable sex hotel, not some trashy place," which is why he keeps a small office here from where he distributes free condoms and lubricant as well as pamphlets about AIDS transmission. He also conducts rapid HIV tests. Of several hundred given during the last month, Chavez told me 7 percent tested positive.

As we talked, prostitutes drifted in and out of Chavez's office to say hello or grab condoms. Blessed with the compassionate patience of a high school guidance counselor, Chavez remembered key facts about each—what state they come from, how old they were, how long ago they'd gotten breast implants—so they felt noticed and cared for. It was brisk outside, but most of the women were dressed in miniskirts and skimpy blouses to highlight their cleavage.

Maybelline, age twenty, told Chavez about spending a night in jail. Jasmine, who was seventeen, wore a bright pink shade of lipstick; when she smiled, I saw braces on her teeth. Fanny, age thirty-seven, had a slightly tougher attitude but was dressed like she'd just stepped off the beach at Acapulco. She wore a turquoise sweater, a white skirt, and a pair of platform sandals.

"Trans usually begin at about age fifteen, but by their early twenties they've usually gotten fat," Chavez said while he gave his own belly an affectionate rub. "People don't pay for fat!"

I was impressed by the beauty of these women. When I asked Chavez if most had undergone an operation to surgically remove their penises, he was shocked.

"No! Why would they?" he replied. "That is their moneymaker!"

The majority of men who hire a trans, he said, want to be anally penetrated. A lot of these clients are Roman Catholic, married, and staunchly homophobic. The idea of having sex with a man is unthinkable to them, yet being fucked by a woman is not.

THE FOLLOWING MORNING, I was back in the café kitchen working with the rest of my crew. We cooked until 5:30 p.m., when we loaded up Kalke's van to take all the food over to Doña Diabla.

Overnight, the nightclub had been lavishly redecorated. There were many vases full of marigolds, the traditional flower for Day of the Dead parties. Votive candles were scattered across the dining tables, and colorful slashes of papel picado (Mexican cut-paper streamers) hung from the ceiling.

Only one problem remained: a lack of guests. At 8:30 p.m., when the party was supposed to begin, there were ten people present. An hour later, thirty. It was obvious the evening was a bust. Pedro Chavez kept muttering about his list of 150 guests who were "definitely" coming.

Yeah, right. And I am Pancho Villa.

It's not like Kalke hadn't warned me. From the beginning, he'd been honest about the challenges we'd confront in throwing a party for people whom life had not treated too well.

That's when I noticed a group of about a dozen young men who had just arrived. Several wore baseball caps with John Deere logos on them; their blue jean pants were dirty and frayed. I couldn't figure out what they were doing at this dinner. To me, they appeared angry and hostile—the sort of guys who are looking for trouble and might like to beat up a gay or transgendered person. Oh, great! On top of everything else, now we were going to have the violence Kalke wasn't concerned about. I rushed off to find him and announced what I believed was the imminent danger presented by these guys.

Kalke told me to relax.

"They are farm boys who've grown up way out in the countryside," he explained. "Often they are the eldest son, and their parents say to them, you need to go to Guadalajara, make some money, and send it home. These young men take a bus for many hours, only to find themselves dropped off in the center of a city with as many people as New York. Uneducated, without any job skills, the only thing they can do to survive is sell their bodies."

Hearing this, my perceptions changed instantly. Some of these boys looked to be barely teenagers. I had judged them as troublemakers, but the trouble was in my mind. I made an instant decision: even if this small crowd was all that showed up, I would do everything possible to make sure these thirty people, and these farm boys, had a night to remember.

Despite the late hour, neither Kalke nor Chavez wanted to serve food until more guests arrived. Instead, they let the show begin.

The show! This was another sore point. When Kalke told me our party would feature three different drag queens, with each doing a set of three songs, I complained that this was too much of a good thing. Kalke brushed me off.

Dressed all in black leather, with boots that had six-inch heels, the first singer was especially kooky. She raced about the club and at one point hopped up on the bar, threading her way through beer bottles and shot glasses of tequila that were littered there. Mexico has its own pantheon of pop divas such as Gloria Trevi, Belinda, and Thalia; it's their music this singer and the two other performers lip-synced. As they did their high-energy acts, more people kept appearing. I now understood that those already present were calling friends on their cell phones, telling them the party was fun and to get over to Doña Diabla.

When the show ended around 10:30 p.m., the crowd had swollen in size to what looked like 175. With every seat in the bar full, Kalke determined it was time to eat.

Amy, Mia, Katie, and I were positioned behind a long table. In front of us were platters loaded with food. Kalke said a short prayer, and his "amen" was like a gun being fired before a horse race. Guests came charging at us from all directions. There was no lining up in a queue or any order whatsoever. We frantically scooped up chicken, meatballs, pork, rice, and salad as plates were shoved at us from every angle and direction. "Buen provecho," I kept saying over and over. People were eating like they'd never seen food before. After everyone had been helped to at least two plates each, the commotion gradually began to subside. Only then did I allow myself to truly experience the party.

I noticed that one table by the wall was taken over by a large group of trans, all sitting together and being watched over by Giovanni. He was a guy I saw the evening before working as a night clerk at Posada San Juan—the "respectable" sex hotel where Pedro Chavez had his office. Giovanni was now behaving like he was Professor Henry Higgins, gesturing to one girl to put a napkin in her lap while she ate and to another to lower her voice a bit.

When I pointed this out to Kalke, once more he let me know that appearances can be deceiving. "I'm not sure sometimes if Giovanni is a good shepherd to his flock or if he's acting as their pimp." He then looked at me and laughed. "But if everything made sense, we wouldn't call it the underworld, right?"

The festivities went on well past midnight, with still more guests arriving and lots more food served.

Sometime in the early morning hours, there was a special award ceremony in which Kalke asked the five of us Americans to step forward. We were handed certificates with gold foil stickers and ribbons as well as gifts. Mine was a figurine of La Catrina about sixteen inches high and made of metal. She was a bony and ugly hag, but it was love at first sight.

When a DJ amped up the music, a couple of trans pulled me into their circle on the dance floor. I was still clutching this skeleton in my hand as I boogied for a while with Fanny and then with Jasmine. In the room's flashing lights, Jasmine's braces were blinking like sparklers. I looked around at one point and saw Kalke smiling at me. He made the thumbs-up sign with both his hands.

18

THE WANDERING
AND THE LOST

D ROP. WAIT NINETY SECONDS. LIFT, DRAIN, AND REPEAT. This wasn't a hard series of tasks to remember. With them in mind, I submerged mesh baskets of flounder filets into sizzling vats of vegetable shortening until I produced a fresh batch of golden, crispy fish.

Drop. Wait ninety seconds. Lift, drain, and repeat.

These brief instructions on how to operate a Hobart Vulcan deep fryer were provided by Rob Rice, executive chef at the Midnight Mission, which is the largest continuously operating social service agency and homeless shelter in Los Angeles. On average, a crowd of one thousand hungry people arrive every day for breakfast, lunch, and dinner. This adds up to nearly one hundred thousand meals a month, or over one million annually.

That's a lot of flounder.

Once I was acquainted with the Vulcan, Rice took a few empty cardboard boxes that had held the frozen filets and flattened them out onto the floor to absorb splatters of grease. Advertising copy printed in bright red lettering on each carton proclaimed the fish to be "Beer-Battered!"

The phrase struck me as unfortunate, since the same might be said, I thought, for many of my fellow kitchen workers. Most were enrolled in drug and alcohol rehabilitation programs run by the mission, and in a typical greeting, each man told me his name, recited what substance he'd used, for how long, and then concluded by proclaiming the duration of his sobriety.

Noe was addicted to amphetamines for most of his life, he said, but had been sober for seven months. Adopted from an orphanage in India by a single woman who lived in Beverly Hills, Noe was hyperactive as a child, so he was put on Ritalin in the second grade.

"Was I born an addict," he asked me, "or was this learned behavior?"

Before I could answer, I was shaking hands with Alex, who had smoked crack cocaine for thirty-five years but was eighteen months clean. "I fell into fear" was his simple explanation for a decades-long drug habit.

These guys obviously respected Rob Rice, who oversaw all meals but was primarily responsible for food served to 250 live-in residents as well as 60 people who are full-time staff members at the Midnight Mission.

A lean, attractive forty-two-year-old, Rice was a marathon runner who taught yoga on the weekends. In earlier jobs, he'd consulted with the actor Mark Wahlberg and his brothers, Donnie and Paul, when they opened a chain of casual dining restaurants called Wahlburgers. Rice had also been a corporate culinary trainer for Wolfgang Puck, interviewing chefs for jobs in Puck's restaurants such as Spago, Chinois, and Postrio. Rice liked to surprise prospective hires with a "grocery bag test" in which the chef wannabe was handed a sack full of unlikely items—maybe sardines, radishes, and chocolate—and told to make something good-tasting in the next forty-five minutes.

"Rarely was anything created you'd call inspired, but even being able to make something edible under pressure like that told me something," Rice said.

Since his own career has had its share of ups and downs, he's sensitive to attitudes he occasionally sees among volunteers who drop by to help serve meals at the Midnight Mission. "Sometimes they'll turn up their noses and say 'people who end up here have made a series of bad choices.' Come on! Let's take the judgment out of it, shall we? We are all human. Everyone's capable of good and bad. Some of us were just luckier to get away with more without getting caught."

Rice continued. "I like to think I have a pretty good understanding of the human condition. I don't baby the guys who work here, but sometimes people need a couple of second chances before they can get it right."

A FEW MEN clustered about Rice as he coached them through a recipe for glazed carrots and chickpeas. He planned to serve this the following day at a special lunch in honor of the Persian New Year, or Nowruz.

"I wish I could add some rose water, but I don't have a lot of that lying around," he observed.

With an expected head count of two thousand guests, Rice was assembling ingredients for chicken marinated in yogurt and Middle Eastern spices; rice with saffron, currants, and apricots; and a mixed green salad.

As he went over all this, Rice offered impromptu lessons on the health benefits of turmeric and ginger root. He explained why poultry's dark and white meat are different in texture and flavor. And he taught an easy way to peel shallots: "Blanche 'em in a little hot water, and the papery skin will just slide off."

Watching this shallot-peeling tip was a guy I hadn't seen yesterday. He looked on with awe as if Rice had done an incredible feat. When I smiled at him, the man grinned back and said, "Hi, I'm Sam. I used to drink a liter of vodka every day, but now I've been clean for sixty-four days!"

Such intricacies of cooking technique might seem effete in the setting of most soup kitchens, yet Rice was trying to show these men how a real restaurant operates. Thanks to his past career, Rice has connections to dining spots all over Los Angeles; many have hired guys who trained with him at the Midnight Mission. In Rice's experience, kitchens are a meritocracy, and restaurant work is often a first leg up for people with criminal records.

"An executive chef shows up one day and discovers one of his sous-chefs has quit," he explained. "He'll go into the dishwashing pit and ask if anyone knows how to roll ravioli. Some Mexican guy will shout 'I do!' and he'll be promoted from dishwasher to prep cook, just like that. This happens in kitchens all over L.A. every day. No one cares if you've ever been arrested. If you know how to make pastry dough, that's your opportunity to advance."

Before he can teach these men how to cook, Rice must contend with health problems they face while transitioning from their former life of substance abuse. He's seen enough to recognize advanced cases of hepatitis C, for instance, where a person's liver stops functioning. "Any time a person's skin is light green, that's not good," he said.

Rice is convinced that nutritious eating eases the pain these guys feel as they detoxify.

"It's a little like a spiritual conversion, or being 'born again,'" he suggested. "It is one day—and one salad—at a time."

Alex, of the thirty-five-year crack-smoking habit, agreed. His cholesterol levels had gone down dramatically since he'd been on Rice's diet. "Before I came here, my idea of fresh produce was opening a can of creamed corn," he said. "Rob changed all that."

Rice must be flexible with his meal planning. In what seems karmic payback for all those grocery bag tests he inflicted, Rice contends with a haphazard food supply at the Midnight Mission. Chickpeas in his glazed carrot recipe came from the Federal Emergency Management Agency. "The beans aren't whole but cracked into pieces, so they can't be sold," he said. "They'll either end up as a food drop to a FEMA refugee camp or get sent to me."

The biggest challenge Rice faced that morning was a vegetable grower from California's central valley who arrived with dozens of wooden pallets, each piled with crates of green beans. It was not only a massive quantity but also on the verge of spoiling. Green beans can last two weeks after being picked, Rice explained, but he guessed these would begin to grow mold in the next thirty-six hours.

"Most of our clientele? You show them a cucumber and a zucchini, side by side, they won't know the difference. They've been raised on fast food, and when I say 'raised,' I mean eating at McDonald's every day practically their whole life. It's a big problem, because unless I smother vegetables with cheese sauce, they don't eat them."

Rice and I stared at the pallets of green beans stacked from floor to ceiling. It would require a tsunami of cheese sauce to cover all these.

THE MIDNIGHT MISSION is located in a part of town tourists rarely see. I have visited Los Angeles dozens of times but never ventured to these blocks just a short walk from the Staples Center, L.A.'s enormous sports and entertainment complex. This downtown district is currently undergoing a renaissance, I learned, with elegantly faded office buildings and boarded-up movie palaces from Hollywood's heyday in the 1920s and 1930s being refurbished and given new life.

Yet, as I headed east on Sixth and crossed over Los Angeles Street, in the space of a few short steps there was a distinct difference in atmosphere, like an invisible line divided wealth from poverty. Civic boosters and real estate brokers may have dubbed this neighborhood Central City East, but everyone else calls it "Skid Row."

The term dates back to the seventeenth century, when it referred to a slippery, muddy passageway through the woods along which felled timber was hauled. This rough path, especially at its shoreline terminus, was the "main drag" of a logging camp; most of the bars and brothels patronized by men working in such camps were built nearby. By the end of the nineteenth century, the name Skid Row was used for any locale—from San Francisco's Tenderloin District to the Bowery in Lower Manhattan—where men who were down on their luck might gather.

Today, Los Angeles contains the largest homeless population in the United States. As a result, a vast section of the city's downtown is nearly impassable, with sidewalks blocked by overloaded shopping carts, garbage bags full of who knows what, and mysterious bundles tied with rope. All of this is jumbled and tumbled together, as if there'd recently been an earthquake or a massive fire and thousands of people were forced to grab whatever they could salvage and camp here, in the open. Buzzing swarms of flies are drawn to the filth and decay.

Improvised as these living situations appear at first, a closer look shows them to be more or less permanent installations. Pieces of blown-out furniture such as sofas, bureaus, and even dining tables were arranged to create outdoor rooms, though plenty of people were also sitting on plastic lawn chairs or buckets that once held Sheetrock compound. They were smoking and drinking beer, talking or dozing. This vista of strangely relaxed misfortune stretched for many blocks around the Midnight Mission, which was founded in 1914.

"FOR THE PAST century, we've been a beacon of light for those with nowhere to turn," said Ryan Navales, the Midnight Mission's public affairs coordinator, who gave me a tour around the facility. "Downtown Los Angeles has long been a magnet for drifters and people hoping for a lucky break. Whole families straggled out here during the Great Depression. Farmers fled the Dust Bowl. Veterans have poured in following every war the United States has fought in."

A third of the homeless in Los Angeles have substance abuse problems, Navales estimated. "At Midnight Mission, our focus is on them. Booze is a bigger problem than drugs because it's cheaper, it's legal, and much easier to get."

He then corrected himself. "We shouldn't talk about the homeless as if they are all the same. 'Homeless' is an adjective, not a noun. It's a homeless man, a homeless woman, or a homeless child. There are 58,000 homeless individuals in Los Angeles and just as many different reasons for how they ended up this way." Putting this number in context, Navales told me that 58,000 people was an over-capacity crowd at the Los Angeles Dodgers' baseball stadium.

Navales shared his own story of living on the streets. He comes from a small town called Pilgrim in the High Sierra of Northern California. Though he made his living as a carpenter, Navales said he was also a "Microsoft-trained tech engineer" who'd been financially successful enough to own a three-bedroom house in Pasadena. After developing a taste for alcohol, however, he graduated to heroin. "I had run amok. My family and parents reached their limits with me. I burned every bridge possible."

Three years ago, a cousin dropped him off at the Midnight Mission. All that was left of his life was in one backpack. Fifty pounds heavier than he is now, Navales said it was hard for him to walk, as he could only shuffle his feet along like an old man. "I was swollen up like a tick from all the alcohol in my system. I had a distended liver. I was pissing blood and addicted to librium."

Navales paused, his eyes having welled up while recalling these memories. He took a few slow breaths before continuing. "I recognized this might be my last chance. I grabbed on to what was available here, and I got busy getting sober. This place saved my ass. My life now is smaller than before, but it's manageable."

During our time together, Navales repeatedly emphasized three things.

First, the Midnight Mission does not take any government money and is completely funded by the donations of individuals, families, and corporations. Lately, some of the largest financial contributions come from wealthy Iranians who live in the Pacific Palisades.

"They wanted to give back to the community, but there really aren't many homeless or needy people in their neighborhood," Navales explained, while smirking at his understatement. (Pacific Palisades is one of the most affluent zip codes in the United States.) "So, three years ago, they decided to hold a Nowruz celebration here at the mission. We cook up traditional Persian food, and we close down Sixth Street, where we arrange tables for an open-air meal. You'll see what it's like tomorrow; it's really great!"

Second, the Midnight Mission is one of America's largest organizers of 12-step meetings for the homeless. In the three days I spent there, I was frequently asked if I was in the "program" or a "friend of Bill's." They were not inquiring about my affinity for President Bill Clinton but rather Bill W., one of the cofounders of Alcoholics Anonymous.

Finally, the Midnight Mission is both nonsectarian and nonreligious. "There is no praying here and no church," Navales said. "You don't have to do anything to get help except ask for it."

THIS LAST WOULD not have pleased the Midnight Mission's founder, Tom Liddecoat, who was a firm believer in the power of prayer. Brother Tom, as he preferred to be called, also made sure his hungry visitors were indoctrinated with the Christian faith before they were offered a single bite of food.

I learned some of this history from Larry Adamson, president and CEO of the Midnight Mission, who is only the fourth director in its one hundred–year history. As an icebreaker when we first met in his office, I asked how it felt to run America's largest soup kitchen. This proved to be an unfortunate blunder.

"We are *not* a soup kitchen," Adamson replied, his voice impatient. "We don't serve soup. I want to banish that stereotype. Our executive chef, Rob Rice, used to work for Wolfgang Puck, so we have some very well-fed homeless people, trust me."

What's more, because of many donations of fresh food, Adamson estimated the average cost of these excellent meals served at the Midnight Mission was less than fourteen cents each. "But the unexpected arrival of food each day puts major demands on Rob," Adamson explained. "When a truckload of broccoli shows up, he has to decide quickly what to do with it."

I thought of those about-to-go-moldy green beans.

"Which, in a funny sort of way, brings us back to our creation a century ago," Adamson said. He then told me the story of Brother Tom.

Thomas Liddecoat was a broker for fruits and vegetables who sold these perishable goods to mom-and-pop grocery stores operating along Main and Los Angeles Streets, the two avenues that defined downtown L.A. in the twentieth century's first decades. In those years, the city's population was growing rapidly, as was its homeless population. When Liddecoat saw how many veterans from World War I and other vagrants were living on the edges of downtown, he had an idea. After work, he began to make return visits to his customers and retrieve whatever food they felt was about to spoil and planned to throw away. Liddecoat brought this salvaged refuse back to his house, where his wife, Mary, and he would cook and serve it to hungry men—but only after they'd listened to one of his sermons.

"Liddecoat was a lay preacher of the Pentecostal faith," Adamson said, "and he could deliver a blazing message! His talks were lengthy too, so by the time a meal was finally served, it was often late at night. Legend has it people would say 'oh, that's the place where you can get dinner at midnight,' and the name stuck."

Intrigued by what Adamson told me, I later did more research only to find accounts of Liddecoat's life are vague and frequently contradictory. He eventually became a celebrity and conducted many newspaper interviews. Whether because of unscrupulous journalists or Liddecoat's own burnishing of his past, certain stories that may or may not be true nonetheless became established facts over time.

Born in 1864 in England, Liddecoat immigrated to the United States and ended up in Colorado because his father caught gold fever. Liddecoat was often quoted as saying that he spent his teenage years being raised by American Indians, witnessed the Wounded Knee Massacre in 1890, rode with Buffalo Bill, and ate wild venison, which he called his favorite meat dish. Liddecoat usually completed this portion of his biography by telling of a promise he made to God. In several printed stories, his wording is nearly identical: "One night, when the moon and stars were shining brightly, I rode on my horse to a secluded spot and promised God I would be his worker if he would let me prosper."

At the turn of the century, after establishing a successful produce business in Colorado, Liddecoat came to Los Angeles, where he expanded into a wholesale operation. Apparently God saw fit to answer his in-the-saddle prayer, because when he opened a shelter for the homeless in 1914, situated at what he called "Hell's Half Acre" on Los Angeles Street, Liddecoat could pay for its construction with $100,000 of his own money.

Liddecoat was soon famous for carrying specially printed tickets in his pocket that he would pass out to homeless people. Each card promised free of charge "One meal, bath, bed, barber, laundry, doctor visit . . . and salvation!"

Though listed first, meals in those early days were pretty much an afterthought and were prepared in ways that were slapdash at best. The mission's food supply was exposed to flies and cockroaches and was prepared by men who might be afflicted with syphilis or tuberculosis.

When in 1929 the Los Angeles Health Department and other city agencies forced the Midnight Mission to "clean up or close up," Brother Tom was unbowed. If city government couldn't be bothered to make any other provisions for these men, he thundered, it was hypocritical for such charges to be levied against his kitchen. Above all, Liddecoat did not want his men to feel coddled. He called them "jailbirds, hopheads, and drunkards" to their faces and insisted that they were wholly accountable for all the bad decisions they'd made. He also never failed to remind his listeners of how much worse off they'd be without him.

Despite such harsh treatment, the number of people showing up at the Midnight Mission continued to grow and soon exceeded Liddecoat's ability to pay for it himself. So, he began seeking out deep-pocketed donors. Among his earliest supporters were Harry Chandler, publisher of the *Los Angeles Times,* and Albert M. Johnson, a millionaire who was president of the National Life Insurance Company. Liddecoat frequently stepped into the pulpit on Sunday mornings at various L.A. churches, including Aimee Semple McPherson's Church of the Foursquare Gospel. Being hailed as "the savior of the unwanted" by community leaders, he took his show on the road as a chaplain for the United Fruit and Vegetable Association, raising awareness of the homelessness problem at produce conventions nationwide.

"No man is safe and no citizen's property is secure so long as any man is either hungry or unemployed," Liddecoat liked to say. "If a man has food, lodging, and a presentable exterior, he will not turn to crime."

As Liddecoat's fame grew, he traveled widely across the United States and even internationally for the next three decades—often accompanied by his daughter Mary. He seldom turned down a request for an interview, and with his well-rehearsed skill for telling heartrending stories about the men of Hell's Half Acre, he was always good copy.

When Thomas Liddecoat died in 1942, obituaries written by appreciative members of the press bestowed upon him such grandiose nicknames as the "Bishop of the Underworld" and "Father of the Poor."

Rob Rice looked glum. He stared at half a dozen stainless steel bins full of what appeared to be pale pink wads of already-chewed bubble gum but was actually mechanically separated chicken (MSC).

"I wish I didn't have to use it," he said. "But we get thousands of pounds of MSC donated to us. It's our biggest source of protein."

Small amounts of meat and tissue from cattle, pigs, chickens, and turkeys once went to waste because processors had no cost-effective way to separate this final residue by hand from animal carcasses after the bulk of their meat was removed. Machines developed in the 1960s automated the process, which made salvaging scraps faster and cheaper. These last bits of flesh, bone, skin, and blood vessels are ground up together, resulting in a substance with the consistency of cake batter that can then be formed into meat by-products such as chicken nuggets, bologna, and hot dogs. Listing all of this led Rice into an embittered rant on why mechanically separated chicken is "damn near poisonous."

At his urging, I reluctantly reached into a pan of cooked MSC and put a small clump into my mouth. I was prepared for it to taste bad, but there was little or no flavor at all. It was like chewing a bunch of rubber bands. To make this goop palatable, each week Rice uses many pounds of black pepper, curry powder, oregano, onions, and garlic cloves.

"I wish I could change the way people eat," Rice said, "but these guys are very aware of their stomachs' real estate. From 8:00 p.m. to 8:00 a.m., there is no food to be found in the mission. You and I are accustomed to going this long without eating. We don't even think about it. But when so much is out of their control and they're trying to impose rules on themselves they've never known before, to have nothing to eat for that amount of time seems scary."

"A big bowl of dal [Indian lentils] and rice would taste better, be healthier, and cheaper to produce than chili made with mechanically separated chicken," he continued. "But this crowd will not eat dal. They want the chili."

Rice's posture, normally so athletically upright, had momentarily drooped. His shoulders and the corners of his mouth slumped downward.

"This place can be dark. It demands a lot. People who come here suffer from mental illness or have been the victims of extreme abuse. I think the whole first month I worked here, I would go home crying practically every night," he said. "But you have to make a distinction between those who are lost and those who are wandering. If they're lost, all you can do is show them love and treat them as nicely as you can. For the wandering, it's about letting them experience success once in a while."

At this last thought, Rice's face brightened. He resumed giving directions and orders to his kitchen staff. Owing to their limited attention spans, he's learned it is best to assign each guy one simple task at a time. This included me. Yesterday I fried flounder; now I was told to peel and dice Bermuda onions. Lots and lots of Bermuda onions. I worked at this for several hours, by which point I was no longer weeping from the fumes and finished the job dry-eyed.

A LARGE GROUP of men and women stood outside the Midnight Mission's kitchen. They were all wearing gaily colored T-shirts that announced an Iranian New Year's Festival. The Nowruz lunch would begin in a couple hours.

A local bakery had donated one hundred lemon meringue pies. Each needed to be cut into eight pieces, and these individual slices had to placed on separate plates. Rice demonstrated his preferred technique, severing the pie in half, then into quadrants, then eighths.

"Got it?" he asked.

"Got it," I replied.

When I tried to communicate this method to a few stylishly thin women from the Pacific Palisades, my lesson didn't go over too well. The prospect of even touching these pies was met with raised eyebrows and pursed lips—as if calories were contagious.

"They've got it under control," Rice said. He wanted me to see something on the loading dock. Here were many crates of food just arrived from L.A. Specialty, which is the Midnight Mission's single largest donor of food. What came that morning was a jackpot of organic produce such as broccoli, snap peas, romaine lettuce, arugula, sweet peppers, fava beans, avocados, and portobello mushrooms.

L.A. Specialty is one of Southern California's most esteemed purveyors of fresh fruits and produce, Rice told me. All the city's finest restaurants order from the company, and most of these customers have arrangements by which L.A. Specialty trucks will bring what they don't use to the Midnight Mission. In other words, a century after Brother Tom Liddecoat had an idea to cook meals from the produce his customers didn't sell, precisely the same strategy was still at work.

I couldn't decide if this was wonderful or woeful.

Grabbing several crates and ordering me to do the same, Rice said that he needed me to get busy cutting carrots. A couple of other guys would wash and peel, while I was to slice them in the French style. Rather than a perpendicular cut, which produces a circular piece of carrot, Rice demonstrated how to hold the knife at a forty-five-degree angle so it severed the carrot diagonally and each resulting piece was an oval. The greater surface area on each oval, he explained, would increase the amount of natural sugars that caramelized as it was stir-fried, resulting in a sweeter, crisper bite of carrot.

Who knew?

I carefully followed his instructions—at least at first. After several hours, though, my wrists began to tingle. The knife was starting to get dull. With this blunt blade and my somewhat diminished enthusiasm, holding the knife at a forty-five-degree angle began to be too much work. I shifted the knife upward and began to slice perpendicularly. This was much easier. Head down, I kept at it, cutting and cutting. Carrots and the color orange soon filled my entire field of vision. This color reminded me of the spicy hot soup I helped cook in South Korea, which made me think of that funny lady who sang "What a Friend We Have in Jesus" while shimmying about. My mind wandering, I lost track of time until I suddenly noticed Rob Rice standing at my side.

He picked up a carrot slice, which was perfectly round, not oval.

"What happened to my French cut?"

I was about to complain about the numbing repetition of this task. Wasn't there something more important for me to be doing? But I thought better of it. What if I were down on my luck, in detox from many years of drug abuse, and this skill Rice was trying to teach me might be the very thing that could get me a job and an escape from Skid Row?

"I'm sorry, Rob," I said.

He didn't smile, pat me on the back, and say, "Oh, that's all right." Instead, he frowned at me for a several uncomfortable seconds. Before walking away, Rice repeated his earlier instructions. "Keep the knife at a forty-five-degree angle, got it?"

He was giving me a second chance. Whether or not I would use this as an opportunity to experience success was up to me.

19

IN HONOR OF CURLY

THE STORIES I'VE SHARED IN PAST CHAPTERS ARE, ADMIT-tedly, something of a patchwork. They're loosely stitched together, but I hope in a way that's made sense. With a patchwork metaphor in mind, it's appropriate I finish off this culinary "crazy quilt" of a book with one more swatch. What follows is a zigzagging tale that begins with the hunt for a special type of bedspread called a suzani, and ends with the slaughter of a ram I roasted and fed to a group of poor farmers in Uzbekistan. Can I thread the needle and stitch these wildly different episodes together? Read on and see.

To start, I might as well acknowledge I'm nearly as enthusiastic for textiles as I am about cooking. I know how to sew, appreciate any excuse to get out my sewing machine, and find following a pattern similarly comforting to being instructed by a recipe. So, when I heard the renowned textile designer John Robshaw was going to escort a few people on a trip where he'd teach about block-printing of fabric, ikat, silk cocoons, and the creation of suzanis, I leapt at the chance to join his group.

If you haven't had the pleasure of encountering Central Asian needlework, allow me to introduce you. The Persian word *suzan* means "needle," and a suzani is a hand-embroidered piece of fabric. They are decorated with vibrantly-colored designs of cotton thread, or silk, and are a traditional wedding gift for brides. A suzani is often passed down from generation to generation, with the expectation of further embellishment by each of its owners. While they are made in other parts of the world—such as India, Iran, and Pakistan—some of the most extraordinary suzanis are sewn in Uzbekistan.

Until I went on this trip, I was unaware this country was located between Russia and India, and surrounded by others of the "stans" like Kazakhstan, Kyrgyzstan, Turkmenistan, Tajikistan, and Afghanistan. Though in the twentieth century Uzbekistan was part of the Soviet Republic, long before, this rugged region was an important link on the greatest trade route in history, the so-called Silk Road between China and Italy, which grew in importance from the second century BCE to the sixteenth century CE. It took two years for a caravan to make a complete journey from east to west, though no one trader made the entire trip. Instead, goods such as suzanis (and spices) were sold and resold across this span of time and distance. Silk Road journeys were like marathon relay races, with the "baton" of merchandise changing hands many times.

Cities in Uzbekistan such as Bukhara, Samarkand, and Khiva became wealthy from commerce, as well as rich with libraries and madrassas where both sacred and secular texts were preserved, and the latest technologies explored. Cyrus, Darius, Alexander the Great, Genghis Khan, and Tamerlane all came to plunder this region of Central Asia, and built elaborate monuments to their own glory.

My visit to this fascinating place was arranged by Indagare, a "boutique" travel agency founded a few years back by Melissa Biggs Bradley, who was travel editor at *Town & Country* magazine at the same time I used to write for this publication. Raisa Gareeva, who runs the Salom Travel company, based in Bukhara, was the local contact for Indagare in setting up on-the-ground arrangements. I got to know Gareeva pretty well in the two weeks I spent in Uzbekistan, and she was always happy to talk with me about her country.

Thanks to John Robshaw's expert guidance, I saw many remarkable suzanis, some made by contemporary artisans, others sold by dealers specializing in more antique examples. Over and over again, I found myself lost inside these vivid fields of color, with their looping symmetries, arabesques, and mysterious geometries. Certain patterns are believed to possess talismanic power to ward off the "evil eye," and maybe even enhance the fecundity of a marriage bed, providing a newlywed couple with the blessing of children. Such magical thinking not only occurs around suzanis; it is also at play in a type of charitable cookery which takes place in Uzbekistan, as I was soon to discover.

After Robshaw and others in our little clique of textile-ophiles left to return to the United States, I stayed on for a few more days. I'd arranged to cook a meal at the burial place of one of Sufic Islam's founders and holiest saints, a fourteenth century man named Khwāja Muḥammad Bahā' al-Dīn Naqshband (1317–1389).

Naqhshband espoused a life of hard work, self-reliance, and modesty. His shrine on the outskirts of Bukhara, is steeped in superstitions, with pilgrims coming from all over Central Asia to genuflect, meditate, and pray before his tombstone. Competition is also fierce to be accepted as one of the 140 young men who study Arabic, Sharia Law, and the Quran at a madrassa located here. Because it is considered such an especially holy place, this spot is organized to facilitate a unique spiritual custom for people who have a special need, or a heartfelt wish, they want answered by Allah. They will arrange an act of gastrophilanthropy which requires the ritual slaughter of an animal, whose meat is then butchered, cooked, and served to the needy.

When I was in Istanbul a few years ago, I'd first heard about this Muslim tradition, and was intrigued. Sacrificing life to gain favor with God sounded like a practice from Old Testament times—a page straight out of Leviticus. Could such an ancient custom still be practiced in the twenty-first century? As time went by, this possibility began to seem unlikely; I wondered if I'd misunderstood whoever told me about it in Turkey. It was with some nervousness, then, that one day I mentioned it to Raisa Gareeva. Worried she, being a Muslim, might consider my inquiry insulting, I haltingly asked if she'd ever heard of....?

I'd barely gotten out my question, before she was in instant agreement. Of course! What did I want to cook with—a chicken, a goat, a lamb, maybe even a cow?

Be careful, friends, what you pray for! Sometimes your request will be answered faster than you expected.

A COUPLE DAYS later, I stood in a fenced-in grazing area behind the house of a man named Safo Nomonov. He was both a shepherd, and a halal butcher for the nearby Sufi shrine to Naqhshband. With Gareeva's help—as well as the assistance of my translator, a patient and wonderfully kind young woman named Madena—I'd just agreed to purchase a ram for $200, and now was being given the opportunity, if that's the correct word, to pick which one I wanted.

Call me the Grim Sheeper! I wasn't wearing a hooded black robe or carrying a crook in my hand, but this did not prevent me from looking over the entire group of furry animals with narrowed eyes, and extending a pointed finger. The ram I'd selected was two years old, during which time it was fattened up for the express purpose of being eaten by humans. Whether or not I picked him, he was destined to become dinner for someone. This state of affairs didn't make the ram any happier to see me, however, and he greeted my presence by violently banging his head against the side of a metal watering trough. Straining against a rope tied round his neck and lashed to a spike in the ground, he then let loose with such a violent piss, its splatter pattern of urine doused my sneakers.

"Does he have a name?" I asked, as I belatedly backed away.

Nomonov, after Madena translated my altogether idiotic question, cocked an eyebrow as he gave me a confused look. If he spoke English, he probably would have replied, "It's not a pet, you silly twit. These are livestock."

This was the first of several awkward moments, mostly caused by my city boy ignorance. Yet, as Madena conversed with Nomonov in a combination of Uzbek and Tajik, and then offered his replies in English, I understood he was trying his best to be graciously welcoming. Mostly, Nomonov appeared incredulous an American had heard of this Muslim tradition of gastrophilanthropy, and wanted to participate by not only buying the animal (mentally, I'd decided to call him "Curly"), but help cook him the following day. The latter is an exceedingly rare occurrence he told Madena, even for Uzbeks, who usually aren't all that interested in the actual mechanism by which their sacrificial lamb will be fed to the hungry.

Nomonov had great charisma. He seemed to me the very definition of robust, what with his solid block of a head, meaty fingers, and bright smile. Later, when I asked if I could take his picture at the slaughterhouse, before he slit Curly's neck, Nomonov immediately struck a pose. He lifted up his knife, while glowering impressively.

After choosing Curly and paying for him, Madena and I drove back to the temple complex, where we were escorted into a small chapel. An imam named Mirzo Karimov was waiting for us. He was pale, thin, and had a pained, nearly haunted expression on his face. Without a word of greeting, he closed his eyes, tilted his head back, face aimed at the ceiling, and started to chant a special prayer of gratitude for Curly's life and impending death. He sang with startling force and with a piercingly nasal tone. Part of the training scholars undergo at this madrassa provides them with the requisite skill to be a muezzin, or a priest who will shout a call to prayer five times a day. It requires tremendous lung power to project loud enough to be heard at a great distance. However, we were seated in a tiled room of perhaps 200 square feet and Karimov had not lowered his voice by one decibel. If he'd been singing in Cleveland, they probably could have heard him in Detroit. Assaulted by this sonic blast, every hair on my body stood up on end.

Thoroughly freaked out by his performance—after which Madena whispered to me I needed to thank Karimov with a "blessing" that was the equivalent of $25—we were next escorted to the actual abattoir. Nomonov waited here, one foot atop Curly, who was laying on his side, panting heavily, eyes popped wide, with his back and front legs trussed together with rope.

"Are you ready?" Nomonov asked me.

I was, though I imagined Curly wasn't.

Nomonov's form of execution was not exactly a guillotine's precise slice. Instead, he dragged Curly by his horns over to a drain in the tile floor and thrust a blade into the animal's neck. A geyser of blood shot out and the ram jerked about, wildly thrusting his tied legs, but to no avail. As if he were sawing at an undercooked pot roast, Nomonov worked the knife deeper, twisting Curly's head for greater leverage, until finally, maybe half a minute later, the decapitation was complete.

Dazed, disgusted, and feeling nearly like I was floating outside my own body, I numbly watched as a tube was shoved into what was left of Curly, and a small boy suddenly entered the room, and began to hop up and down on a floor pump. This oddly comical process—it was like the kid was jumping on a pogo stick—inflated poor Curly's carcass to about twice its size, turning him into a fur balloon, which allowed skin to be separated from flesh more easily. Nomonov managed this process with a few deft swipes of his blade. Then, he slit Curly's chest open and out fell his innards in a sloppy, wet gush. The intestines were squeezed to evacuate any feces lodged inside; these tubes would later be thoroughly cleaned for use as surgical thread to close human wounds. Curly's head, fur, and other organs were scooped up and placed in garbage bags for further processing. What remained, pinkish red meat thickly striped with white fat, was what I'd cook the next day into *plov*, a classic Uzbek dish similar to an Indian biryani, made with lamb and rice.

Though I am not a vegetarian, of course I'm aware the plastic-wrapped pound of flank steak, or boneless breasts of chicken, I toss into my grocery cart were once part of living, breathing creatures. But I didn't grow up on a farm, no one in my family was a hunter, and while I've seen photographs taken inside slaughterhouses, I'd never been this close to such life *and* death. Weak from this gory experience, there was a still more incredible scene to come.

Madena and I needed to buy other ingredients for the *plov*. I was low on cash, however, and unlike the suzani dealers who were only too happy to accept payment in U.S. dollars, I'd been told the vendors at Bukhara's fruit and vegetable market would only take *som*, which is the local denomination. (During my visit, one dollar equaled 10,000 *som*.) In all of Bukhara, there was only one ATM which would accept my Citibank card. When I arrived at this location, a long queue of people were already waiting—at least 20 women and men. Ugh! We'd cut things too close and were short on time.

Before I could ask her what we should do, Madena began speaking to those on line. After she'd said a few sentences in Uzbek, which obviously I couldn't understand, I was shocked to see everyone back up. A guy standing in first place gestured for me to step forward.

"No!" I said, embarrassed. "I can't cut ahead of everybody. I'll wait."

I was a *musofir*, Madena reminded me. It is an Arabic word she'd taught me earlier which means a traveler from a foreign land; these people believe it's good to be especially polite to such visitors, she said.

Oh, please. They didn't want me to cut in, I was sure. How could they? If this were New York, no matter what Madena had said to a bunch of people waiting at a crowded ATM, they would have told her to drop dead. But this wasn't New York, and if I waited my turn, the market would be closed when we got there. Then, I wouldn't be able to get what I needed for a charity meal. What was the right thing to do?

Everyone was staring at me. I was holding them up even longer by my dithering and hesitation. So, I barged ahead, got my money—a stack of bills tall as a brick—and bowed to everyone before leaving.

Once we were outside, I scolded Madena. "You shouldn't have done that. I'm sure they resented me as a bratty American who felt entitled to order everyone around. I heard them grumbling. They probably were cursing me! It could have turned ugly."

Madena smiled. "Stephen, I heard what they were saying, too. I had explained to everyone what you are doing tomorrow, and how you'd arranged to have a ram killed. They all knew what that meant. They weren't cursing you, they were *praying* for you, and asking Allah to give you strength as you cook food for these poor people."

Hearing this was, in its own way, even more upsetting than seeing Curly's head sawed off. Madena's explanation made me feel unworthy and hollow. I am not a Muslim; I'm not a particularly devout person in any sort of spirituality. But I like to cook. If I wanted Allah to grant me anything, it was merely the opportunity to experience what it was like to make enough *plov* for an estimated crowd of 300 elderly people, cotton pickers, and young guys studying at the madrassa—many of them so impoverished, they don't often get a real stomach-filling, soul-satisfying meal. Was this a worthy enough goal to merit the blessings of those on line at the ATM? I can't say.

What I do know is, because of their kindness, Madena and I were able to purchase all our supplies. The next day, I worked my butt off, and did my best in honor of Curly. His flesh—which Nomonov had butchered carefully into chunks—was mixed with 60 pounds of rice, and the same amount of julienned carrots, along with oodles of garlic, cumin, and red peppers, then slowly cooked in an enormous copper cauldron set over a wood-burning fire. It was hard, hot, and sweaty work, but the resulting dish of *plov* was delicious. Spooning it out for a long queue of hungry people was a tremendous joy.

Later that afternoon, after the huge pot was emptied, cleaned, and stowed away—ready to be used for another charitable meal, and someone else's request to God—I walked around for a few minutes on the grounds of the Sufi temple.

Naqhshband's sayings are posted prominently in many places at this shrine, and translated into a variety of languages for all to read. One quote of his particularly caught my eye:

> "Ardency of love essentially requires that the lover persistently remain in the quest of the beloved. The dearer is the beloved, the more woe, anguish, and afflictions will be experienced on the way to Him. On the mystic path, excellent conduct of the aspirant is that he should remain restive and uneasy in His quest."

As if I were reading a poem, I needed to slow down, breathe, and allow myself to linger over each word in these few sentences. Yet, rather than gain understanding, with each rereading, I grew more perplexed.

How could I make sense of what I'd seen and done in the past couple days in Uzbekistan? By what sort of mystical miracle was it that I'd been shown such remarkable generosity and hospitality from strangers

like Safo Nomonov, or those people at the bank? And, was it really possible that Curly's death, and the method by which he was then fed to
others, was looked on with special approval by God?

I didn't have a reply to any of these questions, yet Naqhshband's
words suggested this was not only OK, but as it should be.

Answers are easy. Daring to remain always on a quest is difficult, but
it is truly the only way to feel an ardency of love.

EPILOGUE

Inspired by Père Lachaise Cemetery in Paris, Kensal Green is London's first garden-like burial ground. Located in the royal boroughs of Kensington and Chelsea, to the west of central London, Kensal Green Cemetery is the final resting spot of Anthony Trollope, William Makepeace Thackeray, and Harold Pinter, among many other writers, scientists, and politicians who lived and died in the past two centuries.

It's also where Alexis Soyer is interred, which is why I made a pilgrimage there one summer morning. At least, I thought it's where his grave could be found. To my surprise, a Wikipedia page for Kensal Green believed it important to list Betsy Balcombe ("a close friend of Napoleon Bonaparte during his imprisonment on St. Helena Island") and Charles Blondin ("acrobat and tightrope-walker") among the cemetery's notable burials but made no mention of Soyer.

Another reminder of Soyer's diminished stature came on the Tube to Kensal Green when the subway train stopped at Baker Street. Suddenly, a woman's recorded voice murmured the words "Exit here for Madame Tussaud's." Alexis Soyer's kitchens at the Reform Club were once a much more popular tourist attraction in London than these waxworks, yet today Tussaud's global fame exceeds what it was in the mid-nineteenth century, while Soyer is forgotten.

England's cool, humid climate may be ideal for the cultivation of roses, dahlias, and hollyhocks, but it also makes controlling the landscape of as sprawling a place as Kensal Green nearly impossible. Passing under a wrought-iron gate, I waded through waist-high weeds until I found a plywood cabin, what looked like a hobbit house. Inside, a man was watching a soccer game on television; a cat nestled on his lap. Neither looked pleased to have a visitor.

In my hand was a scrap of paper on which I had jotted down the figures 3698099. How I obtained this number I could no longer recall. "It is the location of a once great chef, Alexis Soyer?" I asked, ashamed by the unlikeliness of my inquiry. How often had this poor fellow been asked where so-and-so was buried? Talk about a needle in a haystack!

While grumbling something unintelligible, he heaved himself up—the cat screeched as it was sent flying—and peered at a tattered map thumbtacked to the wall. After a few moments, the groundskeeper turned to me with a grin. "Oh. Right you are! He's there with his Missus, ain't he?"

Yes! This much I knew for certain. Alexis Soyer had spent an exorbitant amount of time and money meeting with many different designers and stone masons to construct an ostentatious monument for his wife, Emma.

The groundskeeper pointed at a clump of bushes and a leaf-strewn dirt path. "Go through there and along the wall," he said. "Eventually you'll come to a gate. Across from it, there's a tall statue of a woman, with angels flyin' all about. Can't miss 'er."

It was slow going through this overgrown terrain. Tall stone obelisks and even entire mausoleums were blanketed with English ivy nearly as if they were topiary specimens. More disturbing still, every few steps my foot landed on yet another toppled tombstone. Trampling people's graves worried me—as did the likelihood of twisting an ankle. Was there no one to tend these plots? Not a single person still alive who cared about their ancestors?

After trudging along for about five minutes, I came out onto a gravel service road. And there, exactly as I'd been told, stood a stone statue of a woman atop a tall plinth. The passing of many seasons had done its worst, eroding her upturned face and obscuring the features of two winged putti fluttering by the woman's feet. Farther down on the pedestal were two words only: "TO HER." Circling around to the column's rear, I saw this carved into the stone:

To the Memory of Madame Soyer /
Died September 1, 1842 / Aged 32 Years
England gave her birth / Genius Immortality

Below was an oval-shaped recess where I guessed a sculpted likeness of Soyer might once have been. For, under the gaping hole was this inscription:

Alexis Benoit Soyer / Died August 5, 1858 / Aged 48 Years

Had a vandal intentionally defaced this tombstone? Whatever the explanation, I was sorry to find Soyer's burial spot—and, by extension, his legacy—in such a state of neglect. Feeling a tug of melancholy, I sat at the pedestal's base and began to think about what a zigzagging path it took to get to this spot—not just through the tangle of Kensal Green Cemetery, but also to cities and kitchens around the world where I had cooked alongside so many wonderful people.

My life forever changed when I allowed Alexis Soyer to be my guide. He was an unlikely choice of role model, that's for sure. The preaching in Baptist churches I grew up in taught that only people who truly are good can truly do good. This religion repeatedly assured me that I was born bad. Adam and Eve were my actual ancestors, as they were for the entire human race, and their misbehavior in Eden—the original sin— was my heritage. To have any hope of becoming a better person, I needed to ask Jesus Christ to be my savior. Only by praying (and praying!) for the Lord's help would my sins be forgiven, and only then could I gain the selfless compassion to love my neighbor.

Looking at the world this way is helpful for many people. This certainly was The Answer for my parents.

It didn't work for me.

Alexis Soyer's life suggested a few more attainable truths.

To be alive is to be morally muddled. It isn't always clear what is the right thing to do. Sometimes we take a leap of faith and break an ankle. We may aspire to a consistency of purpose, but something will always confound our best-laid plans in ways big and small. We'll improvise and make mistakes; there will be less than perfect results. Being aware of our failings, then, is only honest, but by living in fear of a possible accusation of hypocrisy—"How's it going with your magical misery tours?"— we can easily talk ourselves out of any act of charity.

Or not.

Alexis Soyer deserved no halo, nor was he a self-denying saint. He was a boozy, bawdy bon vivant who enjoyed being famous, loved having money, and spent it freely on both himself and those around him. He didn't alter his outrageous style of dress or rein in his naughty sense of humor even when he was feeding London's poorest citizens or making soup in Dublin during the potato famine. When people mocked him behind his back, Soyer kept on keepin' on, and he comforted tens of thousands of people by doing so. Keeping his example in mind, I had become more forgiving of my own failures, inconsistencies, and the zigzagging juxtapositions of my life.

I was still a wide-eyed kid on Sunday morning, flipping pages of the *New York Times* with a greedy fascination—what's new? what's next? Only now I was paid to write a story about a charred dining room in Texas, a cruise on the Peruvian Amazon, or Cher's line of cruciform jewelry. Is it guilt over this crazy career of mine (and, oh yes, that I am also fortunate enough to have a loving and financially successful husband) that makes me want to spend days cutting carrots at the Midnight Mission, making meatballs in a cramped kitchen in Guadalajara, or skinning tomatoes for a Bolognese sauce in Pittsburgh?

I don't know the answer to this question, but it doesn't matter.

In one of his books, Alexis Soyer wrote "any tainted water is made good, by first converting it into steam." He was talking about cooking here, but I don't think it's too much of a reach to also see this as a comment on our utility as human beings. We are all "tainted" to some degree. Everyone has their guilty secrets and regrets about things done or left undone. But it doesn't require a pure fountain to be generous to others. Goodness will result through the "steam" of our efforts.

William James, the nineteenth-century American psychologist and philosopher, once offered his students this advice: "Don't think yourself into right action; act yourself into right thinking." It's a sentiment Alexis Soyer would have agreed with wholeheartedly. So do I.

THOUGH ITS PURCHASE started me on this journey, I don't own a Lacanche oven anymore. James and I moved from our London Terrace apartment several years ago, and I've had the opportunity to build two other kitchens for us in different houses since then. In a loft apartment where we currently live, I cook on a BlueStar range (made in good old Pennsylvania, I might add), which has eight gas rings on top, whereas the Lacanche "only" had six. Trust me, Alexis, all eight burners are being put to good use. That's because in the past few years, I have found my way into a broader definition of gastrophilanthropy.

My parents liked to welcome into our house Christian missionaries from overseas when they were visiting the United States on fundraising tours—Mom and Dad's way of lending support to a cause they deeply believed in. When James and I open up our apartment to a variety of progressive people and nonprofit groups, for which we regularly host parties for up to 150 people at a time, I'm doing something oddly similar. Rugs are vacuumed with extra care, windows are washed. We fluff up the pillows, and hire the waiters and bartenders. I cook all the food.

In the process, we've helped support politicians such as North Carolina governor Roy Cooper, Senator Tammy Baldwin of Wisconsin, and Cynthia Nixon in her bid to be governor of New York State. There have been many other events too, including for Planned Parenthood; Leadership for Educational Equity, a nonprofit group that addresses inequity in America's public school system; and Housing Works, a New York City–based organization helping people with HIV/AIDS and other life-threatening illnesses.

James and I were honored recently at a charity dinner where we were given a Social Responsibility Award for the fundraising efforts we've done on behalf of these various organizations. After this gala one of our friends remarked, "Only you two could get a humanitarian prize for hosting cocktail parties!"

His joke stung a bit. I understand that spending whole days making lamb kebabs, mini-quiches, or lemon bars may not be everyone's idea of giving back to the universe. Then again, not everyone knows how to cook this way. But I do, and this hard-earned knowledge provides me with an unusual kind of influence.

A few weeks ago, at an event James and I hosted at our apartment for Callen-Lorde, another charitable health care provider to New York's neediest, one of our guests wrote out a check for $25,000 on the spot. This guy, who admitted he'd never given a dime to Callen-Lorde before, later said he was having such a good time drinking Sancerre and eating my recipe for poached shrimp with an arugula pesto that he got "a little carried away."

A good meal can open not only hearts, but also wallets. For the opportunity to learn this peculiar truth about charity, I must also thank my imaginary friend, Alexis Soyer.

THE SKY WAS becoming increasingly gray. Soon I needed to leave Kensal Green, as I had a lunch date with a friend back in London's Soho at Nopi, a vegetarian restaurant created by the Israeli chef Yotam Ottolenghi—someone whose exuberant love of cooking and passionate wish to teach others how wonderful it can feel to make food for others has brought him fame, wealth, and a celebrity comparable to Alexis Soyer's.

A drizzle of rain began to fall, which would cause still more foliage to sprout. I could only hope ivy wouldn't creep up and completely obscure Soyer's grave—a lamentable possibility that reminded me of Florence Nightingale's response when she learned he had died.

"Soyer's death is a great disaster," she wrote. "Others have studied cookery for the purpose of gourmandizing, some for show, but none but he for the purpose of cooking large quantities of food in the most nutritious and economic manner, for great numbers of men. He has no successor."

A century and a half later, Nightingale's pronouncement is still correct. It's true that no single person is Soyer's successor, or has inherited his mantle of charitable cookery. Instead, many hundreds, thousands, and even millions of people, whether they know it or not, are following a gastrophilanthropic path that Alexis Soyer blazed when they cook for the poor. There is Rob Rice, Shon Guy-Ho, the Sauce Boss, Aryeh Cohen, Varda Sohan and Ziva Sharon, Nattie, Adam Graham, Jeff at the Recovery Café, the Band of Brothers, Atilla the Nun, Soup Can Kerry and Can Opener Ann, Biswajit Singh, and all the other people I spent time with as described in these pages.

Oh, and why not *you*? Go ahead, turn up a flame under that fry pan. If you cook it, they will come. Someone, somewhere, is always hungry.

AFTERWORD

A S THIS BOOK NEARED PUBLICATION IN ITS ORIGINAL, hardcover format, the coronavirus was still a vague mystery. In those last months of 2019, it appeared limited to what seemed a few isolated cases in distant China. No one knew at that time how the illness was transmitted, how far it might spread, or what was the best way for the world, America, and each individual to respond. Impaired by the self-important myopia of a first-time author, I'm embarrassed to admit I was so busy making plans to publicize *The 24-Hour Soup Kitchen*, I managed for many weeks to disregard warning signs of a looming contagion.

The marketing campaign I'd come up with was ambitious. After a book launch party in New York, I'd arranged to drive cross country, visiting several dozen cities along the way. At each stop, my plan was to host a dinner that I'd cook to recognize and celebrate those chefs who worked full-time at soup kitchens in places like Atlanta, Houston, or San Diego. I'd reconnect with some of the gastrophilanthropists I met while writing my book, and I envisioned making new friends, and getting to hear their stories, also.

By the end of March 2020, a mere week away from my publication date, however, the pandemic's severity could no longer be ignored. With numbers of infections rising, and hospitals overwhelmed with sick patients, I woke up fast. Suddenly, this book was the least of my, or anyone else's, concerns.

Swinging wildly in the opposite direction, I now became increasingly aware and then afraid. I imagined Manhattan might go into a total lockdown, with all roads, bridges, tunnels, and the subway system closed. Those who lived here would be quarantined away from the rest of the country, something similar to what the city of Wuhan, China, did to contain its outbreak. Panicked by this possibility, my husband James and I decided we would relocate, temporarily, to a weekend house we own upstate in the Hudson Valley. Thus began our quarantine, a purgatory I thought might last a few weeks, or a month or two. Eventually, it stretched to over a year, or until we gratefully, nearly tearfully, rolled up our sleeves, and were given our second dose of the Pfizer vaccine.

In this long, longer, longest stretch of time before vaccination, I was suspended in a weird stasis where every possible decision about the future seemed wrong. On hiatus from my "real" life back in New York City, I found myself with far too much free time, knocked about by terror, then boredom; boredom, then terror. Struggling with these dueling realities, I began to worry about how much more worrying I could stand. And, trust me, my tolerance for worrying is high. In fact, I'm a world-class worrier. It's a "skill" I inherited from my mother.

One sleepless night, though, I came up with an idea. James' retail clients, for whom his P.R. agency handles marketing communications, will sometimes introduce a new line of products by temporarily taking over a space for what's called a "pop up" shop. Maybe it only lasts for a month or two, before closing down. It's a cut flower, not a planted tree. The beauty is the brevity—if the concept doesn't work, there's been no huge outlay of costs or effort. Maybe I could apply this idea to cooking, and form a temporary charitable kitchen: a pop up, better still, a "soup up" kitchen. Something similar, in fact, to what my hero, Alexis Soyer, did when feeding the hungry in Dublin during the nineteenth-century potato famine.

Searching for advice, the following morning, I began sleuthing on the Internet and learned Columbia County, where our house is located, has only one spot that serves a free lunch on weekdays. It was the Salvation Army Community Center in Hudson, a town about ten miles north from where I sat. I dialed a number found online, and a woman who picked up on the first ring, Darcy Connor, sounded as if she'd been waiting for me to call.

When James and I later dropped off a car-load of groceries, Connor gratefully informed us her pantry shelves were completely cleared out that morning. We three shared a warm few minutes together—a pleasant encounter which might have ended with hugs all around. Instead, we laughingly maintained the requisite amount of social distance. As we headed for the door, Connor had one more request. She was in full crisis mode, with numbers of hungry guests rising week to week. The volunteers, mostly retired senior citizens, who used to cook for her were now too nervous about catching Covid-19 to show up at the Salvation Army. Connor didn't know what she would do. If I could suggest anyone who might take on chef duties for one of these lunchtime shifts, she'd be grateful.

"Well, I know how to cook . . ."

The words were barely out of my mouth before Connor replied, "Can you come next Tuesday?"

Um . . . sure. I agreed to show up the following week.

I was really, really, *really* nervous that next Tuesday. James is usually blasé about things; as noted above, I'm the fretful one in our family. However, on this morning, he was jittery, which got me even more torqued up. When my alarm went off at 5:30 a.m., James woke, too, and was rubbing his hands with anxiety as he peppered me with a litany of last-minute demands: You will keep your mask on? You will always wear gloves? You won't touch your eyes? You will stay at least six feet away from others? You won't shake hands or make any physical contact with anyone?

His questions, all lovingly well-meant, felt like pinpricks to my bleary eyeballs. It was as if I'd agreed to go pick up used surgical syringes, barehanded. At a leper colony. In Chernobyl.

That first morning, I brought along several batches of chocolate chip cookies I'd made the evening before. At the kitchen, I was assisted by an energetic volunteer named Ria. In the narrow and tight space, we collided frequently. When not volunteering at the Salvation Army, Ria was an emergency room nurse at the Hudson hospital, where she told me they were starting to see a surge of pandemic patients.

"It's gettin' bad out there," she drawled.

I decided not to tell James about any of this later.

While cooking two big pots of chicken curry, mixed greens, and a fruit salad, I wore gloves and compulsively wiped all surfaces with Lysol. It was a relief when Ria explained this food would be individually boxed, bagged, and put outside on a table for people to pick up. We'd have no contact with any of our guests.

Maybe I was a fool to put my body at risk this way, but I left that kitchen feeling happier and healthier than I had for several weeks. In fact, I'd already committed to prepare next Tuesday's meal. If I was to become infected with the coronavirus, I decided it might as well be while making meals for poor people.

All those chefs I'd met while writing *The 24-Hour Soup Kitchen*, their techniques of mass cookery I'd learned, shortcuts, substitutions, and "hacks," allowed me in a matter of a few hours to produce enough food to feed many dozen people. Quickly, our numbers grew. In late March, we were feeding 50 people a day; by June, it was closer to 100.

I've been at it now, cooking every Tuesday's lunch at the Salvation Army for nearly a year, supported each week by a rotating cast of friends who give up their morning to help me make curries, stews, baked pastas, and other savory things. I've come to deeply admire and respect Darcy Connor, who is such a good Christian, she never ever talks about her faith. She simply embodies it.

Or, better still, she offers it up, fresh every day, on a plate.

RECIPES

THERE ARE MANY DIFFERENT WAYS TO COOK FOR A CROWD. Learning to "scale up" a recipe written to serve four, and using it to feed forty, will take a bit of trial and error. A good rule to follow, however, is you can always add more fluid, salt, or other spices, but once you've placed something into the pot, it can't be taken out.

What follows are five extremely "forgiving" recipes. Meaning, you can easily multiply all ingredients listed by whatever multiple you like and still have a good chance of ending up with something that tastes good.

Best of luck and may the kitchen gods be with you!

EASY CHICKEN CURRY
(Serves 6)

INGREDIENTS

2 tablespoons olive oil

1 large onion, peeled and diced

Salt and pepper (to taste)

6 or 8 cloves of garlic, minced

2-inch knob of fresh ginger, minced

1 red bell pepper, seeded, and chopped into ½-inch pieces

1 teaspoon curry powder

1 teaspoon cumin

½ teaspoon turmeric

2 cinnamon sticks (or ½ teaspoon of ground cinnamon)

1 cup chopped tomato (either fresh or canned is fine)

1 can unsweetened coconut milk (13.5 ounces)

1½ pounds boneless chicken, cut into ¾- to 1-inch pieces

Chopped cilantro (optional)

Chutney, coconut flakes, raisins (optional)

INSTRUCTIONS

Place oil in a large skillet; turn heat to medium-high. A minute later, add onions, along with a generous pinch of salt and some pepper. Cook, stirring occasionally for about five minutes, until onions are very soft and starting to turn golden. Add garlic, ginger, and red peppers.

When above ingredients are all melded (another three to five minutes), add curry powder, cumin, turmeric, cinnamon, and tomato. Cook, stirring, for another few minutes. Add coconut milk and simmer until it thickens slightly, about two minutes, stirring occasionally. Add chicken, stir, and cook until the flesh is no longer pink, in about six to eight minutes.

Add another pinch of salt and pepper. Taste. Adjust seasonings as necessary. Serve over rice, garnished with cilantro. You can also top with chutney, coconut flakes, and raisins, if they are handy.

EVERYTHING COOKIES
(Makes about 2 dozen cookies)
(Adapted from Alex Witchel's recipe)

INGREDIENTS

Softened Butter (optional)

1 very ripe banana

⅓ cup canola oil

⅔ cup sugar

1 teaspoon vanilla extract

¾ cup flour

½ teaspoon baking soda

¼ teaspoon salt

¼ teaspoon ground cinnamon

2 cups oatmeal (not instant)

½ cup chopped walnuts

½ cup chocolate chips

½ cup dried cranberries or raisins

½ cup grated sweetened coconut

INSTRUCTIONS

Preheat oven to 350 degrees. Line baking sheets with parchment paper or grease them with softened butter. In a mixing bowl, mash banana well. Add oil, sugar, vanilla, and blend thoroughly. Add flour, baking soda, salt, and cinnamon, and mix until moistened.

Add oatmeal, walnuts, chocolate chips, cranberries/raisins, and coconut. Mix together, making sure oatmeal is moistened and well incorporated. If it looks too slippery, add a tablespoon more of flour.

Using clean, slightly wet hands, roll dough into balls slightly smaller than a golf ball, about an inch and a third in diameter. (The dough is sticky; moisture on your palms helps in this hand-rolling process.) Place each ball two inches apart on cookie sheet and flatten slightly.

Bake until lightly browned, about twelve to fourteen minutes. Remove from heat and allow cookies to rest for a few minutes before lifting off cookie sheet with a spatula. Then place on on a wire rack to cool completely.

MEXICAN MEATBALLS
(Serves 6 to 8)

INGREDIENTS

3 pounds tomatoes, chopped

1 medium white onion

6 garlic cloves

2 teaspoons canned chipotle
   chiles

½ teaspoon ground cloves

2 tablespoons olive oil

Salt and pepper (to taste)

1 pound ground beef

1 pound ground pork

½ cup bread crumbs

1 egg

1½ teaspoon oregano

3 tablespoons drained capers

INSTRUCTIONS

Puree tomato, onion, garlic, chiles, and cloves in blender. Heat oil in large skillet over medium-high heat. Add tomato mixture. Cover and cook, stirring occasionally until sauce thickens slightly, in about ten minutes. Season with salt and pepper. (This step can be done hours or even a day earlier.)

Combine beef, pork, bread crumbs, egg, oregano, and add a half cup of cooled tomato sauce. Mix well. While forming a generous table-spoon of the meat mixture into a ball, insert three capers into its center; close up, and reshape ball. Repeat with remaining meat and capers.

Bring tomato sauce back to a simmer over medium heat. Add meat-balls to sauce and cook, simmering meatballs and turning them occa-sionally, until they are cooked through, in about twenty minutes. Serve with ice.

MUJADARAH, OR MIDDLE EASTERN LENTILS AND RICE
(Serves 6 to 8)

INGREDIENTS

1 cup brown lentils

2 large onions

¼ cup olive oil, plus two tablespoons more

8 garlic cloves (minced)

¾ cup rice

1½ teaspoons ground cumin

½ teaspoon allspice

Pinch of cayenne pepper (optional)

2 teaspoons salt

1 teaspoon black pepper

1 bay leaf

1 cinnamon stick

1 cup full-fat plain yogurt

Chopped cilantro (for garnish,
optional)

INSTRUCTIONS

Put lentils in a large bowl, add hot tap water, enough to cover beans. Stir fluid a few times to submerge lentils. Let soak for fifteen to thirty minutes.

Peel onions and slice them in half. Then cut each half into quarter-inch disks (or half-moon shapes). Heat a quarter cup of olive oil in a fry pan and slowly sauté the onions, keeping heat moderately low. Stir occasionally for ten to fifteen minutes or until onions are very caramelized, even brown and crispy in a few spots. Turn off heat.

While onions cook, put two tablespoons of oil into a medium-sized pasta pot, add garlic and sauté over medium heat, stirring occasionally so it doesn't burn. Stir in rice, cumin, allspice, cayenne, and sauté two minutes.

Drain lentils and stir into rice. Add four and a quarter cups of water, two teaspoons of salt, one teaspoon of black pepper, bay leaf, and cinnamon stick. Bring to a simmer, then cover and cook over low heat for approximately twenty to twenty-five minutes or until both rice and lentils are softened. Add a little more water if mixture looks dry. Remove from heat and let stand, uncovered, for five minutes.

Serve lentils/rice mixture with a dollop of yogurt and a generous spoonful of the sautéed onions. If desired, sprinkle with cilantro and freshly-ground pepper.

MOM'S APPLE COBBLER
(Serves 8 to 10)

INGREDIENTS

8 to 10 Apples (Granny Smith,
   Golden Delicious, or other
   baking apple)
1 lemon
½ cup dried cranberries
1 cup flour (or, to be gluten-free,
   almond flour)
1 cup sugar

1 teaspoon salt
1 teaspoon baking powder
1 cup oatmeal
½ cup ground walnuts
1 egg
1 stick of butter
1 teaspoon ground cinnamon

INSTRUCTIONS

Peel, core, and cut apples into slices roughly one-third inch thick. Zest and squeeze juice from lemon. Combine apples, cranberries, lemon zest and juice, then spread mixture into a 9 x 13-inch baking dish.

With a whisk, mix together flour, sugar, salt, and baking powder, then stir in oatmeal and walnuts. Add egg and combine thoroughly until dry ingredients are moistened and crumbly. Spoon this topping over apples, making a layer that covers all of the fruit.

Melt butter, then drizzle it evenly over the crumble topping. Dust with the teaspoon of cinnamon. Bake in 375-degree oven for approximately forty minutes or until apples are softened and bubbling up around edge of crumble topping.

Served with vanilla ice cream.

(Note: Other fruits can be substituted for apples, such as peaches, mangoes, mixed berries, or a strawberry-rhubarb combination. If using fruit other than apples, however, don't include the cranberries.)

ACKNOWLEDGMENTS

EVERY WRITER, LIKE EVERY CHEF, HAS MANY PEOPLE TO thank. That's because no book, or meal, can be created as a solitary effort, but requires the collaboration of many people. My deep appreciation goes out to everyone who helped me cook up *The 24-Hour Soup Kitchen,* and especially to the following people:

K. Dun Gifford, the late founder of Oldways Food Preservation and Trust, who taught me that regional recipes are an excellent way to understand different cultures around the world.

Dr. Peter Hawkins, my mentor whose wise counsel not only helped me survive graduate school but also find my voice as a writer.

Early readers of this manuscript who cheered me on, including Brian Nash, Carl Charlson, Cheri Coons, Elisabeth Reed, Raphael Kadushin, and Tod Lippy.

Ruth Reichl, Cynthia Nixon, Dr. Gregory Sterling, and Charles King. These are all very busy people, but they graciously agreed to look at these pages in galley form and offer kind words for the back cover.

The many friends on a mailing list for my annual holiday letter, whose enthusiastic reception for my storytelling gave me the courage to keep writing.

Patrice Tanaka, my former boss and current pal, who has changed my life for the better in important ways.

Mark Fretz, Evan Phail, and all the good folks at Radius who guided me with delicacy and tact through the process of publication.

Henry Carrigan, my editor, who snipped, corrected, and red-lined my paragraphs in the nicest way possible.

All the chefs who graciously allowed me to cook alongside them and learn from their example. And, a special word of gratitude to Bunty and Meet Singh, my friends in Delhi, whose generous introduction to a soup kitchen at the Bangla Sahib Gurdwara launched me on this journey of culinary discovery.

Jean-Jacques Augagneur, who would not allow me to return the Lacanche range I bought from him and so caused me to start cooking more gastrophilanthropically.

Alexis Soyer, my imaginary friend and guide. His indefatigable good cheer and a graceful ability to handle the zigzags of life in nineteenth-century London—high and low, rich or poor, feast or famine—inspired me to follow in his charitable footsteps a century later.

Ruth Cowen, whose remarkable biography of Alexis Soyer allowed me to know this fascinating man in full.

Above all, much love and thankfulness to James LaForce, my husband and life partner for the past three decades. James is the funniest, smartest, and most consistently surprising person I know. He's also a joy to cook for because he's never late to dinner, always cleans his plate, and insists everything I prepare is delicious. Finally, James has never complained about the many nights when I've been away from home cooking for others and he's had to fend for himself with cold cereal or scrambled eggs.

APPENDIX

It's easy to find a way to cook for others in need. Simply type "soup kitchen" into Google, add just about any location in the world, and several choices will appear. All these charitable restaurants could use an extra pair of hands to get lunch or dinner ready.

Below is contact information for some of the places where I volunteered, which I've listed in the same order I've written about them in the previous pages. I've also included several other sources that might help you explore gastrophilanthropy. Each of these organizations will be happy to accept your donation of time, money, or food.

Delhi Sikh Gurdwara Management Committees (India)
Guru Gobind Singh Bhawan
Gurudwara Rakabganj Road
Gokul Nagar
Pandit Pant Marg Area, Central
Secretariat, Gokul Nagar
South Block, Rakab Ganj
New Delhi, India 110001
Telephone: 011-23712580-81-82 /
011-23737328-29
info@dsgmc.in

Restaurants du Coeur (France)
contact@restoducoeur.org

Faith Mission of Elkhart (Indiana)
801 Benham Avenue

P.O. Box 1728
Elkhart, IN, 46516-1728
Telephone: (574) 293-3406
info@thefaithmission.org

Jubilee Soup Kitchen (Pittsburgh)
2005 Wyandotte St
Pittsburgh, PA 15219
Telephone: (412) 261-5417
Jubileesoupkitchen@gmail.com
www.jubileesoupkitchen.org

East End Cooperative Ministries (Pittsburgh)
6140 Station Street
Pittsburgh, PA 15206
Telephone: (412) 361-5549
www.eecm.org

Rainbow Kitchen (Pittsburgh)
135 E 9th Ave
Homestead, PA 15120
Telephone: (412) 464-1892
www.rainbowkitchen.org

Loaves & Fishes (Minnesota)
721 Kasota Avenue SE
Minneapolis, MN 55414
Telephone: (612) 377-9810
www.loavesandfishesmn.org

**Holy Apostles Soup Kitchen
(New York)**
296 Ninth Avenue
New York, NY 10001-5703
Telephone: (212) 924-0167
www.holyapostlessoupkithen.org

**Los Angeles Youth Network /
Youth Emerging Stronger**
P.O. Box 988
Los Angeles, CA 90028
Telephone: (323) 467-8466
info@YouthEmergingStronger.org

Recovery Café (Seattle)
2022 Boren Avenue
Seattle, WA 98121
Telephone: (206) 374-8731
www.recoverycafe.org

Mobile Loaves & Fishes (Austin)
9301 Hog Eye Road, Suite 950
Austin, TX 78724
Telephone: (512) 328-7299
www.mlf.org

Meir Panim Relief Centers (Israel)
5316 New Utrecht Avenue
Brooklyn, NY 11219
Telephone: (718) 437-9100
www.meirpanim.org

Sauce Boss (Bill Wharton)
Telephone: (850) 212-3837
info@sauceboss.com

**The Community of St. Martin
(Guadalajara, Mexico)**
P.O. Box 954
Highland, CA 92346
Telephone: 33 1546 9107
casa 33 3144 6704
Guadalajara, Jalisco, Mexico
www.comunidaddesanmartin.org

The Midnight Mission (Los Angeles)
601 S. San Pedro Street
Los Angeles, CA 90014
Telephone: (213) 624-9258
www.midnightmission.org

World Central Kitchen
1342 Florida Avenue NW,
Washington, DC 20009,
Telephone: (202) 844-6430
www.wck.org

Food Bank for New York City
39 Broadway, 10th Floor
New York, NY 10006
Telephone: (212) 566-7855
www.foodbanknyc.org

No Kid Hungry
1030 15th Street, NW
Suite 1100 W
Washington, DC 20005
Telephone: (800) 969-4767
www.nokidhungry.org

**Worldwide Opportunities on
Organic Farms**
WWOOF-USA
PO Box 22274
San Francisco, CA 94122